Crossing the Threshold

CROSSING THE THRESHOLD

Understanding Religious Identities in South Asia

BY

Dominique-Sila Khan

I.B.Tauris *Publishers*
LONDON • NEW YORK
in association with
The Institute of Ismaili Studies
LONDON

Published in 2004 by I.B.Tauris & Co Ltd
6 Salem Rd, London W2 4BU
175 Fifth Avenue, New York NY 10010
www.ibtauris.com

in association with The Institute of Ismaili Studies
42–44 Grosvenor Gardens, London SW1W 0EB
www.iis.ac.uk

In the United States of America and in Canada distributed by
St Martin's Press, 175 Fifth Avenue, New York NY 10010

ISBN 1 85043 435 2
EAN 978 1 85043 435 1

A full CIP record for this book is available from the British Library
A full CIP record for this book is available from the Library of Congress

Library of Congress catalog card: available

Typeset in Minion Tra for The Institute of Ismaili Studies

Printed and bound in Great Britain by MPG Books Ltd, Bodmin

The Institute of Ismaili Studies

The Institute of Ismaili Studies was established in 1977 with the object of promoting scholarship and learning on Islam, in the historical as well as contemporary contexts, and a better understanding of its relationship with other societies and faiths.

The Institute's programmes encourage a perspective which is not confined to the theological and religious heritage of Islam, but seeks to explore the relationship of religious ideas to broader dimensions of society and culture. The programmes thus encourage an interdisciplinary approach to the materials of Islamic history and thought. Particular attention is also given to issues of modernity that arise as Muslims seek to relate their heritage to the contemporary situation.

Within the Islamic tradition, the Institute's programmes seek to promote research on those areas which have, to date, received relatively little attention from scholars. These include the intellectual and literary expressions of Shiʿism in general, and Ismailism in particular.

In the context of Islamic societies, the Institute's programmes are informed by the full range and diversity of cultures in which Islam is practised today, from the Middle East, South and Central Asia, and Africa to the industrialised societies of the West, thus taking into consideration the variety of contexts which shape the ideals, beliefs and practices of the faith.

These objectives are realised through concrete programmes and activities organised and implemented by various departments of the Institute. The Institute also collaborates periodically, on a programme-specific basis, with other institutions of learning in the United Kingdom and abroad.

The Institute's academic publications fall into a number of inter-related categories:

1. Occasional papers or essays addressing broad themes of the relationship between religion and society in the historical as well as modern contexts, with special reference to Islam.
2. Monographs exploring specific aspects of Islamic faith and culture, or the contributions of individual Muslim thinkers or writers.
3. Editions or translations of significant primary or secondary texts.
4. Translations of poetic or literary texts which illustrate the rich heritage of spiritual, devotional and symbolic expressions in Muslim history.
5. Works on Ismaili history and thought, and the relationship of the Ismailis to other traditions, communities and schools of thought in Islam.
6. Proceedings of conferences and seminars sponsored by the Institute.
7. Bibliographical works and catalogues which document manuscripts, printed texts and other source materials.

This book falls into category two listed above.

In facilitating these and other publications, the Institute's sole aim is to encourage original research and analysis of relevant issues. While every effort is made to ensure that the publications are of a high academic standard, there is naturally bound to be a diversity of views, ideas and interpretations. As such, the opinions expressed in these publications must be understood as belonging to their authors alone.

Table of Contents

My heart has become capable of every form:
It is a meadow for gazelles, a monastery for monks,
A temple for idols, the Ka'ba for pilgrims,
Tablets of the Torah, the book of the Qur'an.
I follow the religion of love;
Where its camels turn, there lies
My religion, my faith.

Ibn 'Arabi, *Tarjumān al-Ashwāq*.

Preface

This volume, which is the outcome of a long period of research on Hindu-Muslim interactions that started in 1990, aspires to be an original contribution to the subject, as well as a synthesis of previous scholarly studies. I submitted my Ph.D. dissertation on the cult of Ramdev Pir among the Untouchables of Rajasthan at the Sorbonne University, Paris, in 1993, and while I was working on turning it into a book by focussing on some specific issues, adding new documents and recent field data, I realised that I was in fact investigating the fascinating issue of plural religious identities. In this way my work which, at first, may have appeared as a specialised study on folk religion, of limited interest for a broader readership, was given a new impetus. What was initially perceived by some as a marginal research project on some minor and obscure sects of north India gradually came to be linked to issues of more contemporary relevance. It was then realised that the data collected during long years of field research and the questions addressed in my subsequent publications were perfectly in tune with the recent works of scholars who were inquiring, from various other perspectives, into the problems connected with modern South-Asian societies: politics, religion and caste, nationalism and regionalism, conflicts and coexistence. And since many other contemporary societies are faced with similar problems, the task of reflecting on the shaping of religious identities in a particular historical and geographical context may ultimately help us to understand issues of universal human significance.

First of all I am indebted to Professor Azim Nanji, Dr Farhad Daftary and to all the scholars of The Institute of Ismaili Studies who encouraged me in this project after having kindly invited me to give some lectures in London.

Without my husband, Abdul Sattar Khan, who not only accompanied me during all my field trips but gave me precious information on the various local traditions that he had been observing for many years, I could not have collected so much interesting and original data.

I would also like to thank Dr. Zawahir Moir who encouraged me to continue with my research project at a time when I felt disheartened and isolated, and generously shared with me her profound knowledge of Muslim cultures, and in particular the Ismaili tradition.

Nor can I forget the constant encouragement and support given by Professor Françoise Mallison. My long discussions with Shail Mayaram were also a major stimulus for which I am grateful.

D.-S. Khan

Note on Transcription and Transliteration

Sanskrit and north-Indian vernacular words have been transliterated according to the standard system with a few simplifications that make the reading easier to non-specialists: the palatal consonant 'c' is rendered as the English ch; nasals are represented by n or m.

Diacritical marks are not used for proper nouns, including names of sects, movements, associations, political parties, etc.

Arabic and Persian words are transliterated according to a system based on that used in the new edition of the *Encyclopaedia of Islam*. However, for words that appear in the English dictionary, as well as some that are frequently used in the text, neither diacritical marks nor italics are used.

Introduction

Accustomed to perceiving Hinduism and Islam as fixed, monolithic and distinct categories, one often forgets that a long and complex historical process precedes the comparatively recent emergence of the two main religious blocs in South Asia. Indeed, popular literature and journalism tend to focus on confrontation and difference, whereas peaceful coexistence and constructive exchange make poor news.[1] Is this because positive Hindu-Muslim interactions are mere exceptions or marginal cases within a context where religious identity was defined once and for all in an ideal and remote past, resulting in the existence of perpetually rival communities?

More often than not, direct observation warns us against such general statements. Better than any theoretical discussion, an anecdote will show the complexity of the subject. The event we are going to describe took place recently and thus belongs to the landscape of modern India. The author of this work heard it from the priest of a Shiva temple located in the old bazaar of Katu Shyam, a peaceful Rajasthani village in the Jaipur area, famous as a local pilgrimage centre.

At that time a low wall separated the Hindu temple enshrining a stone lingam, the traditional symbol of Shiva, from a small mosque presumably built by the Mughal emperor Awrangzib (r.1658–1707). In front of it one could see a few graves, the main one being the *mazār* (tomb) of a fakir known as Shahid Baba or Murli Shah.

The priest of the neighbouring Hindu shrine, affiliated to the Shaiva order of Nath Jogis, told us the following story. One day, while his brother was on duty at the shrine, the priest jumped across the wall and plucked a few flowers in the open courtyard of the mosque. Having returned to the temple he prepared himself for the evening devotions, ringing the bell and offering the stolen blossoms to his deity. But suddenly, instead of the usual mantras, he started unwittingly to recite the *namāz*. Those who witnessed the scene said that he had been possessed by Shahid Baba, the pir of the neighbouring darga. Moreover, during the following days he continued to behave like a Sunni Muslim, reciting his five daily prayers and observing the corresponding rules of purity. His father understood that the Sufi saint was angry because of the robbery committed in his shrine and proposed to offer him in compensation two lemon trees. After this the priest recovered his former 'religious personality'.

The metamorphosis had lasted for a period of forty days, at the beginning of which Shahid Baba had manifested himself to the priest, saying: 'On that day if you had kept the flowers for yourself instead of offering them to Shiva (who is also Baba Adam), I would have killed you on the spot!' Curiously, an oral tradition points to the fact that initially, there was only one shrine. However, the opinion of our informants differed as to its identity: was it a Hindu or a Muslim sacred place? Visiting the same village four years later, we saw that the partition wall between the two shrines had been raised by five feet, but, interestingly, this did not prevent the children of the Hindu priests from continuing to partake regularly of the sacred offerings made to the pir of the darga or shrine.

This temporary transformation of the Hindu priest into a Muslim believer, the legend of a former united or unifying tradition, as well as the persistence of ritual exchanges between the two shrines are far from constituting isolated cases. Numerous examples could be given that would point to the artificial character of religious boundaries, as well as to their relative fragility. While describing two ritual processions which take place annually in Bihar, for example, Peter Gottschalk remarks that they differ only by the heroes they memorialise, Imam Husayn and Durga:

> Attempts to categorize these events as Muslim and Hindu demonstrate both the multiple meanings each term allows and the uncertainty which commonly accompanies their use ... Efforts at labeling such rituals as 'Islamic' or 'Hindu' often rely on unclear definitions and thus overlook the often shared identities and participation in each other's lives.[2]

How, then, can one account for the current perception of Islam and Hinduism as two monolithic, distinct and rival faiths? In the Indo-Pakistan subcontinent metaphors that view history through the oculus of Hindu-Muslim conflict are still very strong. As Carl W. Ernst has it, 'it is often assumed that the conflict between Islam and Hinduism (construed as political entities) is one of the eternal verities', one of the chief reasons being that 'the main distorting presupposition in Indian historical thinking today reads the medieval past in terms of modern religious nationalism. In this view historical events are implicitly seen as prefiguring the partition of British India into an Islamic Republic of Pakistan and an overwhelmingly Hindu Indian Union.'[3]

Although this type of ideological historiography is widespread, it has not prevented a number of more critical writers from asserting the existence of a composite culture emerging out of long-term exchanges; but if some of them go as far as viewing positive interactions as a dominant trait in South Asian history, others argue that in spite of all this the two communities have never ceased to exist as separate religious, or at least, cultural 'enclosures'. Crises, whenever they occur, always reveal the 'fault-line' between them.[4] According to this view, under the pressure of various forces such as orthodoxy, elite culture and state power, the common features that may have earlier emerged start to dissolve into conflicting units. This would prove that 'the composite culture or synthesis is fragile by nature precisely because it is unable to withstand intervention from above.'[5]

Another suggestion is that both the ideas of harmonious coexistence or perpetual hostility between Hindus and Muslims should be rejected as naïve and idealistic constructions, in so far as these communities cannot be defined a priori and once and for all; considerable changes and variations have occurred over time, whether in the form of conversions, sectarian splits or acculturation processes which prevent us from viewing their history as either the convergence or the divergence of two invariable, uninterrupted lines representing 'eternal' Hinduism or Islam.

The exponent of this theory, however, apparently still believes that the traditions represented by Islam and Hinduism, in spite of their multiple and fluctuating forms and the frequent exchanges which took place between them, have never lost their specific features.[6] Again, all these viewpoints are based on the assumption that Hinduism and Islam have always existed as relatively homogenous entities, carefully preserving separate identities.

Which of these theories is nearest to the truth? We would not hesitate to answer 'none of them'. The question seems like one of those riddles to which there is no right answer because the premise itself is false.

Let us address the issue in completely different terms. Instead of trying to decide whether Hindus and Muslims have been friends or enemies, or if they have been so alternately, one should rather ask the following questions: which Hindus have coexisted and interacted with which Muslims; which Muslims have been hostile to which Hindus; and which Hindus have regarded which Muslims as their enemies?

If we assume that religious groups are not defined once and for all, the idea of two compact and uniform blocs can be only a construct. The Hindus or the Muslims whom the question addresses are not real characters; they belong to an 'imagined community' constructed in opposition to an entity perceived as the 'indigenous Other'.[7] Such constructs, in turn, force us to address the question of identity versus alterity, and lead us to re-examine the broader issue of Self and Other – both at the individual and collective levels. Ultimately this should help us to move away from 'the taken-for-granted, naturalised categories of 'Hindus and Muslims'.[8]

If the personal story of the priest of Katu Shyam shows the complex processes that are at work in the individual psyche, at the collective level also the existence of intermediary and fluid categories have been a constant challenge to our usual bivalent line of thought. The embarrassment of the British commissioner who was entrusted with the 1881 census of Punjab may serve here to illustrate our purpose: 'the observances and beliefs which distinguish the followers of the several faiths in their purity are so strangely blended and intermingled that it is often impossible to say that one prevails rather than the other, or to decide in what category the people shall be classified'.[9]

The presence in South Asia of communities and traditions that could not easily be classified as Hindu or Muslim seemed to defy the Cartesian logic to which most Europeans adhered. How should one understand and define them? In the past, the adjective 'syncretistic' has been often used to describe these phenomena, while terms such as 'hybrid movement', 'amalgam', 'blend' or 'fusion' have been widely resorted to. The concepts of 'acculturation' and 'inculturation' were later introduced to explain how 'composite' forms of religion could emerge through mutual exchanges and influences occurring in a more or less spontaneous way.

Syncretistic traditions have been perceived positively as 'bridging the gulf' between communities. Traditionally, Sunni Sufis, Hindu yogis or ascetics and 'non-sectarian' saints and devotees have been credited with a rapprochement which is supposed to have given birth to these movements through the conscious effort of some religious reformers. Negatively, however, they were seen as forms of 'imperfect' Islam or Hinduism, spontaneous and somehow disorderly creations of the 'popular mind'. Curiously, the possible role of Ismaili Islam in this interplay has never been really explored – a gap which we will attempt to fill, at least partly, in this book.

In the *Oxford Encyclopedia of Mesoamerican Cultures*, Hugo G. Nut clearly links the concept of syncretism to folk religion which is practised, according to him, by rural and urban traditional communities. He views this phenomenon as 'interesting and often curious blends of magical and religious elements of several provenences'. Quoting other authors, he goes on to explain that the concept can be used in two ways: one can speak of 'spontaneous' and of 'guided' syncretism.[10] In other words, for him, conscious or unconscious acculturation is a phenomenon that concerns only popular religious beliefs and practices.

Another term, 'transculturation', as Robert S. Carlsen reminds us, was coined in the 1940s by the Cuban sociologist Fernando Ortiz, to describe a similar phenomenon in the same part of the world. Later this term was more widely employed thanks to the writings of Mary Louise Pratt who uses the words 'contact zones' to refer to social environments 'where cultures meet, clash, and grapple', that should also be viewed as dynamic, interpretive and expressive spaces.[11]

Here, however, this interesting concept is used exclusively to describe a discourse that reflects the victory of a dominant power over a subservient one and is perceived as a consequence of colonial rule. However, as we will see in the cases we propose to study here, such phenomena are not always associated with folk religion or conquest.

In recent scholarship other concepts have been suggested in order to account for the complexity of the so-called 'syncretistic' phenomena. Apart from being an alternative to the idea of 'syncretism', the 'border zone', 'contact zone' or 'shatter zone' concept has also provided an alternative to what scholars have called the 'sectarian trope'. In the same perspective, the concept of 'liminality' has been brought forward. The word 'liminal' (from the Latin *limen,* meaning 'threshold') had been used at first in the domain of psychology to refer to in-between structures of consciousness. Later, in his studies of religious practices, Van Gennep resorted to it in order to describe certain rites of passage. And finally Victor Turner[12] enlarged the concept to describe whatever is 'intermediary' in the form of 'bridges, gates, doorways, boundaries or social margins', liminal locations being points of intersection between the theological discourses.[13]

The success of the concept of liminality originates from the fact that it can be applied to a wide variety of human phenomena, including histories, cultures, peoples, etc. As an alternative to 'syncretism', however, it may not be fully satisfactory as it does not totally avoid a Manichaean vision and may even imply the idea of something merely transitional,[14] as it seems that ultimately a no-man's land between the boundaries or a threshold has to be crossed. In addition, the concept of liminality may not describe adequately all the phenomena related to 'syncretism' or 'composite culture'.

Tazim Kassam has conceptualised, in an original and constructive way, the striking duality or syncretic mode typical of South Asian Nizari Ismailism. She views it in the form of a 'figure-ground' which can be read as two black faces or as a white chalice according to the perspective chosen by the observer.[15] The passage to a more monolithic category would not consist in seeing one of the two heads as the 'right' one, but in perceiving their lineaments as forming an entirely new object.

Actually, in order to perceive visually phenomena that are related to the concepts of composite culture, syncretism, liminality or contact zone, one can resort to another metaphor, that of Janus Bifrons, the Roman deity who guards the doorway. He is one, although he has two faces that look in opposite directions. The threshold need not therefore be viewed only as a temporary space, a kind of limbo out of which one would eventually have to emerge to return to normality; it may be regarded as a permanent opening into a world of multiple values. It could also suggest a potential anti-structural questioning of certain fixed categories such as religious identities,[16] 'drawing upon a line of thought that emphasizes "fuzzy" thinking as an alternative to bivalent, either/or logic which has dominated the western philosophical tradition from the Greeks to the Logical Positivists'.[17]

The existence of a threshold may even become a source of revolutionary change based on the idea of 'resistance' implied in the desire to preserve one's original understanding of religion versus normative and orthodox models. Syncretic and liminal traditions or communities can be perceived as cohesive forces in the social fabric, powerful links in the uninterrupted chain of religious traditions. But as they tend to disappear as modern society shapes itself along more monolithic criteria, the open doorways between communities are gradually closed and replaced here and there by boundary walls that rise higher and higher every day. Groups endowed with a composite religious identity are threatened and often obliged to make a drastic choice. The landscape of South Asia and the fate of its inhabitants may have been different if history had not forced so many people to 'cross the threshold'.

1

Who is Hindu, who is Muslim? A Brief Historical Survey

Among Hindus the idiom of Hind is right,
Among Sindhis the idiom of Sindh is right.
Rumi

Who is Hindu, who is Muslim? This is the next question that we should address, paraphrasing a famous *ginān* of the Nizari Ismaili missionary Pir Shams.[1] The issue of religious and social identity cannot be tackled without critically examining the meaning of the words 'Hindu' and 'Muslim' which nowadays seem so unproblematic to most people.[2] The concept of identity is, of course, a recent one, whether it refers to individuals, societies or faiths. According to Harjot Oberoi, the religious identity of a particular human group should not be determined only by its formal beliefs, since it results from 'the whole historical process by which a cohesive community of believers comes to be produced, consolidated and reproduced through a cultural fusion of texts, myths, symbols and rituals with human bodies and sentiments and often under the aegis of religious personnel'.[3]

Dharma: The Law and the Other

Nowhere in the Vedas – regarded as the oldest texts of the Indo-Aryan civilization – in its later commentaries (*Brahmanas*, *Aranyakas* and *Upanishads*), in the mythology of the *Puranas*, or in the classical pan-Indian epics (*Mahabharata* and *Ramayana*) does one find terms that correspond to our 'Hinduism' and 'Hindu'.

In fact, foreigners were the first to use the word Hindu to designate a particular geographical region and its people.[4] In Sanskrit and the languages derived from it, the dialectical variants Sindhu/Hindu, which initially meant 'water stream', became a proper noun for the main river of the north-west, later translated by the Europeans as 'Indus'. The Achaemenians borrowed it and further extended its meaning to the country around the Indus. This name is mentioned in the Avesta, and Darius I, who expanded his kingdom to that river in 517 BC, also used it for the territory and its inhabitants. The term, which was adopted by the Greeks in the fifth century BC, was found also in Aramaic.[5]

In ancient and classical India no religious or ethnic meaning was attached to this word. Similarly there was no word for 'religion'. Dharma, its nearest equivalent – which would be used in modern times to translate the term 'religion' – had a much broader semantic dimension and encompassed a variety of meanings that emerged historically in different texts and contexts. In some passages of the Vedas, dharma refers entirely to the sacerdotal duties and rules associated with sacrifice. In later treatises it linked social to cosmological law. Eventually it came to refer to a particular branch of knowledge and developed an ethical aspect. In any case, it was exclusively connected with a world dominated by Brahmins and, as such, unknown to all those who, being 'outside the pale', practised other forms of religion. Theoretically, at least, the cohesive force of Vedic and post-Vedic society lay in the *varṇa* system – which should not be confused with the concept of *jāti*, or caste, described later in this essay. The *varṇa* system probably originated from the traditional division of Indo-European society into three classes corresponding in South Asia to Brahmins (priests), Kshatriyas (warriors and rulers) and Vaishyas ('others' who would later be more exclusively identified with the merchant class); the fourth *varṇa*, Shudras, included the subservient groups, mainly artisans and menials. The remaining population was later referred to by Orientalists as 'outcastes' since they were not part of the *varṇa* system which they had translated as 'caste'. At this stage it is important to specify that these four socio-ritual categories (a more adequate translation of the word *varṇa*) were not fixed entities. Initially, the three higher groups (*suvarṇa*) may have included only those who called themselves 'Aryas', but it is obvious that they gradually extended to other ethnic and cultural groups – although the convenient fiction of an 'Aryan' (Indo-European) origin was maintained throughout. Conversely, some Aryas may have been included in the fourth *varṇa* after intermarrying with non-Aryas or taking to menial tasks – as is hinted in the famous book of law entitled *Manusmṛti*. Therefore, it would be wrong to conclude that the word *varṇa* has any racial or ethnic connotation. Its literal meaning, 'colour', is to be understood symbolically, white (Brahmins) for purity, red (Kshatriyas) for war and so on.[6]

Dharma, as the divine and human law and order of the three upper *varṇas*, was opposed to *adharma* referring to disorder, chaos and injustice. Some of these rules were codified in the *Dharmashastras*. Much later, as we will see, the translation of dharma as 'law', including both social and religious law (a concept somewhat comparable to that of the Halacha in the Jewish tradition and of the sharia in Islamic thought) would have a strong influence on the legal system imposed by the British in India – and far-reaching consequences for the issue of identity which concerns us here.

In turn, the Buddhists resorted to the concept of dharma, giving it, however, a different meaning. Dharma (symbolised in literature and iconography by a wheel or *chakra*) referred to the teaching of the historical Buddha, based on his own particular vision of cosmic law and ethical philosophy. Needless to say, numerous other learned traditions and ascetic movements, among which Jainism is the best known, emerged in the Subcontinent, which can be traced back to at least the sixth or seventh century BC.

Each religious movement logically viewed itself as the one true path to salvation, referring to its teaching as *satya dharma* (the true dharma) or *saddharma*. In one particular *Upanishad*, for instance, it designates the ultimate reality, the Absolute Brahman.[7] Buddhists and Jains also referred to the message of their founders in that way. Later on, the same words will refer to the Tantric path[8] and, interestingly, the medieval Nizari Ismaili tradition of South Asia was to be mainly known as *satpanth* or *satdharm* – a name which, to this day, has remained connected with its Imamshahi branch in Gujarat and Maharashtra.

Remarkably, none of these movements distinguished itself by a specific name, defining itself only in opposition to the Other. In this way, if the Brahmins had no term to designate their followers, they had one to refer to the 'remaining ones', that is to say, to all those who were not allowed to take part in their ritual ceremonies; the *mlecchas* (literally, 'barbarians') may have been initially Dravidians, Mundas, Tibeto-Burmans, Scythians, Hunas and various other communities supposed to be of non-Aryan origin. Subsequently, it would acquire a still wider, non-ethnic meaning, applying to all those who were not part of the Brahmanical order, such as Buddhists, Jains and later on, Muslims and Europeans.

The word *dāsyu/dās* instead, as used in the *Rig Veda* (the oldest of the four Vedas), apparently designated the indigenes of the north-western plains whose religious and social practices were perceived as opposed to those codified in the Vedas and *Dharmashastras*.[9]

From the fifth century onwards, references found in the Brahmanical literature tell us that Jains were viewed as heretics. The persecution of Jain monks in medieval South India is a well-known historical event. Conversely, Jains made derogatory statements about the Brahmins and their religion was described as 'false' and 'full of lies'. While a blanket term referring to those whom we now call Hindus continued to be absent from the Brahmanical texts, Indian, Greek and Chinese Buddhist sources, as well as Jain sources, distinguished two broad categories: 'Brahmanas' and 'Shramanas'.[10] The latter were ascetics and followers of the movements that opposed the Brahmanical order, such as Buddhists, Jains, Ajivikas and others.[11] In the world of learned religions this divide was of particular significance. The dharma, as defined by the Brahmins and their followers, was indissociable from the traditional division into *varṇas*: this gave birth to the concept of *svadharma*, implying that rules and rituals were not the same for all. Belonging to a particular *varṇa* implied that one had to follow a different social and religious law that was determined once and for all by one's birth and defined in the treatises such as the *Manusmṛti*. The duties and rights of a Kshatriya (warrior), for instance, differed considerably from those of a Brahmin whose main task was connected with knowledge and rites.

Instead, the so-called Shramanas preached a universal system of ethics that did not take into consideration caste or social rank, but they were also characterised by internal diversity. Buddhism developed its distinct schools of thought, broadly known as Hinayana, Mahayana and Vajrayana, each claiming to be the right 'path', whilst the Jains divided themselves into various branches (mainly Shvetambara and Digambara), each having its particular organisation and mode of worship.[12] One can conclude from this that during the ancient and classical periods, the Brahmanas, Shramanas and others probably did not have the feeling of sharing one religion or even of belonging to a broader tradition spanning their differences.

In this way, the self-perception of the local population appears to differ considerably from the later interpretations of the Europeans, whose desire to compare local traditions with monotheistic religions such as Judaism, Christianity and Islam inevitably led to certain misconceptions and misunderstandings. During the colonial period, the tendency was to look for one Indian religion distinct from Buddhism or Jainism. But if it was easy to perceive the latter in terms which were familiar to them (these movements which had crystallised into particular religions had had a historical beginning and founder) the quest for one 'Hinduism' was to lead to very different results. The phenomenon, which belongs to a much later period, will be analysed in a subsequent chapter, but at this stage one should at least mention the existence of a modern debate which revolves around the following question: is there something which can globally be called Hinduism? While a number of scholars assert the existence from the oldest times of one 'Hinduism', others prefer to use the plural and speak of 'Hindu religions', emphasising the diversity of beliefs and practices, as well as the absence of one single religious authority and sacred book.

A long time before efforts in this direction were made – chiefly by Orientalists – the Europeans who sent their traders and adventurers to India, had divided the world into four major religious groups: Jews, Christians, 'Mahometans' and heathens, also referred to as 'gentoos'.[13] The Indian pagans, according to this perception, constituted only one particular sect among them, while for the traditional exponents of the Brahmanical dharma, as we have seen, the *mlecchas* were the 'same undifferentiated Other'.

Caste and Sect: Redefining the People

Jāt panth pūche na koi,
Hari ko bhaje so Hari ko hoi.

Kabir

'Do not ask of caste and sect, whoever sings the praise of the Lord belongs to the Lord.' This famous saying ascribed to Kabir, the great fifteenth-century saint of northern India alludes to the fact that in medieval India people were classified mainly according to the categories referred to as *jāt* or *jāti* and *panth.*

The main historical event of that period is the advent of Islam in the Subcontinent with the formation of states ruled by Muslims, first Sunni Arabs and Ismaili Fatimids in Sindh, then Turks from Central Asia, as well as the penetration of various Muslim religious figures, Sunni ulama and Sufis, Twelver Shiʿi theologians and Ismaili missionaries, later subdivided into Tayyibis and Nizaris. Colonial and, at times, post-colonial histories, in search of clear-cut religious boundaries, generally oppose what they call the 'Hindu' period to the 'Muslim' one which is followed by a 'British' (characteristically not 'Christian') period. Nationalist ideology which draws from colonial writings based on a few selected sources tends to transform history into a 'historiomachy', as Ernst has called it, where the main characters, Muslims and Hindus, are portrayed in a simplistic way, as heroes or villains.[14]

Before going further one should, once again, address the issue of terminology. At what time did the word 'Hindu' start to designate a particular religious group? Was the term 'Musulman' universally used? And if not, how were the newcomers to the Subcontinent and their converts referred to?

Following the Persians and the Greeks, Muslim writers referred to the inhabitants of the Subcontinent as Hindus, since the regions located on both sides of the Indus river were known to them as Hind and Sindh. For them all those people who were not Muslims, Jews or Christians were Hindus.[15] The designation, which was at first purely geographical, was thus broadened, without acquiring a distinct religious meaning. Hindus were not distinguished by their various sects, castes and traditions, and no effort was made to differentiate the Brahmanical classes from the indigenous *mlecchas*. Therefore the category 'Hindu' included all those whom we would define as Buddhists and Jains, as well as the followers of various non-Brahmanical traditions. '"Hindus" became a term of administrative convenience used when the Muslim rulers had to differentiate between the "believers" and the rest of the population. "Hindu" therefore referred to the "rest".'[16] Termed *dhimmī*, they were not considered as being different from the *ahl al-kitāb*, the monotheist Jews and Christians and, like them, they had a protected status. On the other hand, for the Sunni 'mainstream' theologians, the followers of the traditions which apparently derived from Islam, but did not comply with the approved canon, were called *kāfir* (unbelievers), *malāḥida* or *rāfiḍī* (heretics), without any clear attempt to distinguish between them. For instance, Ismailis are never mentioned as such, which makes it difficult to evaluate the particular role they have played in South Asian history.

So far as Hindus are concerned, according to Romila Thapar, the consciousness of being the 'amorphous subordinate other' was already a foreboding of the emergence of the modern concept of 'Hinduism'.[17] Once more, the embryonic formation of a religious identity – as we would understand it today – seems to be closely linked to the image of the Self and the Other.

The exponents of the Brahmanical dharma retaliated by including all Muslims in their equally amorphous category, *mlecchas*, whilst the word *yavana* (initially meaning 'Greek') was later introduced to refer to the foreigners among them. But precisely because the label *mlecchas* also continued to be applied to various indigenous groups that were 'outside the pale', the phenomenon should not be interpreted according to our modern criteria; for those who followed the sacred law of the 'Brahmins', the latter were not fundamentally different from the Muslims. Besides, the extreme diversity of regional traditions, religious beliefs and social customs in South Asia certainly prevented any feeling of unity among the people who did not embrace Islam.

The same could be said of the Muslims whom the modern-day Hindu fundamentalists indiscriminately perceive as 'foreigners' (*yavanas*). Surprising as it may appear at first, by 'Muslims' the British meant only those who claimed descent from the Arabian countries, Iran or Central Asia. The converted population was not taken into account although its numeric strength was obviously much greater.[18] Another word by which Sunni Muslims were designated in South Asia was 'Turk' or 'Turushka' and sometimes even 'Shaka' (Scythian), again pointing to a regional rather than a religious identity.[19] The word 'Musulman' seems to be more recent, although it appears in some devotional compositions of medieval India; but generally these are later transcriptions of older texts transmitted orally.

As reflected in various texts and inscriptions, the *jāti* category starts to play a major role in South-Asian society, although it is impossible to ascertain with accuracy in which period it crystallised. The *jāti*, which can be translated as caste or sub-caste, is an endogamous group consisting of various exogamous sub-units called *gotras* (clans). Logically, there cannot be a fixed number of castes as no *jāti* can be defined once and for all. Sects have crystallised into *jātis*, which have split into smaller exogamous units or, on the contrary, merged to form a new caste. *Jāti* is not connected with a particular religious tradition (even if it often has ritual connotations) nor with a specific region, although it does vary according to region and time. In contradistinction to the more theoretical and ritual category of *varṇa*, it can be viewed as an organic phenomenon, coinciding with an observable social reality. It does not however replace the *varṇas* which remain essential components of the Brahmanical dharma, appearing as ideal structures, abstract frameworks, pigeonholes into which the Brahmins and their followers try to include the numerous *jātis* who, in turn, may accept this classification or oppose it to claim their own distinct place in the prestigious *varṇa* system.

Although the *jāti* as a social category does not constitute a closed system, it tends to become so whenever it is successfully linked to the *varṇas*, hence the concept of *jāti* as a timeless, albeit not immovable, hierarchical structure proposed by contemporary scholars such as Louis Dumont, which enabled them to characterise Hinduism as a social and religious phenomenon.[20] They have reminded us, however, that this hierarchy can exist as a structural entity only from the point of view of those who claim to be at its top, often the exponents of the Brahmanical *dharma*. More realistically, it appears as a somewhat fragile consensus, depending on the particular balance of strength between various groups and the existence of a dominant caste in each particular region or village. Our Western vision of *jāti* is, in fact, contaminated by what we know of the *varṇa* system, and the fact that both *jāti* and *varṇa* were indiscriminately translated by 'caste' (until modern scholars started to distinguish them) has had far-reaching consequences for our understanding of the social system of South Asia.

In this respect, the existence of *jātis* among Muslims, theoretically averse to the idea of social inequality, is a significant phenomenon. The basic division between the so-called Ashrafs ('nobles', claiming to be descendants of foreign Muslims) and the Ajlafs (converts) – somewhat akin to the world vision which emerges from the *varṇa* system – did not preclude the existence of numerous Muslim endogamous *jātis*. Although, unlike the Hindu higher *jātis*, the non-Ashrafs, chiefly represented by the artisan castes, could with a few exceptions eat with the others, they were accorded at different times different positions on the social scale. This depended, among other things, upon their particular religious affiliation. For instance, the Nizari Ismailis always performed their rituals, including the partaking of sacred offerings, together, regardless of their particular caste status.[21]

The present tendency among Hindus to view all Muslims as members of one single *jāti* may be misleading. It is true that, when asked about his caste by a Hindu, a modern Muslim would simply answer 'Muslim', but when an Indian or Pakistani Muslim asks somebody about his *jāti*, he will expect another Muslim to specify the name of his caste. The same could be said of the Jains who are perceived as belonging to one particular Hindu *jāti* in spite of their own sectarian and caste divisions. In medieval South-Asian society, caste affiliation was thus a major identity marker.

Before dealing with the second term of the expression *jāt panth*, we must examine briefly the political landscape of the Subcontinent after the advent of Islam. In South Asia, as elsewhere, states have patronised religious figures and institutions which have, at various times, influenced the culture of the country, generating new syntheses and giving birth to what can be defined as 'state religions'. Non-Muslim rulers had been either combating the groups they considered to be heretics or protecting particular sects according to the historical and social context. Many kings had embraced Jainism and Buddhism which had spread to nearly the whole Subcontinent, but gradually, towards the eighth century, and the Brahmins had regained the favour of local rulers who adopted their dharma. The former legitimised the latter who, in turn, granted them land and privileges. But if temporal and spiritual power was divided between rulers and priests, the latter's control over religion was far from absolute. For instance, during the medieval period, north-Indian Rajputs who claimed to be Kshatriyas, as the descendants of gods and kings mentioned in the Epic and Puranic literature, patronised a wide range of cults and traditions, somewhat spanning the gap between the Brahmanical religion *sensu stricto* and non-Brahmanical traditions, including diverse sectarian movements, popular cults or other religious systems such as Jainism. In this way, they played the role of mediators between the upper caste culture and the low caste or even tribal ones.

At a time when Muslim rulers were building their own kingdoms and empires in the Subcontinent, they had to face not one single unified power but a large number of bigger or smaller kingdoms that were not only independent, but often hostile to one other. The diversity of Muslim rule coincided with the diversity of Hindu rule. The Delhi Sultanate failed to transform itself into one big empire and thus, between the thirteenth and sixteenth centuries, various rival, independent, Muslim-ruled territories emerged in Gujarat, Malwa and elsewhere. Even at its peak, the Mughal empire founded by Babur in 1527 did not spread to the whole of the Subcontinent. Following the short-lived Fatimid Ismaili kingdom in Sindh in the ninth century, Twelver Shiʿi states emerged in the Deccan and around Lucknow.[22] At the courts of the Sunni kings, who were the majority, both 'legalist' theologians and Sufis (some ulama were themselves Sufis) played a major role.

Can we conclude that the formation of Muslim states in South Asia led to the earliest religious conflicts, as reflected in some recent popular history books? This view does not derive from ancient local sources. It was initially rooted in the colonial discourse. Historians like Keene and Titus stressed the militant nature of Islam.[23] Conquest and conversion were linked and said to have taken place by the sword.[24] Besides, the image of the aggressive and intolerant Muslim, whose sole aim was to conquer the 'infidels' of the Subcontinent, was presented by Colonel Tod, the first European historian of India and author of *Annals and Antiquities of Rajasthan*, in opposition to the brave Hindu Rajputs whose virtues, tolerance and sense of honour he described as praiseworthy. The decline of the Rajput kingdoms was also explained by the continuous attacks of the sultans and by their later alliance with the Mughals, viewed as an act of shameful submission.[25] It may be interesting to note that Tod's book, which has recently been translated into Hindi, has met with immense success among middle-class Hindus, including those Hindu Rajputs who pose as enemies of the Muslims but are ready to close their eyes on the spurious chapters where the British Resident attributed to them a foreign origin. Tod's vision was to have a profound impact on the Hindu nationalist perception of history. According to their ideology, which has influenced the discourse of the common man today, Maharana Pratap, the sixteenth-century ruler of Mewar (an important kingdom of south Rajasthan), was a hero of 'Hindu resistance', along with the Maharatha chief Shivaji who rebelled against the Mughal emperor Awrangzib some two hundred years later. Typical clichés emerged in this way: the intolerant Awrangzib versus his brother, the apostle of unity, Dara Shukoh; the fanatic Ala al-Din Khilji (fourteenth century) against the tolerant Akbar.

However, a closer look at the documents of that period show a much more nuanced picture. Awrangzib may have adhered to a strict 'orthodoxy' and leading an austere life failed, unlike his predecessors, to encourage the fine arts; but he also gave donations to various Hindu religious orders and to Brahmins. He never attempted to convert the Rajput kings who were his faithful allies and he admired the strong character of his main ally, Maharaja Jai Singh of Jaipur, to whom he gave the honorific title 'Sawai' (literally, 'one and a half'), proudly held by all his successors to the present day. Akbar did take a deep interest in other religions and cultures, but this did not prevent him attacking the ruler of Mewar, a southern kingdom of Rajasthan, ruthlessly destroying the fortress of Chittor and killing most of its inhabitants.

It is not difficult to demonstrate that battles between Muslim and Hindu rulers were mostly fought over territory and power rather than religious issues. The eleventh-century Turkish conqueror, Mahmud of Ghazna, is often viewed as a hero or villain symbolising the victory of Islam over Hinduism, but sources from his own time show that 'his raids on temples were motivated more by lust of gold, slaves and jewels than by intolerance of idolatry'.[26] In his case, Islam served to legitimate his regime and conquests, securing thus the support of the ulama.

Regarded by Hindu nationalists as the protector of Hinduism against Islam, the rebellious Maharana Pratap, was helped by a considerable army of Muslim Pathans, noblemen of Afghan origin, as well as by the Sufi Suhrawardi qadis (judges) of Roll, a village near Nagaur.[27] Similarly Akbar did not directly fight his adversary but sent for this purpose his faithful ally and commander-in-chief, Man Singh, the Hindu ruler of Amber kingdom.

The Mughal-Rajput alliance was instrumental in the development of the strategic region later referred to as Rajasthan. Most Rajput states grew into rich, powerful and prestigious kingdoms. Their rulers, who had acquired considerable wealth during the campaigns, fought on behalf of the Mughals, and drew inspiration largely from the Mughal courts without abandoning their own religious and social practices. Indeed, the encounter between these Muslim and Hindu elites created a refined culture which included architecture, painting, music and literature. Mughal and Rajput art, for instance, have wrongly been termed

'Muslim' and 'Hindu' by a number of writers for whom the entire history of that period is based on the Hindu/Muslim sectarian trope. In fact, Hindu artists were employed at the Mughal court and Muslim ones worked in the Rajput palaces. Hindu epic and mythological scenes are to be found in Mughal painting, in the same way that Turko-Persian elements became an integral part of Rajput architecture. This synthesis continues in the modern period. Even the Hindu nationalist Birla recently built his Institute of Technology in the style of Rajput/Mughal palaces inspired by the *liwan* (entrance gate) of Persian mosques.

It is, therefore, clear that the expressions 'Mughal' and 'Rajput' styles are indicative of patronage and do not have any religious connotations. On the whole, Muslim rulers were much closer to the Hindu ruling classes than the latter were to the low caste and indigenous groups who, in turn, were closer to the artisan communities converted to Islam.

The repressive measures taken by some Muslim rulers against indigenous kings or nobles and even their occasional attempts at conversion were aimed at punishing the rebels. Their primary motivations were not religious but political.[28] Interestingly, as Ernst has reminded us, religion-based expeditions – although the underlying motive was still booty – were directed mostly against Muslim groups considered as heretics. We would add that the Ismailis who, organisationally, were the strongest among them, most probably constituted the main targets of their attacks.[29]

Similarly, the alleged 'resistance' organised by some Hindu rulers was not in defence of 'Hinduism' – a concept which in a 'monolithic' form was non-existent at that time – but was motivated by the desire for independent power. Whenever alliances were considered to be profitable, as for example in the case of Rajputs and Mughals, inter-caste marriages were not banned. From the time of Jahangir onwards (that it is to say, from the beginning of the seventeenth century) Mughal emperors were the offspring of Akbar's Rajput wife. Actually Rajput rulers considered that they belonged to the same *jāti* as the Mughal.[30]

All these interactions have sometimes been perceived as giving birth to a 'composite' cultural model, whereas those who wish to emphasise the divide between Hinduism and Islam often declare that the desecration of temples by Muslim soldiers at various times in history has been a trauma from which the Hindus have not yet recovered. For instance, the destruction of the Somnatha shrine in Gujarat by Mahmud Ghazni, an event that occurred in 1026, has become a symbol of all the so-called 'humiliations' suffered by a people portrayed as innocent, and intrinsically mild and tolerant. As Thapar has it:

> This would certainly have been traumatic. But the question arises as to which Hindus were thus traumatised? For the same temple now entered by *mleccha* soldiers was in any case open only to the caste Hindus and its sanctum would have been barred from the larger population consisting of the indigenous *mleccha*. The feeling of the latter was of little concern to the caste Hindus who worshipped at these temples. The trauma was therefore more in the nature of the polluting of the temple rather than the confrontation on any substantial scale with another religion.[31]

Ritual pollution was indeed a concept entirely alien to the non-Brahmanical religions. As stated in the *Dharmashastras*, for example, for the higher castes and for all those who at various times have adopted their dharma, the slightest damage done to a stone image renders it unfit for the cult. Hundreds of broken statues (*murtis*) and parts of temples have thus been discarded in different sites. Nonetheless, the practitioners of folk religions who do not share this belief regularly gather these broken fragments under a sacred Banyan or Pipal tree in order to worship them in their own fashion.

The 'which Hindus, which Muslims' question is, therefore, essential for a proper understanding of religious identities in South Asia.

Thapar has also shown that the present perception of the Somnatha raid was shaped only during the late colonial period,[32] the first recorded mention of the debate having been made in 1943, in the House of Commons in London. Examining thoroughly the various sources which refer to this event (Hindu, Muslim and Jain) she concludes that, in reality, perceptions vary widely according to the time and the author. For instance, one learns from a Somnatha inscription dated 1264 (in both Arabic and Sanskrit) that a Muslim trader has acquired land from some neighbouring temples with the approval of Hindu priests – an event which happened only 200 years after the raid. In turn, the Jains show some interest in the event for entirely different reasons. For them the destruction of the sacred site of the 'Brahmanas' proves the superiority of their religion, since their own shrines were spared.

Besides, one should not forget that many Hindu rulers themselves did not hesitate to demolish temples to loot their wealth. King Harsha of

Kashmir is a famous example,[33] but there are many others. The shrines built by the Jains – in spite of their proud declarations – were often desecrated by rulers who transformed them into Hindu places of worship. Similarly Hindu kings, such as the famous fifteenth-century Maharana Kumbha of Mewar, did not hesitate to demolish a number of mosques. R.V. Somani says of the deeds of Maharana Kumbha: 'Kumbha after capturing it (Chanderi) successfully carried out depredations and collected a large amount. He, at the same time, had demolished several mosques and palaces'.[34] Richard M. Eaton explores this issue taking into consideration the political and economical motives: 'Which temples were desecrated in India's pre-modern history? When, and by whom? How, and for which purpose?'[35] As he himself concludes, this approach will facilitate a responsible and constructive discussion that this controversial subject needs. As a whole, the recently published volume contains remarkable contributions to the issues raised here.

It is necessary to insist on the fact that the destruction or desecration of shrines was not primarily motivated by religious considerations. The aim was to acquire wealth or to assert one's military superiority. This is also true for the modern period. Although 'Operation Blue Star' launched under Indira Gandhi's rule in 1984 has sometimes been regarded as a religious offensive, it is obvious that the attack on the Amritsar Golden Temple was a purely political move.

Those who claim the existence of a single Hindu religion view the numerous traditions and schools of thought which cannot be classified, such as Jain or Buddhist, as mere branches of Hinduism, on the model of Christian sects. But even if the different sects, cults and traditions have influenced each other and share common traits, does it prove that they are mere divisions within one religion? Following this argument one could come to the strange conclusion that Islam is a sect of Judaism or Christianity since the Prophet Muhammad established his new message by borrowing some elements from the old Semitic religions (the name 'Allah' for example) and was deeply inspired by the Hebraic and Christian scriptures and customs. Of course, the use of the singular expression 'Hindu religion' (coinciding with the modern *Hindu dharm*) or of the plural 'Hindu religions' is ultimately a question of vocabulary, depending on our definition of the concept of 'religion'. What is important for us here is to try to grasp the huge diversity that characterises the religious beliefs and practices prevalent in medieval India.

In the world of indigenous traditions, along with the Brahmanical dharma, the local/regional cults and caste or family religions continued to develop independently, although not necessarily in isolation, among certain low-caste, Untouchable and tribal communities, whilst distinct traditions were founded by learned spiritual masters (gurus, *āchāryas*). These were generally referred to as *sampradāys* (Sanskrit *sampradāya*). The term *sampradāy*, meaning 'what is handed down' (tradition or transmission) will in modern times acquire a broader meaning, as the equivalent of our word 'religion' (*hindū sampradāy*).[36] To translate it as 'sect' can be misleading, because the word in its Western use, conveys the meaning of dissent and heterodoxy. The Vallabha *sampradāy* or *Puṣṭimārg*, for instance, founded in the sixteenth century, claims to follow the old Brahmanical dharma, and so does the much older *sampradāy* founded by Shankara in the eighth century.[37] According to Daniel Gold, the word *sampradāya* refers to a Brahmanic movement, whereas to designate the non-Brahmanic traditions the term *panth* is used.[38] This seems to be contradicted, however, by the fact that the Virashaiva movement founded in twelfth-century Karnataka refers to itself as *sampradāy*, although it openly goes against the Brahmanical dharma, advocating radical social change and forbidding image worship.[39]

But if the term *sampradāy* seems to have a wider range of meanings, the word *panth* is definitely connected with traditions 'that were not able to find their roots in the Veda'.[40] *Panth*, which means literally 'path' also implies a *paramparā*, or transmission from guru to disciple and, when connected with the Sant movement (*sant mat*), is also referred to as *sant panth*. Among them the fifteenth- and sixteenth-century Kabīr, Nānak and Dādū *panths* are the most famous. Preceding the emergence of the 'path of the saints', the Nāth *panth* had gradually crystallised into various orders connected with Tantrism and yoga. Besides, within certain traditions the word *panth* serves to designate secret rituals that can only be performed by initiates (Kuṇḍā *panth*, Bīsā and Dasā *panth*).[41]

At the same time we see that the term *mārg* (way) is used with a wide variety of meanings. *Puṣṭimārg* (the path of grace) refers to the *sampradāy* founded by Vallabha, *Vāmmārg* to the left-handed Tantric tradition as a whole and *Kanchlīmārg* to a particular Shaktic-Tantric ritual. It seems, therefore, useless to attempt to draw a sharp line of demarcation between the words *mārg*, *sampradāy* or *panth*. Suffice it to say that all these denominations point to the existence of numerous guru-disciple lineages, each proposing a different path to salvation, through a distinct system of beliefs and practices.

Both *sampradāy*s and *panth*s or *mārg*s are often connected to a particular religious current referred to as *bhakti*. The advent of Islam is often seen as the major cause of the emergence of this devotional movement focused on the worship of a personal God with or without qualities (*sagūṇ* or *nirgūṇ*) and on an essentially emotional approach to religion. It flourished in the northern part of the Subcontinent, roughly from the beginning of the fourteenth century onwards – although it started much earlier in the south, having older roots in the *Bhagavad Gita*.[42]

Some have perceived the *bhakti* current of north India as a reaction and a resistance movement against the threat of Islam. By creating a greater solidarity and allowing more devotees to participate in religious gatherings, irrespective of their caste, and regional or family traditions, it is assumed that the *bhakta*s enabled many 'Hindus' to escape conversion. But once more, this theory is based on recent perceptions of 'Hinduism' and 'Islam' as two homogenous blocs and on the colonial myth of forcible conversions.

The constant obsession with finding one main characteristic common to most Hindu traditions which could be the basis of a religion called 'Hinduism' had led most scholars to believe that *bhakti* was a single and uniform religious current with minor variants. A detailed analysis of the texts ascribed to the different exponents of *bhakti* and of the sects which derived from it would show to what extent this is erroneous. Surdas and Tulsidas, for instance, do not share the same ideals, while Raidas, the Untouchable saint, and Mira Bai (in spite of later attempts to connect them through a *guru-śiṣya paramparā* or master-disciple transmission) have understood religion in distinct terms. In our opinion, however, if any broad distinction should be made within the medieval *bhakti* tradition, it is not, as most scholars have it, between its *nirgūṇ* form (devotion to a formless God without image worship) and its *sagūṇ* form (image-worship including temple cult), but rather between the movements which take into account exclusively indigenous elements and those which incorporate Muslim beliefs or practices. In this respect a careful study of the evolution of the *panth*s which emerged after Kabir, Dadu and Nanak would be essential for our understanding of the religious identities in South Asia.

Those three *bhaktas* referred to as Sants – along with other less-known figures – should be distinguished from the remaining *nirgūṇ* saints, precisely because the religious message expressed in their poetry is not only initially non-sectarian, but transcends what modern authors see as 'the Hindu-Muslim divide' or 'cultural faultlines'. It is to their teaching that various scholars have attached the label 'syncretism' which, whenever it was perceived as positive and creative, was termed 'synthesis'.

For this reason, many think that the *panths* that emerged, for example, after Kabir and Dadu, were founded against their will. These two religious figures are generally regarded as non-sectarian, while the *panths* associated with their names are viewed as later developments which distort or even contradict their original teaching. After having examined in detail the phenomenon of 'liminal' sects and communities, we will see that this opinion, shared by a majority of scholars, does not necessarily reflect the complex historical reality.

At present we will limit ourselves to tracing alternative definitions of the words 'Hindu' and 'Muslim' in the *Sant paramparā* as markers of identity. Partly contradicting the opinion of some authors like Thapar, Frykenberg and von Stietencron,[43] Wagle attempts to prove the existence of a strong awareness of Hindu/Muslim difference in sixteenth-century Maharashtra – a supposed gulf which the local Sants like Eknath tries to bridge. As an example he quotes the interesting composition attributed to this poet, entitled *Hindū-Turk Samvād* (Debate between a Hindu and a Turk).[44] Similarly, one finds in the poetry of Kabir, Dadu and Nanak the Hindu/Turk dichotomy, also present in the devotional songs of less-known sectarian traditions of Rajasthan, Gujarat, Sindh and Punjab, such as the Mahamarg, Barmati, Bishnoi, Jasnathi and Ai *panths*.[45]

It would be useless to deny that these words, as used by the above-mentioned Sants, point to some kind of radical difference and are indeed categories of a binary type. But once more we fall prey to our modern prejudice in concluding that they cover the same range of semantic values as in present days.

Let us have a closer look at the *Hindū-Turk Samvād*. Eknath observes that the Turk terms the Hindu *kāfir*(unbeliever) while the Hindu expresses his fear of being 'polluted' by the Turk. The Turk then characteristically addresses his adversary as 'Brahmin' and the Hindu defines his opponent as 'devoting five times a day only to God' which clearly points to his 'orthodox' Sunni affiliation.[46] For the Turk, Hindus are those who revere the Vedas and the *Shastras* (sacred scripture supposed to be based on the former), perform image worship, follow the sadhus and observe caste rules connected with purity and pollution, referred to as *jāti dharma*. Apart from the fact that one does not find the expression *Hindū dharma* which is replaced by *Maharashtra dharma*, it is obvious that although the term 'Hindu' is in this context something more than a vague geographical designation, it refers exclusively to the upper-caste Brahmanical dharma current that flourished in medieval South Asia. Similarly, Kabir addresses himself to pandits (learned Brahmins), sadhus (ascetics) and qadis (Sunni judges).[47]

Additional evidence can be drawn from a poem ascribed to Gorakhnath, one of the alleged founders of the Nath *panth* (thirteenth century?) where the author, very much like Jambha, founder of the Bishnoi *panth*, distinguishes between the categories 'Hindu', 'Musulman' and 'Jogi', the latter referring to a member of the Nath tradition, thus clearly not classified as 'Hindu'. In an interesting text of the Kabirpanthi tradition, which is in the form of the debate between Raidas and Kabir, both Sants quarrel and abuse each other by pointing to their low origin. Raidas says to this rival: '*Terī māī turaknī, terā bāp julāhā*' (Your mother is a Turk, your father is from the Julaha or weaver community). And Kabir replies: 'Your mother is a Chamar (Untouchable leather-worker), your father is a Chamar.'[48] In the first utterance 'Turk' is distinguished from 'Julaha', although we would classify both as Muslim communities (like his adversary Raidas, Kabir never refers to himself as Turk but as Julaha). Now, Julaha is the name of a *jāti* and not of a *panth* or *sampradāy*. Although ultimately it is not known which religion was followed by Kabir's family, one can at least infer that his tradition was, at that time, considered to be different from that of the 'Turks' or Ashraf Sunni Muslims. In the same way, although his poetry and tradition do not incorporate any Islamic elements, Raidas is not labelled a Hindu, but a Chamar, and seems to have a distinct identity. Consequently, during that period, social and religious categories (*jāt-panth*) do not appear as watertight compartments but tend to overlap.

As in the case of the term 'Hindu' applied exclusively to the

Brahmanical upper castes, the category 'Turk' then appears to have been restricted to the higher class Ashraf Sunni Muslims strictly adhering to the sharia. Consequently, if the words 'Hindu' and 'Turk' do refer to the followers of particular and 'opposed' or contrasting religions, they are certainly not used for the entire population; instead, they can be viewed as 'extremes' in the religious continuum of South Asia, something comparable to blue and red in the colour spectrum.

The image of the spectrum, as we will see further, will seem more relevant than the binary opposition of 'black and white', because of the existence of 'intermediary shades'. During the medieval period, if 'Hindu' and 'Turk' or 'Musulman' point to those easily contrasted and defined extremes of the spectrum – which evidently appear as antagonistic – it seems that the identity of the remaining groups remains 'fuzzy' or vague.

If the controversy about the existence or the essence of 'Hinduism' is a comparatively recent one, the scholarly debate concerning the religion founded by the Prophet Muhammad, although not new, tends to be ignored or downplayed by historians and anthropologists. Since it could be unambiguously defined as one religion with a historical founder and a sacred book, it has sometimes been surmised that there existed one 'true' Islam and that all other forms and sects should be regarded as 'dissident' or 'heterodox' movements. For Aziz Esmail:

> ... each sect or school of thought took it for granted that it was the only true understanding of Islam. In fact it was not presented as an 'interpretation' (for which term, in this general sense, there is in any case, no Arabic equivalent). For the relativity implied in this term is a modern conception. Each school presented its doctrine as the truth, with a supporting rationalisation, and a polemical refutation of its antagonists ... Throughout the history of Islam, a pluriform rather than uniform culture has been characteristic of the reality of Muslim societies.[49]

If our present vision of Hinduism is the result of a complex evolution, so is the image of one 'orthodox' or 'universal' Islam. Farhad Daftary, among others, has shown that this conception has mainly been the construct of Orientalists basing themselves exclusively on the writings of Sunni theologians.[50] Instead, according to Esmail, 'what many textbooks on Islam assume to be the standard definition of Islam is by and large an uncritical assumption. It assumes an orthodoxy when, in fact, the orthodox definition was the outcome of a long historical process.'[51] Islam is not a 'closed' and 'finished' system; its extreme diversity regarding both time and region has been amply demonstrated.

Although the Muslim rulers of South Asia had been mainly Sunnis officially associated with the learned ulama, the diversity of Islam continued to be an important factor. Sufism, of course, played a major role in modifying their perspective. And, if we can talk of the various *panths* flourishing within the indigenous tradition, one should also mention the existence of different Sufi orders or *ṭarīqa*s and remark that this term, like *panth*, also means 'path' or 'way'.

However, one should avoid thinking of Sufism and Sunni 'orthodoxy' in terms of two contrasting or opposing categories, as has too often been the case. There were actually a great variety of doctrines and attitudes among the Sufis themselves. For example, a number of Sunni mystics may have had a spiritual interpretation of Islam as the 'inner religion', and at the same time presented themselves as guardians of a certain orthodoxy at the court of local rulers. A few Sufis were also ulama and their idea of Islam may have led them to fight those whom they regarded as heretics; this could be contrasted with the position of other shaykhs or pirs who kept a neutral position or even attempted to engage into some sort of dialogue with the 'heterodox' groups.[52]

There were also many groups of Qalandars, or wandering dervishes, some of them of the so-called *beshar* type that did not follow – as their name indicates – the Sunni sharia.[53] The fact that the fakirs of the Malang, Rifa'i and Madari orders appeared more similar to Hindu ascetics than to other Sufis may, however, be misleading. One should not forget the existence of similar groups in countries other than India.

Finally, if the Shi'a were probably always a minority in the Subcontinent, one should not underestimate the influence they have exerted in various domains. Among them the Ismailis, in particular the followers of its Nizari branch, deserve particular attention. While it cannot be doubted that their religion was Islamic by origin and nature, its distinct system of belief as well as the historical circumstances in which it developed led to a considerable rapprochement with the indigenous communities. If Nizari Ismailism – owing to its philosophy and organisation – is at present viewed as a *ṭarīqa* of the Shi'i-Sufi type, it appears to have already been the case in medieval India. Most Sunni rulers and the Sufis who stayed at their courts have attempted to eliminate or convert them. Thus to avoid persecution, the Ismailis have resorted to the Shiʿi practice of *taqiyya*, or precautionary dissimulation of their true beliefs. Even at the time when it had spread to many parts of the Subcontinent and had a strong organisation with its main seat at Ucch-Multan, the Ismailis lived as discreetly as possible and mostly as 'separate pockets of followers'.[54] Due to its particular encompassing nature, it could have appeared as one of the numerous indigenous *panths* which had emerged during the medieval period. As such it was often called *satpanth* or *satya panth* in a more Sanskritised form (literally, the 'true path'). This reminds us of the fact that for a very long time Ismailism – even before its division into various branches – had been referred to, among other names, as *dīn al-ḥaqq*.[55] Similarly, if the name '*satpanth*' was regarded as a translation of the other Arabic denomination *Ṣirāṭ al-muṣtaqīm*, one should not forget that in the South-Asian context it was but another form of the old formula *satya dharma* or *saddharma* (true dharma) which, as we have seen, was used by nearly all the exponents of rival indigenous movements. It is easy to conclude, at this stage, that we have a remarkable point of intersection between Islamic traditions and original religions of the Subcontinent.

There is also reason to believe that the Nizari Ismailis who had to conceal their faith under vague denominations such as *satpanth*, also appeared outwardly as the followers of distinct sects, such as the Nizar Dharm or Mahamarg, the Prahlad (or Bishnoi) *panth*, the Barmati, Jasnathi and Ai *panths*.[56]

Besides, the South-Asian Nizari converts had kept their *jāti* affiliations (often linked with specific professional activities) which were also convenient for concealing their actual religious identity. Some of these communities, such as the Bishnois for instance, came to form a caste-cum-sect group, whereas the Jasnathis, as members of a particular *panth*, still consist in various endogamous sub-*jātis* which, due to their particular religious affiliation, do not intermarry with their caste fellows following various Hindu traditions.

Until recent times, certain communities, now openly recognised as Nizari Ismailis, appeared as separate *panths* or as *jāti* groups, a fact which has led many writers unfamiliar with the Ismaili tradition to believe erroneously that all Khojas, Shamsis, Maulais, etc., were members of distinct branches or sects.[57] Recently, the term 'Agakhani Khoja', initially applying to only one particular caste group of South-Asian

Nizaris, has come to refer to all of them. In turn, shifting religious allegiances have split the Khoja *jāti* into two groups, a Muslim group including 'Agakhanis', Sunnis and Twelver Shiʿa on the one hand, and a Hindu group including Hindu Aryasamajis and Swaminarayanis on the other.[58] Actually, conversions and changing *jāt-panth* identities have been dominant features in the history of the Subcontinent.

In the subsequent chapters we will attempt to throw some light on the particular role played by the Ismailis in medieval and modern South Asia and on their relationship with various religious traditions and social groups – phenomena that have remained to this day largely unexplored.

This chapter may be concluded by recalling that the formation of religious identities in South Asia was a long and intricate process. Sometimes merged with social categories, they were neither fixed nor sharply defined entities. Besides, the many changes that occurred over time should not be perceived exclusively in terms of 'conversions' or 'shifting identities'. They may also have had to do with the reinforcement of notions such as 'orthodoxy' versus 'heterodoxy', as well as with the much later emergence of the concepts of 'great' and 'little' traditions.

2

'There is no Hindu, there is no Musulman': Standing on the Threshold

I am neither Hindu nor Muslim.
Bullhe Shah, *Kāfī*, 153

'There is no Hindu, there is no Musulman.' This astonishing declaration of Guru Nanak, which symbolises the emergence of Sikhism as a new path to salvation in the fifteenth century, and the still more surprising utterance of Bullhe Shah, the eighteenth-century Sunni Sufi saint of Punjab: '*hindū nā nahī musulmān*' (I am neither Hindu nor Muslim) – actually an echo of Kabir's words – may serve as an introduction to this chapter.[1]

After having briefly examined the social/religious categories prevalent in medieval India, which were mostly determined by the combined categories *jāti-panth/ṭarīqa*, and ascertained the meanings of the words 'Hindu', Turk and Musulman, in that particular context, we will draw attention to the interface between Hindu and Islamic communities in traditions past and present. In doing so, instead of the usual image of two distinct blocs, we will picture on the one hand the wide spectrum of Hindu/indigenous religions, and on the other the rich continuum of Islamic traditions which gradually penetrated into the Subcontinent from the eighth century onward. The Hindu-Muslim interface should not, however, be viewed as the convergence of two fixed straight lines, but rather as the encounter between various fluctuating sets of lines representing the religious movements which have their historical roots either in the Muslim countries (prior to the penetration of Islam in South Asia) or the Indian subcontinent.

Colonial and sometimes post-colonial writers tend to view this encounter as one single phenomenon indiscriminately labelled 'hybrid cults', 'syncretism', 'symbiosis' or 'composite culture'. A careful study would instead reveal the existence of distinct modes of interactions that have different causes and sometimes quite opposite consequences.[2] A tentative classification does show that if we want to understand the phenomenon in all its complexity, these modes must be carefully distinguished, even if they can be, at times, closely connected.

During the colonial and even post-colonial periods, encounters between Islamic and indigenous religious cultures were believed to occur exclusively at the level of 'popular' beliefs and practices; more recently, scholars' attention has been drawn to the active exchanges which took place between Bhaktas, Jogis and Sufis and are supposed to have led to mutual borrowings. What scholars believe to be Sufi influence has been traced, for instance, in the Nath *panth*, while the impact of the latter on some Sufi poets and saints has been brought to light. In this way it has been shown that points of intersection were also to be found at a higher level, connected with learned poets and mystics.

Yet little attention has been paid to the specific role that the Nizari branch of Ismailism, itself a particular tradition within Shi'i Islam, may have played in the Subcontinent. This is obviously due to the lack of Ismaili written sources referring to that period and to that part of the world,[3] and scholars having drawn nearly exclusively from 'official' Sunni, often medieval and post-medieval, Sufi records. In these documents Ismailism is altogether absent or, at least, never mentioned as such. One can only find allusions to various groups globally labelled heretics (*malāḥida, rāfiḍī*, etc), between whom no clear distinction is made. Actually, until the middle of the nineteenth century, if one relies exclusively on written documents, it would be no exaggeration to say that Nizari Ismailism was, from the point of view of written history, a nonentity.

The general opinion among scholars, who base their judgement on the size of the present Nizari Ismaili community globally, is that having always been a minority in South Asia, it can have played only a negligible part in the social and religious fabric of the Subcontinent. The fact is that most specialists of South-Asian Islam have a scanty knowledge of the Ismaili tradition, while very few specialists of Ismailism are familiar enough with the Indo-Pakistani context.[4] Another reason is that Ismaili studies in the Indo-Pakistani area have been nearly always limited to Khoja traditions (mainly to their literature referred to as *ginā̄ns*). We know that the term 'Khoja' initially applied to one particular community, namely a group of Lohanas, a merchant caste said to have been converted by the fifteenth-century Ismaili missionary (*dāʿī*) Pir Sadr al-Din. The traditions of other converted groups (whether they now claim Ismaili origin or not), such as the Shamsis, Maulais, Imamshahis, Barmatis, Nizarpanthis, etc., have remained largely unexplored,[5] a common presupposition being that the Khoja heritage represents in itself the whole tradition of Indian Nizari Ismailism, and that communities can be proved to be, or to have been, Ismaili only if they openly declare this affiliation. Obviously, the role played by the complex phenomenon referred to as *taqiyya* or precautionary dissimulation – resorted to extensively by persecuted Shiʿi communities – has been largely ignored or underestimated.

In fact, a detailed study would reveal that Ismaili elements are present in a particular configuration in the rituals, literature and organisation of a number of South-Asian communities, who may not admit openly, at present, any former connection with them. If those elements cannot be considered as definite proofs, they should certainly be regarded as 'traces', pointing to the greater significance that Ismailism may have had in the past and, in particular, to the role it has played in the Hindu-Muslim interface.[6] The main difficulty lies, of course, in trying to distinguish the specific influence of the Ismailis from that of other Islamic (mainly Sufi) and non-Islamic traditions.

A careful analysis of the different ways in which Hindus and Muslims have interacted will enable us not only to make such a distinction, but also to shed new light on the issue of religious identities in South Asia.

Interactions of this type could be classified as two broad categories, the first including modes of 'alliances', 'sharing' and 'borrowing', and the second referring to a process which may be termed 'overlapping', that is connected with 'liminal' traditions and communities. We will illustrate these modes through a few carefully selected examples and attempt to see their bearing on the issue of religious identities.

Alliances: Protecting, Healing and Being the Other

Protecting or healing the Other in a specific ritual context can be regarded as a sacred covenant struck between two different communities. Recently, an interesting phenomenon has attracted the attention of social anthropologists and historians of religion. Practically all over the Subcontinent one finds Hindu and Jain shrines guarded by Muslim saints or martyrs whose graves are generally located at the entrance or on the periphery of the sacred site. A local tradition often accounts for the presence of a Muslim shrine in a non-Islamic sacred complex.

Little known as it is outside of its own region, the legend of an anonymous mystic of Kalawad (in Saurashtra, modern Gujarat), simply referred to as 'Pir Baba', provides a good illustration of this phenomenon, The saint is said to have prevented, through his miraculous intervention, the destruction of a temple to Shitala Mata, the goddess of smallpox, at the hands of the fourteenth-century Malik Kafur who was commanding the army of the sultan of Delhi, Ala al-Din Khilji. His darga is located in the vicinity of the Hindu shrine and the sacred alliance has given birth to a particular tradition: the service of the temple is performed jointly by a Hindu and a Muslim priest.[7]

Belief in the healing or prophetic power of some sacred figures also helps people to transcend religious barriers. Both Muslim and non-Muslim devotees continue to flock to the famous darga of Shakarvar Shah at Narhar in Rajasthan to seek a cure from possession by evil spirits, while others go to the Hindu shrine of Mehndi Balaji, within the same state, for a similar purpose.

The contemporary case of a female Hindu devotee of Rajasthan claiming to be endowed with healing powers when possessed by Pir Baba, identified with the son of Imam Husayn, paralleled by the story of a Muslim woman of the same village whose body and mind are regularly inhabited by the spirit of a goddess, are other examples of the same phenomenon.[8] People belonging to different religious communities come to seek their help, regardless of the outward religious affiliation of the healer. As Shail Mayaram has shown, 'possession demolishes a series of dichotomies, and among them that of appearance-reality', compelling us to 'renegotiate the taken-for-grantedness of the distinction between Self and the Other'.

A case drawn from my own fieldwork will provide another example. While grazing a herd of goats in the vicinity of a famous darga located in the city of Malpura, south of Jaipur, a young Hindu belonging to one of the former-Untouchable castes used to partake of the sacred offerings that were made to the tomb by various devotees. One day he was possessed by the pir who, through his medium, expressed his wish to appoint him as his *sevak* (attendant of the shrine). Annoyed, the young boy's family asked the saint to forgive them if their son could not abide by his request. Pir Baba consented, but declared that he would continue to possess the boy unless he came to his darga once a month to make sacred offerings. Once settled in Jaipur the young Hindu made regular visits to the shrine of the Muslim saint. But when his work prevented him from doing so, the pir immediately possessed him; his whole body was shaken and he seemed to be in a state of mental confusion. But if five elders (of whichever community) were present, they could control the situation, ask questions and hear predictions uttered from his lips.

Let us now briefly examine the cases described above from the point of view of identities. Alliances struck for protection are generally connected with the belief in one single 'power' whose 'religious identity', as we would have it now, is of no concern to the devotees. The faith in supernatural deeds performed by sacred figures during their life and after their death (called respectively *baraka* and *parchā* in Islamic and indigenous traditions) has been somewhat linked with the belief in spirits which is by no means a privilege of the Indian indigenous traditions. In folk religion the dead pir who remains all-powerful is easily identified with the nearly homophonic *vīr*/*bīr* (spirit of a deceased hero, saint or a deity like Bhairava and Hanuman). Besides, the fact that Hindus sometimes resort to the help of Muslim pirs to protect their shrines, to effect a cure or to grant them a boon, must not be regarded as different from the numerous cases where, for instance, members of the higher caste (Brahmanical) communities require the assistance of lower caste shamans and exorcists. In such cases it may be said that a 'divine covenant' is made between the two parties, but both retain their respective identities which – it should be repeated – before the nineteenth century at least, is to be seen as connected with a particular sectarian or caste tradition rather than globally as 'Hindu' or 'Muslim'.

The cases of possession we have examined under the same heading lead us, however, to somewhat different conclusions. A Hindu devotee who is possessed by a Pir Baba does not only strike an alliance with him, the fact that he lets his body and mind be temporarily inhabited by a power belonging to a different system of beliefs, leads us to question, to a certain extent, the idea of personality and personhood. Undoubtedly 'possession suggests how corporeality is envisaged as a permeable site' and shows how 'body boundaries are rendered fluid'.[9]

This is perfectly illustrated by the story of the young Hindu goatherd mentioned above.

However, the cases described by Mayaram have a particular configuration and specific historical background which should not be ignored. Both female shamans described by her belong to the Mer caste, one of the communities which we would term 'liminal', and whose two main sections, Merats and Rawats (now respectively claiming to be Muslims and Hindus) appear to be the result of a later division. Even now, as confirmed by the phenomena described earlier, the Mers – whether Rawat or Merat – have a common heritage which includes indigenous and Islamic elements.

In the Introduction we had told the story of a Shaivite priest possessed by the Shahid Baba of a neighbouring shrine. The power of the pir asserted itself over his body and mind not to punish him for having encroached on his territory – as could be wrongly surmised – but to convince him that he had committed a wrong deed in stealing the flowers. The ease with which the Nath yogi assumed a Muslim personality (in this case that of a sharia-abiding Sunni) and relinquished it after a few weeks reveals the same 'permeability' as well as the fragile and artificial nature of the so-called Muslim/Hindu 'cultural faultline'. But, here also, the 'original' identity of the tradition is unclear. Legend has it that before the boundary wall was raised, there was but one sacred site at Katu Shyam. Was it a Hindu temple, as the Naths claim, or a darga as the Muslim caretakers claim? The difficulty we have in answering this question only shows that we are unable, at present, to understand the historical meaning of 'liminal' identities.

Consequently, the cases of the Mer healers and of the possessed priest of Katu Shyam rather point to an 'overlapping' process through which so-called 'syncretic' traditions and communities have emerged.

Sharing Sacred Time and Space

The 'divine covenant' that binds together two spiritual powers implies the human alliance of supposedly distinct communities but also points to another mode of interaction which I have referred to above as 'sharing'.

In villages as well as in cities, it was – and often still is – customary for most communities to participate in each other's festivals. Muharram, a Twelver Shiʿi festival, was celebrated not only by Sunnis and Ismailis, but also by a number of indigenous groups. Similarly, Jains and Muslims took an active part in Holi, Diwali and other Hindu festivals such as Shitalashtmi. As we will see further, this picture gradually changed, as festivals came more and more to be regarded as markers of communal identity. At that time the sharing of sacred time, related to agricultural and fertility symbols, had more to do with social than with religious considerations.

Similarly, many sacred sites connected with particular traditions did not traditionally constitute tight enclosures. Some Sunni and Twelver Shiʿi mosques may have been closed to the 'unbelievers', just as entrance to Brahmanical temples was long forbidden to all *mlecchas* from lower caste and tribal communities, as well as to Muslims, Sunnis and Shiʿa, both Ashrafs and converted groups (with the exception, as will be shown further, of some Ismaili Guptis); but this represented the extremes of the continuum, the religions of those whom Kabir and others referred to as 'Hindus' and 'Turks' or 'Musulmans'.

It is a well-known fact that the most famous Sufi shrine of India, the darga dedicated to the twelfth-century saint Muʿin al-Din Chishti of Ajmer, is still visited by a great number of Hindu, Jain and Sikh devotees. This is the case for many other Muslim shrines all over the Subcontinent.

In villages even now Muslims rarely shun the sacred places belonging to other traditions. Many of them participate fully in certain temple festivals. For instance, in many villages of Shekhawati (Rajasthan), such as Mundawara, Losal and Kachriawas, near Sikar, Manihars (Muslim bangle-makers) and other artisan castes make vows and offerings to deities, such as Bheruji or the seven goddesses locally referred to as 'Sat Mamai'. A particular clan of them established near Sikar even accept Shitala Mata, the goddess of smallpox, as their lineage deity and celebrate her annual festival in the same way as the Hindus. For these people Shitala is the protector deity of their clan. The 'covenant' signed with this sacred power alien to their tradition has led to a regular 'sharing' of sacred time and space.

Numerous Muslim shrines, as well as temples dedicated to various goddesses or other non-Brahmanical deities, continue therefore to be shared spaces. Besides, there are many places, in Rajasthan and elsewhere, where the service of a shrine is performed by both Hindu and

Muslim priests, or where a temple has only Muslim caretakers and a darga is served by Hindu priests (*pujārīs*).

In the above-mentioned cases, sharing a sacred space does not seem to involve any merging of identities or confusion of personalities. The Hindus, Jains or Sikhs who visit these Sufi dargas do not generally view their pir as a saint belonging to their sect or family/caste tradition.[10] Most do not believe, for instance, that the tomb of Mu'in al-Din Chishti is a Hindu, Jain or Sikh temple. The devotees have simply struck an alliance with a divine figure whose power they acknowledge, as do the Sunni Manihars who benefit from the grace of the goddess Shitala Mata. Similarly, most Sunni Sufi saints have not tried to appear to the non-Muslim population as Hindu gurus or deities, even if they have incorporated elements from the indigenous traditions or, further, asserted that Hindu religions were not essentially different from Islam. Rather than a change of identity, all this implies the recognition of the fundamental unity of the Divine and of the Sacred that knows no boundaries. Like the Sufi teachers, the devotees, and even at times the *murīds*, apparently remain within the limits of their respective traditions.[11]

Instead, the phenomena we are going to describe introduce a new element in the mode of interaction referred to as 'sharing'. In these cases the devotion for a sacred figure belonging to the other tradition results in a partial or temporary shift of identity.

There is an interesting custom connected with the darga dedicated to Davalmalak, a fifteenth-century Maratha saint who 'is known to cure the eye disease of both men and cattle'.[12] The non-Muslim devotee who is afflicted by some eye disease and visits the shrine for a cure has to undergo a curious transformation. Clad in the blue cloth of a fakir and bearing a wooden hoe, he has to shout '*Dom dom Dāvalmālak*', and to beg for food. In this way 'Hindu believers in Davalmalak, without giving up their own Hindu identity, were willing to assume temporarily the Muslim identity of fakir, if this would help them to alleviate physical deformities and pains'.[13]

Similar traditions are found in Ajmer among the followers of Mu'in al-Din Chishti (d.1236), the famous Sufi saint and founder of the Chishtiyya order. It is said, for instance, that a number of Hindu female devotees, who claim to have been granted the boon of a son, have vowed to visit the shrine each Friday, dressed in green saris. The author of this essay also knows a Jain lady who, believing herself to have been blessed with a male child by the intercession of the Sufi saint, has given her child the Muslim name 'Chirag' (holy lamp).[14]

The case of the Shekhawat Rajputs, who worship the fifteenth-century dervish, Shaykh Burhan, as their patron saint, should also be mentioned. A particular historical event accounts for the fact that these Hindus have adopted a number of Muslim customs. In the fifteenth century Hindu Rajputs and Sunni Pathans, both disciples of the Sufi saint, fought together against the ruler of Amber to preserve the independence of the new kingdom of Shekhawati. In order to consolidate the alliance, both communities decided to make a number of compromises: the Pathans publicly renounced killing cows and eating their flesh, whilst the Rajputs swore that they would never eat pork nor the meat of any other animal not killed according to the halal ritual.[15]

Finally, the darga of Diwana Shah Baba, built between 1958 and 1968 and located at Kapasan in south Rajasthan, constitutes another fascinating object of study.[16] The pir, who was born in Gujarat in a Kasai (butcher) family and was affiliated to the Rifa'i order of Qalandars, had two Hindus among his first followers. The main disciple after a Brahmin named Sharma (who died in 1986), was H.M. Kumawat, a Kumhar (potter) by caste, who died one year later. Although the 'official' hagiography of the Kapasan darga claims that the pir never converted him to Islam,[17] the Hindu *murīd* had left instructions according to which he should be buried in the Muslim fashion after his death instead of being cremated or interred in the lotus position like a Hindu ascetic. The tomb of H.M. Kumawat was therefore built according to Islamic tradition.

Now, what does the wearing of a green sari or the choice of a Muslim name mean for the Hindu/Jain women who have been blessed with a son by Mu'in al-Din Chishti? Why do the worshippers of Davalmalak assume the dress and behaviour of a fakir? What could prompt the Shekhawats to adopt Muslim customs and food habits, and the Hindu devotee of Diwana Shah to have himself buried according to Muslim rites? These cases should be contrasted with the stories of devotees who have changed their religion as a result of the fulfilment of a vow. Formal conversion is a phenomenon that the modern mind understands more easily.[18]

What causes the devotees to assume temporarily, or partially, the identity of the sacred figure whom they worship may simply be devotion, or better, *bhakti*, a word which in South Asian terminology, literally means 'participation'. The devotee could be compared to those Krishnaite male saints who assume the persona of a *gopī* (the legendary milkmaid in love with the divine incarnation) or to the Sufi poets who fictively assumed a female personality to be able to worship God as a woman loves her husband. In all these cases, the affective compulsion that induces them to 'participate', generates a kind of imitation as, for example, when the young today tend to mimic the behaviour, dress, and so on, of their favourite actor or singer.[19]

Reverence for a common saint and sharing sacred spaces are generally regarded as symbols of communal harmony. One should stress the ecumenical role played by many of these shrines. In all the above-mentioned examples, the religious identity of the shrine was not in question, but if that is not the case, the same configuration can result in communal conflict. Such a conflict has recently developed at the shrine of Pirana (near Ahmedabad) which is the seat of the main branch of the Imamshahis, an offshoot of the Nizari Ismailis.[20] Devotees have widely divergent opinions regarding the origin and sectarian affiliation of this sacred spot. Some consider it a Sunni Sufi darga, others as a shrine belonging to the Twelver Shi'i tradition, while yet another group views it as a 'purely' Hindu place of worship. There are even people who are aware that its tradition is rooted in Ismailism, and a few others who insist on its 'syncretic' nature, refusing to call it by the name of any known religious tradition.[21] But these reflections have brought us into the domain of specific modes of interaction that result in the emergence of liminality within religious traditions and communities: a phenomenon that will be analysed in the last section of this chapter.

Borrowing: How to Bridge the Gulf

'Borrowing' will be the next mode of interaction examined in this section. Shaykh 'Abd al-Quddus Gangohi, the fifteenth-century Sufi saint from the Sabiri branch of the Chishtis was born in 1456 in Rudauli, near Lucknow in modern Uttar Pradesh. His main work, entitled *Rushdnāmā* or *Alakhbāṇī*, is a collection of his own verses and of some of his pir's which 'identify Sufi beliefs based on *waḥdat al-wujūd* (unity of being) with the philosophy and practices of Gorakhnath, one of the original founders of the Nath *panth*'.[22] Inspired by its doctrines, the shaykh uses many of its terms and concepts such as *omkār*, *sabad* (the 'divine verb'), etc., and identifies, for instance, Alakh Niranjan (the formless and immaculate God of the Naths) with Khuda (Persian for 'God') as creator of the different worlds. Actually, in borrowing terms and concepts from an alien tradition, he stresses their profound similarity with his own mystical conception of Islam. The Nath theory of creation is, in his eyes, a replica of Ibn 'Arabi's vision.[23] The fact that the Shaykh, who wrote in Hindi, used the name 'Alakh' as his *nom de plume* should also be mentioned.[24]

Another interesting case exemplifying the borrowing of Hindu elements by Muslim mystics is the poetry of the Punjabi Sufi Bullhe Shah (d.1758) mentioned at the beginning of this chapter. As Denis Matringe has shown, Krishnaite and Nath elements have found an important place in his poems referred to as the *Kāfī*.[25] In some of his verses the Sufi saint advocates 'devotion to Krishna as opposed to Vedic ritualism, thus indicating the superiority of inner faith to outward religious manifestations'. Nath symbols also are frequently found in his poems, where God is called 'the supreme yogi'. However, according to the same scholar, the *śabdī* attributed to Gorakhnath and the *kāfī* of Bullhe Shah differ at least in one important point: the Sufi saint's verses are full of loving devotion, which is alien to Nath Shaivism but is characteristic of Krishnaite poetry and can also be found in the famous Punjabi legend of *Hir-Ranjha*. Besides, the extent to which Hindu elements are integrated into his poetry is unique. Actually, Bullhe Shah's mystical vision of God is that of a transcendent and immanent Being at the same time: 'He can be Kṣṛṇa and the yogi, the thief and the banker, the mosque and the temple, the Muslim and the Hindu, the lover and the beloved, and so on. This perception of the 'uniqueness of beings' leads Bullhe Shah to reject the diversity of the constituted religions'.[26] This is actually what makes him exclaim, as we have seen at the beginning of this chapter: 'I am neither a Hindu nor a Muslim'.

In the two examples we have selected it is clear that 'borrowing', as a specific mode of interaction, is a conscious process through which elements from a different tradition are integrated into one's own worldview to stress the profound unity of the Divine despite the plurality of vision. In these cases the result is obviously not innovation or creation of a new religious movement. Even when he calls himself 'Alakh', 'Abd al-Quddus does not cease to be a Sunni Sufi in the eyes of his readers; as far as we know, there has never been any doubt about his being a Muslim saint representing one of the multiple currents of Islamic mysticism existing at that time, and no attempt has been made to identify him with a Nath yogi or another Hindu ascetic. The same can be said of Bullhe Shah. Even the fact that he goes so far as to exclaim, 'I am neither Hindu nor Muslim' has not led people to question his identity, which remains unambiguously that of a Sunni Sufi saint.

Although it has been totally ignored by Rizvi and by most authors who have dealt with the Hindu-Muslim interface, one should not forget that the exponents of South-Asian Nizari Ismailism, those who composed the devotional poems known as *ginān*s, have gone even further than Bullhe Shah in borrowing from indigenous sources. References to Vaishnava *bhakti*, both *nirgūṇ* and *sagūṇ*, and to the Nath *sampradāy* pervade these compositions which, from the medieval period onwards, became the primary expression of Nizari religiosity. However, it is only from a contemporary viewpoint that they fall into the category described here as 'borrowing', in so far as the specific historical development of the Nizari community has become known only recently to non-Ismailis. From a pre-nineteenth-century point of view, the *ginān*s are a typical example of the 'overlapping' process which resulted in liminal phenomena, and it is from this perspective that we will consider them in the next section.

While dealing with the issue of exchanges and mutual influences, an important question remains to be answered: if Indian Muslims have borrowed from various indigenous religious traditions, do we know of Hindu saints and poets who have integrated Islamic elements into their religious message?

Those who have studied the Bhakti and Sant movements would probably quote Kabir, Nanak and Dadu as the best illustration of this process. Indeed, a number of specialists regard them as belonging to the Hindu tradition in the broader sense of the word. Guru Nanak (d.1539) is believed to have been a Hindu by birth and education – though his movement was destined to become a separate religion – and although Kabir (d.1518) and Dadu (d.1603) did originally belong to Muslim communities, they are generally perceived as more 'Hindu' than Muslim and are often compared with Guru Nanak. Two factors lie at the root of such a perception: firstly, the vague, encompassing meaning of the word 'Hinduism', and secondly, the rapid re-Hinduisation of the sects which developed after these three famous saints of medieval India.

On the other hand, the specialists of Indian Sufism who have examined these traditions, and acknowledged the influence of mystical Islam on the life and work of their founders, are not inclined either to give them a 'full-fledged' Sufi identity (if one understands Sufism as a mystical current associated mainly with Sunni Islam). According to one scholar, Kabir, for instance, may have frequented the Chishti religious centres or *khānaqāhs* where, apart from Muslim mystics, he probably met the Nath yogis who occasionally visited these Sufi centres;[27] at any rate, he seemed more familiar with the Nath doctrines than with Sunni Islam.

The author's opinion is that the compositions attributed to the three famous saints, as well as the communities who took their names, should not be hastily viewed as examples of 'predominantly Hindu' traditions borrowing from the Islamic context. If such a configuration exists, it would probably result from a complex mechanism of identity shifting. For instance, a community initially following a particular indigenous tradition who, having embraced some form of Islam and then come under the influence of a particular Shaivite or Vaishnavite sect, would most probably have preserved traces of its former religious affiliations, while appearing as 'predominantly' Hindu.

The three famous medieval saints, along with similar lesser-known religious figures labelled 'Nirgun Sants', indeed belong to an entirely different sphere. Their apparently 'dual' personalities may be the result of a more intricate process of identity development. Can we, for instance, regard the Maharashtrian sant Eknath (d.1599) as a 'predominantly' Hindu figure influenced by Sufism? Let us briefly examine his case. In spite of his efforts to show the futility of the Hindu-Muslim differences (as in his 'Hindu-Turk Debate'), Eknath has indeed generally been perceived as a Hindu saint. His guru, Janardan (whose name he always adds dutifully to his own in signing his compositions), is said to have been affiliated to a sect referred to as Dattatraya *sampradāy* – a tradition which, because of its name, is commonly believed to be a Hindu religious movement centred on the worship of Guru Dattatraya, a sacred figure revered by Shaiva Naths and Dasnamis as the combined incarnation of Brahma/Vishnu/Shiva. However, according to the latest research, Janardan's spiritual master was actually a Sufi. Eknath is said to have been initiated by his guru through a strange vision where Dattatraya appeared as a Muslim fakir.[28]

The case of Lal Ded, the fourteenth-century Shaivite mystic of Kashmir, is equally intriguing. She is considered to have been a Brahmin who incorporated certain Sufi ideals and inspired – or even initiated the Muslim saint Nur al-Din Rishi, himself deeply influenced by Hindu ideas.[29] Another opinion is that she may indeed have become a Sufi herself, as some elements of her poetry seem to indicate. Curiously, she is remembered in Kashmir as 'a great apostle of Islam'.[30] Of course, those who see her as 'primarily' Hindu would explain away this intriguing fact by suggesting that she has been 'appropriated' by the Muslims.

As far as the Nath tradition is concerned, the situation does appear to be different. Can we say that the Punjabi saint, Ratan Nath (whose dates are unknown but who was probably a historical figure, with some legends claiming that he was born before the Prophet and lived many centuries after him) for instance, has been 'appropriated' by the Sufis as Ratan Haji, or is it the reverse?[31] 'Appropriation' of a sacred figure by the 'other' tradition is too hastily perceived by modern scholars as a convenient way to account for the presence of combined Hindu/Islamic elements. But has an attempt ever been made to understand the reason why a saint should be 'appropriated', and in what cases, which particular context, the process occurs?

We can now find an answer to the question raised earlier. In the context of South Asia, why does the domain of conscious 'borrowing' in religious philosophy and poetry seem to go only one way? Bringing their traditions from outside, the Sufis and the Ismailis, for instance, wished to be integrated and accepted by the local population, if not always to convert them. They could easily do so by revealing the similarities which existed between their spiritual message and some purely indigenous concepts – a method already adopted by Sufis in other regions of the world and one which coincided with their inner vision. Indigenous religious teachers and saints, on the other hand, had no need to develop such a philosophy to integrate Sufism or any form of Islamic school. The local traditions were rich in various systems of beliefs and practices, ranging from polytheism to monotheism, sacrifice, image worship, *nirgūṇ bhakti*, yoga, dualism and non-dualism, etc. In this respect the Sufis and the Ismailis, at least, had understood that while some Hindus were similar to polytheists found in other parts of the world, there were others who largely shared the views of Muslims and other *ahl al-kitāb*. But no indigenous preacher would have wished or sought, at that time, to 'attract', 'convert' or even 'convince' the Muslims, other than in purely intellectual or religious debates. While the very idea of making Muslims 'Hindus' was then alien to the local traditions, the reverence for the Sufi and Ismaili pirs was natural at the popular level of shrine worship, as well as in the sphere of the *pīrī-murīdī* (master-disciple) relationship which was akin to the indigenous *guru-śiṣya paramparā*.

Liminality: Janus Bifrons, the Guardians of the Threshold

We have chosen to illustrate the Hindu-Muslim interface through the image of an open 'doorway'. Alliances, sharing and borrowing bring together different traditions on a threshold that can be described, in Matringe's words, as 'that sublime point where all religions meet'.[32] This is the domain where universality, recognised as the supreme value, prevails over sectarianism, although devotees preserve their distinct religious affiliations.

Liminality, however, is a distinct phenomenon, where identities become blurred. Liminal figures and communities could be regarded as the sacred custodians of the threshold, comparable to the ancient Roman deity Janus Bifrons, the god of doorways, with two faces pointing in opposite directions. This image is, in a sense, the reverse of the two black faces looking at each other, delineating the white figure in the background in Tazim Kassam's symbolical representation of syncretism.[33] In the cases we are going to examine, the two faces do not 'hide' a third object. They are parts of a single head and look in opposite directions: one towards the wide sphere of Islamic movements, the other towards the complex continuum of indigenous/Hindu religions.

We will argue that contrary to what the British census officers thought, liminality does not emerge spontaneously as a 'popular' phenomenon arising from the 'ignorance of the masses', nor does it reflect a pious and somewhat naïve attempt at 'reconciling the two religions'. It is the result of complex factors that can be analysed with accuracy. A critical study of the medieval Nizari Ismaili traditions of South Asia can help us to understand the reason why a particular religious movement can appear 'liminal'.

Resorting to the practice of *taqiyya*, or precautionary dissimulation, the Ismaili preachers and their followers never disclosed to the non-initiated the real origin and nature of their faith which looked outwardly, according to the context, either as one of the numerous medieval *panth*s prevalent in the northern part of the Subcontinent or as a Sufi *ṭarīqa*. The Ismaili *dāʿī*s (missionaries) and pirs themselves worked in various guises and seemed to be endowed with a dual identity. From outside, the 'syncretistic' nature of their faith could be perceived negatively as a heterogeneous 'mixture' (as Kassam has it, the somewhat uneasy co-existence of foreign elements 'demanding resolution'),[34] or, positively, to use Maclean's terms, as an 'innovative synthesis'.[35]

In certain popular traditions, the Nizari Ismaili pirs active in the Subcontinent were seen as simultaneously embodying the personality of a pir and the character of a Brahmanical sadhu, as in the case of Pir Shams Sabzwari who was also referred to as Samas Rishi. In some Khoja and Nizarpanthi traditions Sadr al-Din and Sahadev are one single character.[36] Pir Hasan Kabir al-Din is said to have preached also as a Hindu ascetic, clad in white or saffron and remembered as *Anant jo dhanī*, 'the Lord of innumerable (devotees)'. In a long *ginān* entitled 'Conversation between Guru Hasan Kabir al-Din and Kanipa Nath', although he is portrayed as a kind of yogi, his teaching clearly shows that he is neither a Sunni Sufi nor a Nath. However, he does not refer to his religion other than by the vague term *satpanth* (lit. 'true path').

The practice of *taqiyya*, we should explain, was not, however, the only factor which generated this type of 'ambivalence'. The Ismaili *dāʿī*s had developed a particular strategy of conversion by accepting and integrating a certain number of beliefs and practices of the people they wished to convert.[37] Besides, their doctrine was presented as the culmination and not the negation of all earlier faiths, including the Indian religions, in the same way that Islam as a whole was said to complete and supersede Judaism and Christianity.

Ramdev Pir and Guru Jambha, the alleged fifteenth-century founders of two liminal communities in Gujarat and Rajasthan, the Nizarpanthis and Bishnoipanthis, are other sacred figures whose identity is unclear. A legend will serve to illustrate this phenomenon. One day the Muslim governor of Nagaur, who posed as Guru Jambha/Pir Jambeshvar's disciple, quarrelled with the Raja of Bikaner, also claiming to be his follower. Pointing to a number of customs, rituals or beliefs connected with the sect, the former asserted that his spiritual teacher belonged to the Islamic tradition, while the latter insisted that he was a Hindu. Eventually, both went to see the saint. According to a Bishnoi tradition, Jambha had replied that he was neither Hindu nor Muslim, since he had raised himself above all castes and sects (*jāt-panth*). Till recently, Jambha's tomb was referred to simultaneously as *samādhi* by his Hindu devotees and by his Muslim devotees as *mukām*, and his shrine was likewise viewed as a temple or a darga.

Baba Ramdev is still called – especially in Gujarat – Ramdev or Ramshah Pir, and the sacred place where he is buried near Pokaran in Rajasthan is described, in his devotional literature, both as a darga and as a *samādhi*. The same ambiguity can be observed in many other figures. In fact, they are so numerous, that is nearly impossible to mention all of them.[38]

These enigmatic saints bear striking similarities to the Nizari Ismaili *dāʿī*s of medieval South Asia. The theory earlier suggested by this author regarding their connection with Ismailism was first rejected as fantasy, but the re-discovery of nineteenth-century Gujarati texts has enabled scholars to re-examine this hypothesis.[39] In fact, recent research based on these texts has confirmed that the Nizarpanthis and the Barmatis, both of whom nowadays identify themselves with Hindus, had once been secretly converted to the Ismaili faith. We are now in a position to understand that their apparent ambiguity is the combined result of a strong claim to universalism, precautionary dissimulation, and some strategies of conversion practised by Ismaili *dāʿī*s and pirs in the Subcontinent.

Liminality, as a specific phenomenon where religious identity (in the modern sense) appears ambiguous, should thus be carefully distinguished from other interactions that belong rather to the sphere of 'composite culture'.

Let us return to one of the key issues related to liminality. Some Khojas, Shamsis and Imamshahi Satpanthis, whose Ismaili origin is openly recognised today, were later referred to as 'Guptis' (lit. 'secret') owing to the fact that they had concealed their affiliation to Nizari Ismailism. But very little was known about their actual faith as late as the end of the nineteenth century. The Shiʿi-Ismaili practice of *taqiyya* and the phenomenon of the South-Asian Nizari communities later referred to as Gupti deserves, at this stage, separate treatment, as it has not been studied in depth, still less understood properly. In Ismaili studies, a certain amount of confusion arises from the fact that the term 'Gupti' is supposed to refer only to a section of the Shamsi community, that is to say, to those followers of Pir Shams who had chosen to conceal their affiliation under a local guise.[40] Actually, our personal research into the Imamshahi tradition of Pirana has shown that the local Sayyids referred to the Patidar disciples as *murīds* (thus resorting to the Sufi idiom) and when asked if they were Hindus or Muslims unhesitatingly replied that they were Guptis. Initially, the communities that were converted at the turn of the nineteenth and beginning of the twentieth centuries also formed 'Gupti *jamāts*'. Some of them, as we will see in the next chapter, have even remained so to this day, whilst others have merged into the Khoja *jamāt*.

On the other hand, an ex-Ismaili writer, Khaki Khoja, author of an undated work entitled *Gupt panth ka Shajra* (probably published in the mid-nineteenth century) proposes an interesting, although rather extravagant, theory concerning the origin of the 'syncretic' Nizari *satpanth* and of the Gupti communities. According to him, one Sohodev Joshi, descendant of an ex-disciple of the Nizari Pir Satgur Nur, who had supposedly created his own Nizari-like sect referred to as Mahamarg, secretly met Pir Sadr al-Din (the Ismaili *dāʿī* who had converted the Lohanas and given them the title 'Khojas') and engaged in a dialogue with him. The two religious leaders 'decided to put away their religious differences and forge a new Ismaili-Hindu synthesis, referred to as the *satpanth*'. Those who would choose to follow it openly were later known as Khojas, whereas those who preferred to continue outwardly as Hindus became Guptis, the Mahamargis (Nizarpanthis) being among them.[41] However, the belief that before British rule, there could have existed Khoja or Shamsi non-Gupti communities, that is to say, openly following Nizari Ismailism, along with Gupti groups following it secretly, is erroneous. History clearly tells us that from the beginning of Muslim rule in North India and in some other parts of the Subcontinent, Ismaili communities could not survive if they disclosed their religious affiliation. They could occasionally be protected by Hindu local kings, but it is highly improbable that they chose to practise their religion in broad daylight. Sunni persecution of the Ismailis was a perpetual menace, as proved by numerous allusions in Indo-Muslim sources to 'heretics' being discovered and exterminated if they did not embrace Sunni Islam.[42] We must surmise, therefore, that for quite a long period all the Nizari Ismailis were 'Guptis' in the broad sense of the word, whether they chose some Hindu sectarian guise or concealed themselves as Sunni Sufis or Twelver Shiʿa. This extensive practice of *taqiyya* can be compared with the phenomenon that gave rise in medieval Europe to the Marranos (Spanish or Italian Jews outwardly converted to Christianity for fear of persecution) or the Nicodemites (Protestants simulating a Catholic affiliation for the same reasons). The consequences also were similar. Some crypto-Ismailis, like a number of crypto-Jews or crypto-Protestants, gradually came under the influence of the local environment and ended up identifying themselves fully with the followers of the simulated faiths. This is what happened to a number of Khojas, Shamsis, Nizarpanthis and others during various phases of their history.

Liminality is also a characteristic of the medieval Sants. For this reason their cases must be briefly examined. Since most of the so-called 'syncretistic' sects that have emerged in their name have evolved and transformed themselves over time, we will try to examine them in their older forms, as preserved through oral or written tradition.[43] Reference has already been made to the Kabir, Dadu and Nanak *panth*s. The Rishi movement in Kashmir and a great number of lesser-known sectarian movements in Rajasthan, Madhya Pradesh, Maharashtra, Punjab, Sindh, Gujarat and Bengal also fit into this category.[44] Many obscure facts remain to be elucidated regarding these traditions, the 'syncretic' character of which has been too hastily viewed by scholars as the result of either 'spontaneous' processes or conscious attempts at 'reconciling the two religions'.[45]

Recently, a number of authors have drawn our attention to the striking affinities of the Nizari Ismaili faith with the *Sant paramparā*, in particular with its *nirgūṇ* version,[46] suggesting that the Nizari preachers may have imitated the 'syncretic' Sants. But the 'priority' could well belong to the Ismailis. In particular, the compositions of Kabir seem to echo the religious message conveyed in the *ginān*s: they incorporate elements reflecting a wide range of beliefs and practices.

It is important to remember that, according to the latest research, as early as the twelfth century, this Ismaili influence spread not only to Sindh, Gujarat and Punjab, but also to Rajasthan, Malwa and Maharashtra.[47] Ucch-Multan (in Punjab) was the centre of the so-called 'main' branch of Nizari Ismailism (following the Kadiwala Sayyids), while Pirana (Gujarat) and Burhanpur (Khandesh in modern Maharashtra) were among the seats of its Imamshahi offshoots. It is, therefore, logical to surmise that the Nizaris interacted extensively with local religious movements, although, owing to *taqiyya*, this interaction may not be clearly traceable as such.

The sharp criticism levelled by the Sants at certain Muslim theologians and judges (mullahs and qadis), 'orthodox' Brahmins or hypocritical ascetics of all sects, is strongly reminiscent of the attitude of the Nizari pirs. Like them, the Sants seem to have consciously associated a number of Sufi concepts and terminologies with elements drawn from the Nath heritage or from the indigenous idiom of *bhakti*, without identifying themselves with any of these traditions.

Kabir, as has been often said, is called a Julaha (a member of the weaver community) and never assumed for himself the name 'Turk' or 'Hindu'. In his case, it is clear that as a 'Turk' (a representative of 'official' Sunni Islam) he would have been considered a heretic by the ulama who were not favourable to this brand of Sufism, while, for the same reasons, he could hardly be accepted as a Brahmanical Hindu. Much has been said about the supposed religion and conversion of the Julahas. According to one author, these low-caste weavers would have been householder Nath yogis recently Islamised.[48] Similarly, what we know of the present Pinjara (Dhuniya) community, to which the saint Dadu is linked, can lead us to the conclusion that, by birth, he was a Sunni Muslim. But none of these hypotheses can be proved. As far as Nanak is concerned, the accounts of his life being entirely based on hagiographic and sectarian texts referred to as *Janamsākhis*, it is extremely difficult to trace his real family background. Not only the hagiographers but the scholars seem to take for granted that he was born in a Hindu family because he is said to have been a Khatri by caste and bears a Hindu name. Bearing a Hindu name and following certain non-Islamic practices and customs does not prove anything. In fact, even today, it is common practice among Muslim members of the Merat, Manganiyar, Bahurupia, Molesalam and other communities to give Hindu names to their children. So did the Khojas until a recent date, and it is still the case with the Pirana Satpanthis. Besides, the meaning of the word 'Hindu' in the context of fifteenth century-Punjab has not been properly re-evaluated. All that we know regarding

Nanak, the founder of the Sikh *panth*, is that he could appear, according to the context, as a sadhu or a fakir, and was sumultaneously called Guru Nanak and Nanakshah.[49]

The presence of typically Satpanthi elements and terminologies in Sikhism (and, maybe to a lesser extent, in other similar *panths*) has curiously remained unnoticed. The liminal nature of the Sant Paramparā should therefore be examined in a new light, and the idea of its possible connection with the Nizari Ismailis should not be rejected a priori.[50]

As we have seen, for a long period religious faith in South Asia remained closely connected with caste/family traditions and the following of a particular teacher, guru or pir. The existence of open 'doorways' had an obvious consequence. It permitted the smooth passage of ideas, doctrines and practices in all directions. If the different forms of 'composite culture' permitted these exchanges, as well as varied interplay with the Self and the Other, occasionally leading to formal conversions, it did not give birth to 'syncretistic' movements, nor did it result in ambiguity. Instead, liminality, as a distinct phenomenon, generated 'overlapping' identities, further challenging our notion of religion which appeared, to use Aziz Esmail's expression, as 'a territory with indistinct borders'.[51] There is ample reason to believe that in this respect the Ismailis of South Asia have played a distinctive role, favouring a rapprochement between different faiths and communities.

This does not mean, however, that the existence of liminal sects, communities and gurus necessarily prevented conflicts, competitions and rivalries,[52] but it certainly checked the formation of tight enclosures, whether cultural or religious. Identities, in the sense that one could give to this word during that period, were obviously not fixed. They were continually shifting. Changes of allegiance, conversions, splitting or merging of religious traditions occurred at different sectarian and caste levels.

In the two remaining chapters, we will analyse the recent historical processes which gradually led to the formation of the two opposing blocs called 'Islam' and 'Hinduism', with particular reference to the largely unexplored role of Ismailism.

3

Creating Orthodoxies

The Musulmans said, 'we will bury him',
and the Hindus said, 'we will cremate him'.
Janam-Sakhi of Guru Nanak*

As mentioned earlier, it has sometimes been argued that the crisis which led to the emergence of two antagonistic blocs revealed a 'faultline' in the apparently firm ground shared by Muslim and indigenous traditions; this would prove the fragility of that continuum and the existence from the very beginning of two separate 'cultural' – if not religious – 'enclosures'.[1] In the second and last part of this essay, we shall further challenge this view and try to demonstrate that the present 'enclosures' called Hinduism and Islam did not emerge as the result of an organic or natural process. Rather than a 'faultline' or chasm – to use the geological simile – we see the phenomenon as an artificial, man-made boundary or partition wall which has been built up slowly over time, and which to this day is not fully complete.

In this chapter we will examine the phenomena referred to as 'Sanskritisation' and 'Ashrafisation'; the part played by the local states in creating orthodoxies; the role of the British colonial power in the formation of clear-cut religious identities; and finally the emergence of reformist/revivalist movements, with particular reference to Nizari Ismaili and related communities.

The Metaphor of the Disputed Body: 'Sanskritisation' and 'Ashrafisation'

The enthusiasm of Mughal emperors Akbar and Dara Shukoh for Kabir does not seem to have been dampened by the legend which was already popular one century or so after his death. As far as we know, the first author to mention it is the great Shiʿi scholar Abu'l Fazl, Akbar's chronicler and favourite adviser. In his *ʿAin-i Akbari* he reports in the following terms the quarrel that arose even before the saint's death: Brahmins wished to cremate him and Muslims to bury him'.[2] Both Mughal emperors interpreted the event – true or legendary – in a constructive way. Kabir had friends and admirers among all kinds of people, regardless of their beliefs, practices or rank in society He was not the follower of any particular religious tradition, having carved out an original path by himself, a movement we would refer to as liminal.

Later on, the legend appears to have been misconstrued. The quarrel proved the fragility of the 'composite culture' or of the initial existence of a faultline, which gradually deepened into a chasm. In order to challenge this view, we shall have to re-examine the legend more critically. First of all, let us remember that similar stories have been circulating about other 'ambiguous' saints, although the episode connected with Kabir is by far the most popular. Sikh hagiography has it that before his death, Guru Nanak's body was the object of the same dispute.[3] In Kabir's case the quarrelling parties who lifted the cloth covering the body found that his mortal remains had disappeared, or rather, had been transformed into flowers. Those flowers (incidentally, the word *phūl* for flowers also refers to unburnt bones, often wrongly called 'ashes', traditionally immersed in sacred rivers after cremation) were then divided among his followers who chose to cremate or bury them. In Nanak's case, knowing that he was going to leave this world, the saint had ordered each party to place flowers on either side of his body, declaring. 'If those of the Hindus keep green, cremate me; if those of the Muslims keep green, bury me'. But none of the flowers withered and 'the Hindus took away theirs, and the Musulmans took away theirs'.[4]

Attention should now be drawn to a few details. The term used by Abu'l-Fazl to refer to those who want to cremate Kabir is 'Brahmins' and not 'Hindus'. Cremation, at least till the turn of the twentieth century, was practised exclusively by high-caste householders, while most ascetics, Shudras (artisans) and Untouchables were buried. Apart from the fact that it was their ancestral custom – a custom which is still prevalent among many of them – they would not have been allowed by the Brahmins to burn their dead had they wished to. In conformity with the *Shastras*,[5] this funerary ritual was the privilege of the 'twice-born', that is to say of those whom the Brahmins included in the three upper *varṇas* (socio-religious categories); this rule applied to all sacred ceremonies connected with Brahmanical sacrifice, as well as the recitation and listening of the Vedas.

Therefore, even if Kabir had been a non-Muslim weaver (belonging to one of the Untouchable communities who practised this occupation, such as the Kohlis and Bhambis), neither his family members nor his caste-fellows would ever have thought of cremating his dead body. Consequently, if the 'flowers' had indeed been divided between the two groups, none of these metaphorical parts of his body could have possibly been burnt. We do not know what really became of Kabir's mortal remains, but contrary to the legend, the actual result of this symbolic division is perfectly logical. Two funerary monuments have been erected side by side at Maghar, near the present Varanasi, at a place referred to as Lahartara in modern Uttar Pradesh. They are in memory of the saint, and both are thought to be real tombs (containing the saint's mortal remains). They are built in a similar style, the main difference being, as we shall see further, that one is called *samādhi* and the other darga.

Similarly, Guru Nanak's *Janam Patrī* mentions the division of the fresh flowers between the two contending groups, but most Sikh texts do not tell us what happened to them.[6] A later Sikh tradition (regarded as the 'normative' one) tells us that Guru Nanak was cremated. If true, the cremation was probably in conformity with the custom then prevalent among his caste-fellows, the Khatris – whether worshippers of Brahmanical gods or Ismaili Shamsi Guptis.[7] In fact, the funerary monuments erected in memory of Sikh saints and martyrs (referred to as *samādh*, a variant of the term *samādhi*) are strangely similar to Sufi dargas. The interior does not contain the mortal remains which have been burnt, but the cenotaph consists of a canopy under which stands a raised structure covered by ornate draperies (*chādar*) donated by priests or devotees. The other Sikh temples enshrining the scripture, *Guru Granth* (known variously as *dharamsālā, darbār, gurudvārā*), look exactly like these *samādhs*. Guru Nanak did not himself specify whether Sikhs should be cremated or buried after their death. This detail may thus point to a later 'split' in the original tradition. In any case, the evolution of Sikhism was to be very different from the direction taken by the movements founded after Kabir and Dadu.

But what do these legendary traditions tell us about identities? Rather than being the consequence of a misunderstanding or of some pre-existing religious disagreement between two distinct communities, these episodes point to a gradual transformation of Indian society.[8]

Ultimately the myth of 'dividing the Divine', this medieval war of relics, leads us to examine the changes which took place in South-Asian society, from roughly the seventeenth century onwards. The two phenomena referred to as 'Sanskritisation' and 'Ashrafisation' account for the way in which various sectarian movements have sought, more or less successfully, to transform the personalities of Kabir, Nanak and of other liminal religious teachers such as the Ismaili preachers. In other words, the stories of the divided body do not tell us of a pre-existing faultline between Hindus and Muslims, but rather point to the process through which liminal figures have been appropriated by Sunni, Twelver Shiʿi, Vaishnava or Shaiva traditions. As this appropriation takes place, the original traditions (which anyway have no written history, the devotional poems having been transcribed at a later period) tend to sink into oblivion, being replaced by new, invented ones. For the Sunnis, Kabir becomes an 'orthodox' Sufi while Brahmanised Hindus claim he was a Brahmin.

Srinivas was the first to propose the term 'Sanskritisation' to describe the process through which a number of communities (generally of lower status) sought to adopt – or come closer to – the customs, beliefs and practices of the higher castes who claimed to be the repositories of the Brahmanical dharma, as embodied in the Vedas and *Shastras*.[9] Sanskritisation, of course, is not a closed historical event, but has been a continuous process that can be still observed nowadays. If on the one hand, Sanskritisation enabled upward mobility, bringing the lower classes closer to those who claimed to be at the top of the social ladder, on the other hand acquisition of wealth and power by those who were not regarded as 'twice-born' generally led them to adopt the Brahmanical model in their social and religious life.

Of course, the religion which, for the sake of convenience has been called 'Brahmanism' should not be considered as a fixed entity. It grew by absorbing various local traditions, as well as beliefs and practices from rival movements which were transformed and legitimised so as to become a part of the Vedic heritage. A few scholars who believe in the existence of a global entity called 'Hinduism' have explained the difference between the Brahmanical model and the regional, village or low-caste religions, by distinguishing a 'great' and a 'little' tradition. Further, they have described a continuous process of 'universalisation' and 'parochialisation' through which each model seeks to come close to the other. The picture which emerges is, therefore, that of an uninterrupted tribal/Hindu and low-caste/high-caste continuum.[10]

After the anti-Brahmanical movements represented by Buddhism and Jainism had lost ground in the Subcontinent, other prestigious models emerged during the early medieval period, among which the *bhakti* and Tantric currents were the most important.[11]

By the twelfth century, in the south, popular 'vernacular' devotion had already been Sanskritised by high-caste Bhaktas, such as Ramanuja.[12] This was also the fate of the initially non-Brahmanical Ramanandi sadhus who sought to link their tradition to the prestigious figure of Ramanuja. In turn, certain religious teachers who could not reject Kabir owing to the great aura of sanctity that surrounded him, attempted to raise the status of the saint by ascribing to him a Brahmin origin[13] and claiming that he was a disciple of Ramananda.[14] By creating fictitious lines or guru-disciples, all the exponents of the Bhakti and Sant movements were therefore soon Sanskritised, as can be seen in the seventeenth-century hagiographic text entitled *So vaiśnav kī vartā* (The story of one hundred Vaishnavas).

Another question arises: why did non-Brahmanical religious currents – Sant Paramparā, Tantrism or Nath yoga – fail to impose themselves as alternative religions? The answer lies in the evolution of the regional kingdoms and of caste society as a whole. In the south, for example, the Buddhists and Jains who endangered the Brahmanical dharma were eliminated from all key positions and at times they were brutally killed.[15] The Brahmins and those who followed their ethos had become indispensable at the court of the local rulers. Apart from being eminent ritual specialists, they were instrumental in legitimising the power of the kings. As is well known, Buddhism rapidly disappeared from the Subcontinent, while the Jains, who remained a minority, were later integrated into the Brahmanical society, for instance in medieval Rajasthan. At the court of the Rajput rulers they often acted as ministers and, most of them being traders, contributed to increasing the wealth of the kingdom. Jainism, by that time, had also largely Sanskritised itself.

The constant battle for hegemony fought by the Brahmins and the astonishing success of their social and religious model is one of the early factors which accounts for those Kabirian 'wars of relics'.

In the nineteenth century Sanskritisation also gave birth to what we perceive as 'Hinduism' in modern times. If strong counter-currents of Indian religions had survived and been powerful enough to oppose the hegemony of the Brahmanical model, the construction of clear-cut religious boundaries and consequently the Hindu-Muslim dichotomy would not have been possible.

The second factor which should now be examined is the evolution of Islam in India. First of all, mention must be made of the social and religious phenomenon referred to as Ashrafisation. It has been rightly stated that 'birth as a principle of status and honour was considerably important in the early Muslim society in India'.[16] The first distinction established after the advent of Islam in South Asia was a binary one. Those who claimed descent from the Muslims from Arabia, Central Asia and Afghanistan constituted the nobility and were divided into the four *ashrāf* categories known as Sayyids, Shaykhs, Mughals and Pathans. The rest of the population, coinciding with the converted groups, were regarded as inferior and referred to as *ajlāf*. The latter were mainly represented by the artisan castes, although other groups such as the Rajputs continued to claim a higher status by virtue of their origin. As said in the previous chapter, the terms 'Turk' and 'Musulman' referred exclusively to the Ashrafs. The local Muslims, Sunni or Shi'a, who could not claim a foreign origin were essentially designated by the names of their respective communities. Whereas the Ashrafs could be regarded as social classes or ethnic groups, the Ajlafs constituted real *jāti*s. While they could generally eat together they were not allowed to intermarry. The religious specialists were divided along the same lines. Both the Sufi shaykhs living in *khānaqāh*s and the ulama belonged to the nobility, whereas fakirs, qalandars, barbers (*hajām*) and butchers (*qasai*, Ar. *qaṣṣāb*), etc., formed the lower ranks. The religious beliefs and practices of the two groups were often at considerable variance, owing to their different way of life and different environments in which they lived.

In the same way that non-Muslims attempted to enhance their social status by adopting some of the practices of the Brahmins, the Ashraf society constituted a model which certain Ajlafs sought to imitate. The upward mobility of the 'low' Muslim castes is too complex a subject to be dealt with at length in this essay, so we will limit ourselves to a few examples: the introduction of clan names (*gotr*) such as Mughal, Pathan, Shaykh, Ghori, etc., among the manihar (ritual bangle-makers) and dhuniya (cotton-carders) communities; or the tendency of *qasais* to regard themselves as belonging to the prestigious Arab Quraysh tribe and so change their name into 'Kureshi'. The converted artisans, thus denying their origin, started to claim descent from the Ashraf Muslims, and consequently sought to conform themselves to their behaviour. At the basis of this phenomenon was the assumption that the Ashrafs who introduced the Muslim faith into the Subcontinent were the representatives of a 'higher', more 'pure', 'true' or 'original' Islam which was exclusively Sunni.

However, as we have suggested earlier, this was not the case. Arabs, Mughals and Afghans had not 'imported' Islam as one single bloc. In fact, the desire for Ashrafisation was originally more a social than a religious factor. But, as we have noted, in the case of low Hindu castes imitating the Brahmins and the Rajputs, religion for the Ajlafs could be a powerful element of social promotion.

It is important to remember that in medieval India, 'Islamic doctrinal structures and orthopraxis were fluid enough to allow for a number of competing normative systems, each claiming to represent hallowed "orthodoxies". No consensus existed as to which system was the "true" one'.[17]

Of course, this must not lead us to over-simplify the issue in assuming the existence of a binary system of beliefs: the Sufi mystical *ṭarīqa* as opposed to sharia textual rigour. Actually, the relations which existed between the Sufis living in the *khānaqāh* and the ulama in the service of the state were not always of opposition. Not only was there much mutual tolerance, but in many cases both – recruited from the same Ashraf groups – shared the same ideals and cooperated with each other.

Besides, there were many more competing systems. The hostility, but also the mutual accommodation, which existed between the Sunni Sufi orders and the Qalandars, or wandering dervishes, is reflected in the Persian literature of the Delhi Sultanate. They had something in common, as Digby points out,[18] because both, in a sense, had 'opted out' from the demands made on them by high medieval Muslim society.

However, the Qalandars expressed elements of 'social deviance' and led an 'antinomian existence', whether they were recruited from 'low' caste Muslims or from all those who sought to escape punishment or oppression.[19]

In modern times, the social and psychological difference between 'more orthodox' Sufi orders and the Qalandars would be expressed by the binary opposition of *beshar* and *bashar* – those who conformed to the Sunni sharia and those who did not. However, the later evolution of the Qalandars shows that, with their integration into the regular Sufi *ṭarīqa*s or into mixed orders such as the 'Chishtiya Qalandarya', they were gradually Ashrafised. As Digby has it, 'at the end of the fourteenth and beginning of the fifteenth century the Qalandars had lost something of their initial force and charisma'. Formerly, the garb of a Qalandar was often respected because of the belief that it might hide a true saint who wished to remain unknown.[20] But it could also provide an effective guise for some non-Sunni saints. This is corroborated by occasional references to the Nizari Ismaili preacher Pir Shams as 'Shams Qalandar'. The Ashrafisation of the famous mystic Lal Shahbaz 'Qalandar', whose tomb is at Sehwan (in Sindh), through his incorporation into the Suhrawardi *silsila* (Sufi lineage), might be interpreted along the same lines. His liminality has not been properly understood and it has been too easily surmised that he was a Sunni Qalandar.[21]

Through a similar phenomenon, a number of well-known Ismaili missionaries have been 'appropriated' by Sunni traditions. Ali Asani writes, referring to Wladimir Ivanow: 'Some of these [Ismaili] *pir*s were so successful in representing themselves as spiritual teachers that until today the non-Ismailis of Punjab and Sind revere them as Sufi masters of Sunni persuasion'.[22] Actually, the apparent 'appropriation' of Ismaili pirs by Sunnis or Twelver Shi'a is not so much the consequence of precautionary dissimulation, as of 'Ashrafisation' (read 'conversion to Sunnism or Twelver Shi'ism') of the pirs' disciples and descendants. For instance, the sixteenth-century Nizari missionary Pir Dadu's Sumra *murīds*, who are today the custodians (*mujāvar*s) of his tomb, regard their *murshid* as a Sunni saint. In fact they have embraced Sunnism together with the present *sajādda-nishīn*s (pirs of a Muslim shrine who generally claim descent from the buried saint) who claim to be his descendants.[23] In other words, at some point after the death of an Ismaili preacher, when his followers come to embrace a different form of religion, they cause the saint himself and his shrine to change their religious identity.

This detail brings us back to the appropriation of Nizari Ismaili pirs by some prestigious *silsila*s, a phenomenon which has failed to attract the attention of most scholars. Even now, many a Sunni devotee of Hasan Darya or Haji Sadar Shah, believing them to be pious dervishes of the Suhrawardi *ṭarīqa*, do not suspect that they were, historically, Ismaili preachers.[24] According to an Ismaili tradition, Lal Shahbaz of Sehwan, who is now generally recognised as a Suhrawardi saint, was a Nizari *dāʿī* who hid himself in the garb of a Qalandar. This saint is indeed endowed with the 'dual' personality that is a typical characteristic of the Ismaili pirs in the Subcontinent.

Before going further, another essential fact related to the process by which religious identities were shaped and shifted in South Asia should be underlined. It must be recalled that before 1866 – the date of the famous Aga Khan court case in Bombay to which we will refer at the end of this chapter – there was no distinctive official Nizari Ismaili identity as such in South Asia. The communities which had been converted by the pirs who came from Iran and established their centre in Ucch-Multan, appeared, as Nanji has suggested, as isolated pockets of followers, belonging to particular castes, professional corporations and/or specific sects. Even the term *satpanth* (which sounds like a self-appraisal rather than the name of a sect) was not extensively used. In the same way that the Ismaili pirs, and the missionaries working under their guidance, never showed themselves openly for what they were, but lived in the guise of yogis, sadhus, Sufis of various *ṭarīqa*s, Qalandars, etc., the Ismailis concealed themselves under labels such as Satpanthis or Piranapanthis, Khojas, Shamsis, Guptis, Maulais and, as my personal research has shown, Prahladpanthis, Aipanthis, Jasnathis, Nizarpanthis, Barmatis, Mahamargis, Lalbegis, Laldasis, and so on. It seems also that communities such as the Julahas and Khatris had been disciples of the Ismaili Pir Shams.[25] This tactic, which was meant to enable survival in a hostile environment, has been so efficient that not only during the colonial period, but even in modern times, some writers have perceived these various groups as following distinct religious movements.[26]

Aziz Esmail has shown in his *Poetics of Religious Experience* that a careful study of historical Islam reveals the great variety of traditions of thought: 'One has only to glance at the differences in the ways of thinking of traditionalists, theologians, philosophers, and mystical thinkers (like Ibn 'Arabi) to appreciate a phenomenal variety of points of view … Moreover, the official belief and practice in any tradition – whether de facto or de jure – is bound to differ from the reality on the ground. Muslim societies, with their historical and geographical span, are no exception to this rule.[27]

This was also the case in the Subcontinent, even at the time when various 'reformists' or 'revivalists' attempted to impose their view of what we would call an 'orthodox' form of Islam. Shaykh Ahmad Sirhindi (d.1624), the Naqshbandi Sufi who called himself the *mujaddid* or 'renewer' of the second millennium of Islam, was far from being approved by all the ulama in the time of Akbar and Jahangir. As we will see later, the creation of orthodoxies, represented by various reformist movements, was to gain momentum only at the end of the eighteenth century.

However, it should not be forgotten that from an early period, some Sunni Sufis deliberately associated with the local powers to eliminate various movements which they regarded as 'heresies'. The struggle may have become stronger from the fifteenth century onwards, when certain orders such as the Suhrawardis, the Qadiris and later the Naqshbandis, seem to have made a systematic effort to eradicate Ismailism.[28] For example, the great fourteenth-century Suhrawardi saint, Makhdum-i Jahaniyan 'Jahangasht', settled at Ucch, is said to have converted the Ismaili Sumra community to Sunnism. He was the grandson of a *murīd* of Baha' al-Din Zakariyya, another Sufi famous for his legendary contest with Pir Shams and Guru Nanak.

Historical and hagiographic records bear testimony to the fact that, following the example of earlier rulers such as Iltutmish (thirteenth century) and Ala al-Din Khilji (fourteenth century), Sikander Lodi, the fifteenth-century sultan of Delhi and his contemporary Mahmud Begra, the independent ruler of Ahmedabad, and later the Mughal emperor Awrangzib, asserted their authority by fighting against the *malāḥida* and *rāfiḍīs* – a common denomination for 'Shi'i heretics', among whom the Ismailis were regarded as the most threatening owing to their success with many agricultural and lower castes. For them, Ismailism was not so much a religious antagonist as a dangerous potential rival in the political and social sphere. To the majority of the rulers of the Subcontinent, being of Sunni persuasion and, of course, of Ashraf lineage, 'Ashrafisation' and 'Sunnisation' were practically synonymous.[29]

As mentioned, the lower Muslim castes who had adhered to non-Sunni religious sects (or to *beshar* orders in the modern sense) could raise their status and were Ashrafised by integrating themselves into the prestigious 'orthodox' Sufi orders. But liminal sects which, from the point of view of Sunni Islam, were regarded as heterodox by the Sufis and the ulama, could, for a much longer period, conceal themselves under the cover of indigenous religious movements. The state power of the local Hindu rulers had not yet sought to create a single local religion which would have condemned all other *panths* or *sampradāys* as 'heretical'. In other words, Hinduism had not yet been conceived as a norm. This will help us to understand what happened to liminal traditions such as that of Kabir.

Textual references tell us about the controversy surrounding this saint. Was he a 'true' Muslim? While the literalists among the ulama could condemn Kabir as having turned into an infidel, those who were inclined towards esoteric knowledge could see him as a *muwaḥḥid*, a practitioner of *waḥdat al-wujūd* (the doctrine of the unity of being). In order to explain Kabir's originality or what could appear as the 'deviant' aspects of his thought, even to the most tolerant Sunnis, they sometimes referred to him as a *malāmatī*, one 'who tried to conceal his spiritual achievement'.[30] Very much like the Qalandars (among whom some more orthodox Sufis thought true saints may have hidden themselves), those who practised *malāmatiyya* were supposed to violate religious laws on purpose, as a kind of asceticism, a pious exercise to provoke the wrath or indifference of the people. Sufi sources, in any case, attempt to connect Kabir with regular orders such as the Firdawsiyya or the Chishti *ṭarīqa*.

Much has been written on Kabir's poetry, although few studies have been dedicated to the *panth* created in his name; but curiously, no effort has been made to analyse in depth the myth of his 'divided body' nor to explore the part of his tradition which has been 'Islamised' to present him as a Sunni Sufi. The study of his darga at Maghar (modern Uttar Pradesh) would certainly provide interesting clues in this respect.

Our knowledge of the 'Hindu' part of his tradition is greater, even if many facts are still shrouded in obscurity. The main seat of the oldest branch of the sect founded in Kabir's name is located in Benares where he is said to have lived and preached. However, it is the place where he died which gives us a clue. One author at least has shown some curiosity about this place which he describes in his work on Kabir: 'In early days it is said there was only one shrine, which both Hindus and Muhammadans visited, and a *melā* was held which lasted over a month. Later on a friction arose.'[31]

At present, the most interesting feature at Maghar is a high wall dividing the sacred place on the bank of the river Ami into two portions: a darga which is taken care of by a family of Muslim Julahas who regard him as a pir, and a *samādhi* where the service is performed by a sadhu of the Kabir *panth*. Keay surmises that this original shrine was of the Sufi type, while the Hindu one was built later. Whether this is true or not, the striking fact is that both sacred structures look very much alike and both enshrine, among others, the tomb where the saint is said to be buried. Even according to the so-called Hindu tradition, the saint has not been cremated, and nowhere in the *samādhi* complex is there any idol, since image worship is strictly prohibited in the Kabir *panth*. A careful study of the sect shows that Islamic elements can still be traced, although they are closer to the Shiʿi Ismaili tradition rather than to the Sunni Sufi one. To give but one example, a particular sadhu of the Chhattisgarh branch of the *panth* is simultaneously called Pramodh Nam and Bala Pir. In fact, a good part of the doctrinal and ritual structure of the Kabir *panth* seems to be modelled on the South-Asian Nizari Ismaili *satpanth*. Even the custom of giving one-tenth of one's earnings (*dasondh*) to the guru is still prevalent in the sect.[32] The typically Shiʿi Ismaili source of authority vested in the figure of the Imam, has been shifted to the guru/pir, that is to say, to Kabir himself, who is viewed – again in the characteristic Satpanthi way – as the divine avatar of the Kali Yuga preceded by other avatars in previous cosmic eras.

It is probable that this connection between Kabir and the Ismailis, if it is not illusory, could be traced through a systematic study of the oral tradition of the Julahas of northern India, the cotton-weavers caste among whom Kabir was born. Our preliminary enquiries in Rajasthan have shown that even when the Muslim weavers belonging to this caste regard themselves as Sunnis or Twelver Shiʿa, they claim to have Pir Shams as their original *murshid*, and account for their conversion to Islam by the same miracle which is ascribed to the Ismaili saint in the *ginanic* literature.[33] For the Twelver Shi'a, Pir Shams was a Twelver and for the Sunnis a Sufi saint.[34] This seems to suggest that a number of the Julahas, originally Nizari Ismailis, were converted to Sunnism by some Sufi orders, while others, probably at a later date, embraced Twelver Shi'ism.

Let us note another interesting fact: the Momin Julahas of the Aligarh region (in present-day Uttar Pradesh, the area where Kabir lived) are now Sunni. They have changed their name to Momin Ansar or adopted the Arabic name Ansari to 'escape the pejorative status implication of their trade names, to dissociate themselves from an ancestry of indigenous conversion, and to align themselves with a high status ancestry linked directly to the sources of Islam'.[35] This testifies, once more, to the process we have referred to as Ashrafisation. As for the other disciples of Kabir, whether they were originally Julahas or not (some seem to have originated from higher castes, for instance from among the merchant classes or Banya) they strove to transform the Kabir *panth* into a purely Vaishnava tradition.

As if inspired by the legendary disputes over the saint's mortal remains, nineteenth- and twentieth-century scholars seem to have been desperately searching for Kabir's or Nanak's religious identity, and while recognising their 'encompassing' or 'syncretic' vision, attempted to classify them as 'primarily Hindu' or 'primarily Muslim'. In his *Fatimi da'wat-e-Islam*, Khwaja Nizami[36] observes that Kabir's and Nanak's movements may well have had their origin in the missionary activities of the Nizari Ismaili *dā'īs*. He states that Sadruddin Dargawala, the caretaker of the Navsari shrine dedicated to the Ismaili missionary Pir Satgur Nur, knowing that Nizami, among others, had been studying the Nizari connection of the Pranami sect, wrote him a letter in which he suggested the Ismaili origin of the traditions founded by Kabir and also Nanak.

The case of the Sant Dadu (sixteenth century) is also of great interest. In order to account for his 'syncretistic' character, most scholars assume that he was Kabir's follower. The same has been said of Guru Nanak to account for the Islamic elements that are traceable in his tradition. But whose follower was Kabir? Actually, Dadu's family and caste background have not been sufficiently explored. This Muslim cotton-carder (Dhuniya, Pinjara) came from Gujarat and settled in Rajasthan where he had many disciples, among whom the most famous was the poet Rajjab, who was regarded as a Muslim. From the seventeenth century onward, one can trace the progress of Sanskritisation in Dadu's tradition. For example the seventeenth-century Hindu saint Gopaldas denies Dadu's Muslim origin, claiming that like Kabir, he was in reality the son of a Brahmin. Higher castes have gradually been attracted into the orbit of the Dadu *panth*, which at present appears outwardly as a 'full-fledged' Hindu tradition, without having lost some of its original characteristics. Although Dadu is considered to be an incarnation of Brahma, image worship is prohibited and his main temple at Naraina (traditionally referred to as *dādūdvārā*) enshrines only a book, the *Dadu Vāṇīs*, supposed to be the saint's mystical compositions. Regarding the guru and pir as an avatar of Brahma was one of the typical Ismaili Satpanthi Nizari patterns; on the other hand, the Dadupanthi shrine strongly recalls the Sikh *gurudvārā* where the *Adi Granth* (another name for the *Guru Granth* above) a collection of hymns, is the only object of worship.[37]

The controversy surrounding Nanak's personality and the nature of his *panth*, is also revealing. Following some hagiographic accounts, Rizvi suggests that he was often seen in the garb of a Sufi, and that in particular, as for Kabir, he could well appear as a *malāmatī*, although the author after a few bold assertions of this type, concludes that the founder of the Sikh *panth* was not necessarily inspired by Sufism.[38] Writers from the British colonial period do not agree on his identity. Hughes wrote that Trump, the first translator of the *Adi Granth*, thought Nanak a full-fledged Hindu, owing nothing to Islamic ideas, while he himself, in his *Dictionary of Islam*,[39] suggests, albeit hesitantly, that Sikhism could be viewed as a Muhammedan sect which, although close to Sufism, was heterodox from a strictly Sunni point of view.

The execution of Arjun, the fifth guru of the Sikhs, by Jahangir in 1606 is said to have been motivated by political factors. That may be true, insofar as politics and religion have always been closely linked, but the satisfaction expressed by Shaykh Ahmad Sirhindi, who claims that it was a great victory for Islam, does probably mean something else. It was not as Hindus that the Sikhs were persecuted (in which case all Hindu religious leaders would have been condemned in the same ruthless way), but as Muslim 'heretics' from the Mujaddid's 'orthodox' point of view. Later wars fought with the Sikhs in the eighteenth century had the same motivations, both political and religious, in the eyes of Muslim reformers such as Sayyid Ahmad Shahid. These wars were regarded as jihad against this heterodox community, guilty of *bid'a* (innovation) and for this reason inimical to the progress of Sunni Islam in the Punjab.[40]

The Sikh *panth*, however, had been gradually Sanskritised after the death of Guru Arjun and, again, could be easily identified with one of the numerous *bhakti* movements. Later, as we will see, the majority of the Sikhs followed a different direction which did not compel them to choose between Islam and Hinduism, thus enabling them to remain 'on the threshold'.

We have seen that by identifying themselves, willingly or not, with Sanskritic/Brahmanical or Ashraf/Sunni models, a number of communities ceased to appear as liminal. But this was done at the cost of 'dividing the Divine', a process which has been symbolically illustrated by the disputes which occurred regarding the disposal of the saints' mortal remains and can have, therefore, a different interpretation from the usual Hindu-Muslim divide.

Religion and State: the Role of Local Kingdoms in the Decline of Mughal Rule

Although Muslim Turko-Persian rule (represented by the Delhi sultanate, the Mughal empire and some independent Sunni or Shi'i kingdoms) had been established over a great part of the Subcontinent, conversions were far from extensive, and most local kings, whether loyal or not to the Muslim rulers, retained their former beliefs and practices.

We have already pointed to the tendency of ritual specialists such as the Charans and the Nath Jogis, to Sanskritise their traditions, so as to align themselves with the prestigious Brahmanical pattern. We will now examine how religion, at the court of some non-Muslim rulers, sought to constitute itself as a model and a norm, in particular after the death of Awrangzib. The activities associated with the founder of Jaipur city may illustrate our purpose.

One of the most the faithful allies of the Mughal emperor, Jai Singh II (1699–1740), had been honoured with the titles 'Maharaja' and 'Sawai' by Awrangzib. Religion at the court had always played a central role: 'it encompassed the Brahmanical tradition (centred on the observation of caste hierarchy and the correct execution of rites) and Vaishnava sectarian traditions (which maintained that universal salvation was possible through the divine grace of different forms of Vishnu). Thus the Crown of Jaipur sponsored a wide range of Hindu cults and rituals, and did so with great liberality.'[41]

In the twilight of Mughal rule the Maharaja of Jaipur attempted to assert his power by constituting a kind of state religion. He did so by trying to reconcile his devotion to Vishnu with respect for Vedic and Brahmanical norms, integrating Vaishnava doctrines with the philosophical system of the Vedanta.[42] In fact the eighteenth-century ruler of Jaipur built a whole, complex, 'religio-political edifice' to legitimate his regal identity. The performance of the long-abandoned horse sacrifice (*aśvamedha*) and the construction of a very unusual temple to Kalki, the tenth incarnation of Vishnu, can be understood as the expression of Jai Singh's ambitions. Through the former symbol he was claiming hegemony on the model of the legendary kings of *Bharatvarsha* (one of the ancient names for India found in old texts) and through the latter he was identifying himself with the future avatar of Vishnu whose mission on earth was to fight against all *mlecchas*,[43] 'barbarians' who did not belong to any Brahmanical caste or tribe.

For instance, in 1725 the Laldasis of Sanganer (near Jaipur) sent a letter to the Maharaja in which they promised to give up their *panth* and follow the Vaishnava Dharma of the Chaitanya *sampradāy* (tradition). Similarly, in 1733 some Dadupanthis of Naraina (the main centre of the sect) replied favourably to Jai Singh's plea requesting them to break all relations with the Muslims and follow the principles of the *Shastras*. Both, as has been shown earlier, were liminal sects, incorporating Sufi/Ismaili and Nath/Vaishnava elements, while sharply criticising Brahmins and Mullahs, and denying the value of idol worship and pilgrimages.[44]

In this way, either by shifting their affiliation from one tradition to the other or by modifying their religious practices, the followers of these movements were gradually Sanskritised. Jai Singh thus deserved to be compared by a chronicler to the tenth avatar of Vishnu, as depicted in the *Kalki Purana*. He also fought a battle against the *mlecchas*, although in his case, they are no more exclusively represented by Buddhists and Jains, but by the religious teachers of all the traditions connected with Islam and the low castes.[45]

Besides, the ruler of Jaipur sought not only to reconcile the Brahmanical tradition with the devotional currents of Vishnuism, but also to demonstrate that various sectarian traditions, whether Vaishnava or Shaiva, were not fundamentally different, while *sagūṇ* and *nirgūṇ bhakti* were not contradictory. On the whole, this policy contributed to 'creating an orthodoxy' and to laying the foundation of a unified movement that would, much later on, in the nineteenth century, globally come to be referred to as 'Hinduism'.

Although the Sanskritising trend that had started gradually in the seventeenth century was thus reinforced, on the whole this energetic policy bore little effect on the actual religious life of the people. Documents dating from the period of British rule, prove that liminal sects and anti-Brahmanical movements were still flourishing in the nineteenth century. Besides, the crisis known as the '*tilaka* quarrel',[46] which took place in Jaipur during the reign of Maharaja Ram Singh II demonstrates that the time had not yet come for the formation of one single religious bloc grouping all the Hindus. Giving up the traditional Vaishnava affiliation of his ancestors, a little more than one century later, the nineteenth-century ruler of Jaipur not only 'converted' to Shivaism, but condemned the practices of the four main Vaishnava sects which, according to him, were against what he called the 'eternal religious law' (*sanātana* dharma). In 1866, he even convinced an assembly of learned pandits (*dharma-sabhā*) to excommunicate the Vaishnava Brahmins of the capital who refused to submit to the new state religion. The interpretation of Vishnuism as a heresy was, of course, inseparable from the definition of orthodoxy; but also the 'true dharma' (*satya* dharma) that had to be imposed upon the Vaishnavas had to do with the political as well as the religious order.[47] Although, in a sense, Ram Singh can be said to complete the religious policy of Jai Singh, by seeking to legitimise his kingship through the order of the dharma, the supra-sectarian character of which he reasserts, his choice of a particular cult and his violent rejection of all Vaishnava traditions reflect a situation which has not much changed since medieval times. As Catherine Clémentin-Ojha has it: 'Indian society would have to undergo many more transformations before the descendants of the protagonists of the *tilaka* quarrel realise their community of interests, before they manifest together and not one against the other their attachment to the "eternal dharma".'[48]

Inventing Hinduism: Orientalists and Anglicists during British Rule

At first the East India Company, founded in 1599, was exclusively engaged in the development of trade and the protection of the British citizens settled in India. But gradually, these commercial activities led the British to involve themselves in the affairs of the various kingdoms and principalities of the Subcontinent.

With the appointment of Warren Hastings (1773–1785) as the first governor-general of British India, the colonial powers started to be concerned not only with the South-Asian educational tradition, but also with local cultural and religious traditions. By accommodating themselves to the laws and customs that were prevalent in the Subcontinent, the British followed the policy of the Indian, Hindu and Muslim rulers, hoping in this way to consolidate their power. Hastings, who was sympathetic to Indian culture and had a special interest in Islamic art and literature, 'established orientalism as the official policy and unofficial mood of the fledgling British government in Bengal'.[49]

First a madrasa was founded at Calcutta in 1780, then a Sanskrit College at Benares in 1791. Between 1811 and 1833, H.H. Wilson, a brilliant Sanskrit scholar, acted as the secretary of the Asiatic Society of Bengal founded in 1784 by William Jones and others with the support of Hastings.[50]

One element is characteristic. The focus on classical or court culture, which, at that time, was exclusively connected with the upper castes, in particular with the Brahmanical elites. This bias would not only have consequences in the educational sphere, it would end by influencing the whole perception of religion.[51]

In the eighteenth century Charles Grant was one of the first to suggest an alternative vision, later referred to by historians as 'Anglicism'. His vision, which was rooted in evangelical convictions, inspired the nineteenth-century secular utilitarians and free-traders,[52] all of whom believed in the superiority of British models and strongly opposed the Orientalists. Rather than accepting and supporting local traditions, they sought to abolish and replace them by European ones. Anglicists perceived local religions as devoid of any value. The beliefs and practices of the inhabitants of 'Hindoostan', as well as their social customs, were characterised by meaningless rites, obscure cults and worthless superstitions. For example, the whole civilisation was termed 'primitive' and 'barbaric' by James Mill, the author of *The History of British India*, published in 1817.

On the other hand, the admiration of Orientalists for South-Asian culture did not prevent them seeing the local beliefs and practices in the light of their own civilisation. As Oberoi has it: 'By importing a Judeo-Christian and Islamic understanding of texts and scriptures into discussion in Indian religions, we could end up establishing religious identities that do not exist beyond the scholar's imagination. Early Orientalist scholarship and administrators fell victim to similar selective definition.'[53]

Census Reports and Gazetteers: The Creation of Religious Categories

Apart from activities related to culture and education, the imperial project included the preparation of census reports and gazetteers which were meant to supply administrators with the necessary information about the vast regions over which they wished to exercise their power.[54]

'The difficulty of an Indian census springs mainly from two sources: the infinite diversity of the material to be dealt with, and our infinite ignorance of that material.' With these words, Denzil Ibbetson, the commissioner of the 1881 census of Punjab, expressed his doubts concerning the task he had been entrusted with.[55]

The author of the *Panjab Ethnography* (1883) which would remain an invaluable source of information to the modern scholar, was literally overwhelmed by the variety and the complexity of the social and religious patterns. He considered that the previous census report established in 1868, a meagre document consisting mainly of dry figures, was of little avail. His ambition was to provide extensive information about local society. Although he had openly admitted, 'it is almost impossible to make any general statement', even for that single province of British India, and was therefore not fully satisfied with his own work, pressed by an order from the Punjab, the census commissioner had to publish the report as early as 1883.[56]

This type of report implied that South-Asian society should be divided into 'Cartesian' categories familiar to the British mind. Even more than the caste system (about which Ibbetson, in his original introduction, provides a lengthy discussion, indeed remarkable for that time), religion seemed to be a factor difficult to reduce to exact figures. But the census commissioner had to submit to rules and standards that were prevalent in nineteenth-century Europe, and in doing so he and his fellow-countrymen contributed to manipulating the social sphere in a very specific way.

The Western (Christian) idea about the 'great faiths' of the world was instrumental in creating the clear-cut categories 'Hindu' and 'Muslim'. Islam and Hinduism were supposed to have 'pure' or 'pristine' forms which were defined as the norm, while the forms that could not fit into these pigeonholes were termed 'deviant'. The British, including Ibbetson, were particularly puzzled by the existence of systems of beliefs and practices which they perceived as located somewhere 'on the border lands' of great religions, and where elements from Islam and Hinduism, perceived as homogenous blocs, were 'strangely blended and intermingled',[57] as Oberoi has it.

In spite of their shortcomings, census reports still provide, as has been said, invaluable ethnographic data to modern scholars, enabling them, among others, to measure the changes which occurred from the end of the nineteenth century to the present day. In this way, we can evaluate not only the transformations of the communities themselves, but the change in our perception of South-Asian society. A few examples will serve here to illustrate the way in which the British, at that time, regarded the communities and sects referred to by us as liminal.

In 1911, H. Rose compiled *A Glossary of the Tribes and Castes of the Punjab and Northwest Frontier Province*, based on the above-mentioned document established by Ibbetson and on the 1892 *Report for the Punjab* by Maclagan. The Chajjupanthis or Parnamis are defined as 'a sect which exhibits a curious combination of the Hindu and Muhammadan creeds among the lower orders'.[58]

The census commissioners were particularly annoyed by the fact the number of Sikhs increased or decreased without logical reason, until it was discovered that some of them returned themselves as Hindus, while others who 'should' have been classified among the Hindus (according to a particular bias, of course) were listed among the Sikhs.[59]

The case of the Sarais, also referred to as Sultanis or Sarwaris, who recognise Sultan Sakhi Sarwar as their spiritual teacher and the founder of their tradition, is of considerable interest and, to this day, as far as we know, no attempt had been made to study it in depth. The British had remarked that they bore some striking similarity to the Sikhs, although they were 'all Shi'is'.[60] Sakhi Sarwar was also traditionally worshipped by the Shamsis, to whom is devoted one of the most interesting headings of Rose's glossary.[61] They are described as 'a curious sect, followers of Pir Shams Tabrez, worshipping no idol but reverencing the *Bhagavad Gita*, passing as "ordinary Hindus" although despised by the "orthodox" ones' (that is to say the followers of the Brahmanical dharma). Further, the author suspects that the Shamsis are 'closely connected' with the Khojas of Bombay and writes that, according to one local source, they are actually Shi'i Ismailis secretly revering the Aga Khan as their living Imam. The Khojas themselves, it goes without saying, were regarded in the same light, as a 'syncretic' community. But, curiously enough, and probably owing to his ignorance of the literature and rituals of South-Asian Nizari Ismailis, the same author does not establish any link between them and the Lalbegis or Balmikis among whom the Chuhras (an Untouchable scavenger caste), are the most numerous.[62] A careful study of their devotional songs, which appeared to the British as a 'confused jingle' indiscriminately mixing Hindu and Muslim elements, would reveal exactly the same patterns of ideas as in the *ginān*s. This is also the case for the Bishnois of Punjab and Rajasthan, the Mahamargis (also suggestively referred to as Nizarpanthis), Barmatis, Jasnathis, Aipanthis and Pranamis.[63] The Imamshahis of Gujarat and Khandesh, whose connection with the Nizaris is well known, also challenged the attempt at creating sharply demarcated religious categories. For instance, in the 1899 *Gazetteer of the Bombay Presidency*, the Matia Kanbis, an agricultural community following the Pirana tradition and recognising Imamshah as their pir, are listed twice, among the Hindu and Muslim castes.[64] This was, of course, an original response to Ibbetson's complaint that it is often impossible to 'decide in which category the people shall be classified'.[65]

At that time, the British limited themselves to stating the facts which puzzled them, expatiating on what they perceived as a meaningless blend of elements belonging to different religions. They attributed this phenomenon to the ignorance of the mass whose faith, in their eyes, 'is seldom more than a superstition and a ritual' as Ibbetson had it. More worrying, instead, is the fact that the British vision continued somehow to influence post-colonial attitudes. Aziz Ahmad's *An Intellectual History of Islam in India*, published in 1969, is a good example of the deep imprint left by this particular 'mapping' of South-Asian society. The author has divided the part of his work devoted to religion into five chapters entitled: Sunni Orthodoxy, Shi'i Sects, Messianic Movements, Folk-beliefs, and Orthodox Sufism, the latter being subdivided into 'Bi-shar' (also known as 'Beshar' mentioned above) or 'irreligious Sufism' and 'Popular and Syncretistic Beliefs'. The so called 'Bi-shar' orders are termed 'heterodox', and the beliefs connected with them 'superstitious' and 'syncretistic'; the fact that *bi-shar* is translated by 'irreligious' is also highly significant. As far as the Nizari Ismailis are concerned, one finds the same confusion as in census reports and gazetteers. Shamsis are said to be a 'sub-sect' of the Khojas, together with the Pira'is. The Imamshahis are listed among 'minor Ismaili sects', as well as the Guptis, while, curiously, the Krishnaite Swami Narayan *panth* is regarded as a 'very Hinduised group of Khojas'.[66]

There is no clear understanding of the links that exist between various groups, nor is the meaning of the different names explained in any way. The author is apparently unaware of the fact that the process through which the Nizari Ismaili community came to be fragmented may account for the apparent existence of various 'sub-sects'.[67]

The recording of the religious figures of the Hindus was to be stopped in 1941, but, as Oberoi rightly states, 'By then it was too late; for all purposes the damage had been done'.[68] In 1947 the cartographic line drawn across the Subcontinent still relied on data obtained from these census reports. And even after 1947, when India and Pakistan began their existence as independent states, the census in India would not stop asking people about their religion. The results were surprising. The allegedly Muslim Mers, endowed with a liminal identity, for instance, sometimes returned themselves as Muslims, but sometimes simply as 'Merats'. In 1954 Lohia had adopted an original classification in his book entitled *Rājāsthān kī jātiān* (The Castes of Rajasthan) mostly based on the previous British census reports and on the 1891 Census of Marwar, but eliminating the category 'syncretic'. For example, Bishnois and Mers are classified as '*musalman*' together with the Kayamkhanis, the Sindhi Sipahis, the Malis, the Minas and Girasias. Later classifications in more recent publications would keep Meos, Sindhi Sipahis, Kayamkhanis as 'Muslims' and 'shift' all the others to the category 'Hindu'.

In 1911, curiously enough (at least for those who are used to binary categories), a few communities of Gujarat, mainly Imamshahis, had returned themselves as 'Mohammedan Hindus'. Gait, the census commissioner, suggested therefore a separate set of tables to list 'debatable Hindus'.[69] The category 'Muslim Hindu' is still used nowadays, as shown by Shafique Virani's latest research on some Gupti communities of Bhavnagar (Gujarat). The Imamshahi Kachias (vegetable sellers) who have shifted their allegiance to the Aga Khan, still referred to as Imamshahis, admit that their religion is Islamic, but nonetheless regard themselves as Hindus.[70]

In the last section of this chapter we will see how this denomination, as well as the 'hybrid' religion of a number of other communities, was understood by the British, their learned subjects and later, by some post-colonial authors.

Laying the Foundation of a Boundary Wall: Separate Laws and Electorates

It has been rightly remarked that Hastings' 'judicial plan' of 1772 setting up new civil courts in the province of Bengal for the East India Company was double-edged. While seeking to respect the local culture, instead of imposing a foreign law, it ended up creating a simplistic vision of South Asia based on the Hindu/Muslim dichotomy, insofar as the Bengali model eventually became the standard for the whole of Imperial India after the direct assumption of rule by the Crown. As an admirer of Eastern civilisations and promoter of Orientalism, Hastings has probably been unjustly accused of using the 'divide and rule' stratagem. He may not have intended to split the population in this way in order to reinforce British control over the provinces but, influenced by the particular perception prevalent in that period among Europeans, he thought, as did many of his contemporaries probably, that South Asia had two great faiths which should be exclusively identified with the classical, 'higher' traditions: the Sanskritic and the Arabo-Persian.[71]

The harm done by gazetteers and census reports – in spite of their undoubted value as a source of information – in introducing a hasty binary classification, was thus to be consolidated by the institution of two separate systems of personal law. In Bengal, Hastings had decided that 'in all suits regarding Inheritance, Marriage, Caste and all other religious Usages or Institutions, the Laws of the Koran with respect of the Mahometans, and those of the Shaster with respect to Gentoos, shall be invariably adhered to'.[72] The new provision meant concretely that, before deciding which law was to be applied, the membership of each social group should be defined along these binary lines. When the Bengali model came to be applied to all the provinces administrated by the British Crown, the diversity of South-Asian communities, customs and languages was gradually underestimated and even later denied, creating the image of two homogenous blocs – which, in turn, would be the main source of inspiration for the 'two nations' theory about which more will be said in the next chapter.

As Amrita Shodhan has stressed, Hastings' views, however, differed greatly from the opinion of Justice T.M. Perry of the Bombay Supreme Court. The latter believed that the simplistic classification of the population as 'Mohammedans' and 'Gentoos' was erroneous and should not therefore encourage the court to adopt two uniform systems of laws; he was rather in favour of preserving the diversity of local customs and usages, and of letting as much as possible the various communities resolve their own disputes.[73] Therefore, in 1847, at the Bombay high court, Justice Perry ruled that the Khojas would be submitted to their own customary law which was at that time akin to the law of some Hindu communities.[74]

In this way, Shodhan has shown that in matters of administration and personal law, two periods must be clearly distinguished: the earlier, when under Company administration different experiences were made in different regions, such as Punjab, the Bombay Presidency and Bengal, and the later after 1858, when a uniform Bengal-style judiciary was established in Bombay and Madras as India becomes a part of the British Empire.[75] As far as the first period is concerned, in the Bombay Presidency as we have seen above, the diversity of customary law being recognised, all Muslims, for instance, were not treated as one single community. This is exemplified by the Khoja-Memon case tried by Perry in 1848. The recognition of the specific customary law of Nizari Ismaili Khojas as distinct from that of other Muslim groups was not perceived, at that time, as threatening their religious identity; later on Justice Conch (1867) would continue this trend.[76]

In other words, we could say that at least during that period and in that region, caste (*jāti*) was still prevailing over religion (in the modern sense), as a marker of identity. This permitted, as we have seen, the existence of liminal communities and traditions as those represented by the Khojas. But liminality was not to remain acceptable for long. Shodhan also reminds us that in 1866, during the famous 'Aga Khan Case', when, the Islamic origin of the *satpanth* having been determined, and it had to be decided which category, Shiʿi or Sunni, was applicable to them, 'ambiguous' statements were simply ridiculed. The declaration of a Khoja who explained first that he was a Shiʿa, then hesitatingly said he was a 'Sunni' (meaning that the religious doctrine adhered to by him was Shiʿi but that he followed the Sunni customary law) is characteristic of the difficulty with which liminal communities have had to accommodate themselves to binary categories. So was it for the affirmation of another witness concerning the fact that a particular Nizari text was neither Sunni nor Shiʿi but simply 'a good book'.[77]

Anticipating the modern period, it may be interesting to note that the author of this essay has found a similar configuration within the present Pirana Imamshahi community. When summoned to declare themselves unambiguously Shiʿa, Sunni or Hindu, our informants gave various elusive answers. They could simultaneously return themselves as Shiʿi and Sunni or as Hindu and Sufi. Characteristically, this was felt as an embarrassment only by 'categorising' judges applying the binary Hindu-Muslim legal system, who had to resolve disputes within the community. Ordinary devotees and disciples appeared little concerned with the religious identity of the Imamshahi tradition, or rather were satisfied with the category 'Satpanthi'. Like the witness mentioned above by Shodhan, they were inclined to assert that the *satpanth* (lit. 'true path') was neither Sunni nor Shiʿi, neither Muslim nor Hindu, but simply 'a good religion', 'the right way' of worship and devotion.[78]

To come back to the case of the Bombay Khojas, the decision to apply a Hindu-like customary law was contrary to the wishes of the Aga Khan's group. However, it was only after the passing of the Sharia Act in 1937 that the Khojas who had decided to follow the Imam started to be submitted to the same law as all other communities classified as Muslim.[79] This uniform Islamic law would raise new issues, since, traditionally, Ismailis had never adopted the four Sunni schools of *fiqh* or jurisprudence.

The binary concept of personal law, later applied in a uniform way by the British in the Subcontinent, as has been remarked, mainly originated from a 'semantic' misunderstanding, which itself was the result of the Orientalists' attempts to grasp South-Asian civilisation along the familiar lines of Judeo-Christian thought.[80] The ancient – and universal – connection between law and religion was perceived as a possible basis for the establishment of a local judicial system. According to this view, the Jews had their Torah, a sacred book where religious and social rules were defined, the Muslims had the sharia established on the basis of the Qur'an and the Sunna, and the Hindus their dharma, as described in the famous *Dharmashastras*. It was not realised that Islamic religious law comprised various schools and tendencies, whether in the Sunni world where four main systems of jurisprudence of *fiqh* had emerged in the course of history, or among the Shi'a, who were themselves divided into divergent groups, and that the *Dharmashastras* were very far from being applied to all non-Muslims. In many cases, while there was in each kingdom a legal system applicable to all, particularly for criminal cases, at the micro-level, community councils or *panchāyats* (so called because they usually include five members) had their own system of personal law which varied considerably from region to region and from caste to caste.[81] This also applied to other parts of the Muslim world ruled by a colonial power, such as Afghanistan.

The reductionist attitude which prevails in that period applies not only to religious communities but also to social groups, as we will see, with the subsequent attempts at simplifying the de facto caste system (*jāti*) by equating it entirely with the division into four *varṇas* – a move which will continue to influence the modern perception of India and Pakistan.

The religious and social division of the country through the categorising activities of the census operations and the post-1857 personal law system could not but be reflected in the political world. When the time came to actively involve the 'natives' in the administration of the British provinces, the reforms decided by the government in 1909, establishing separate electorates and reservations for the Muslims, 'gave birth to a religio-political community, sections of which began to see themselves in the colonial image of being unified, cohesive and segregated from the Hindus. 'An otherwise diverse "community" was thus homogenised, like a "caste" or a "tribe", in order to be suitably accommodated within political schemes and bureaucratic designs'.[82] Even if this provision was to be short-lived, it would not only give birth to the concept of two separate nations but, like the rest, was to leave indelible traces on the attitude and mentality of the population.

Reformists and Revivalists: Defining Islam and Hinduism

Like Shaykh Ahmad Sirhindi, Shah Wali Allah (1703–1762), who lived in Delhi to witness the decline of the Mughal empire, paved the way for the future reformist movements of Sunni Islam which would, more often than not, refer to him and regard his work as a source of inspiration and authority. However, Marc Gaborieau has made it clear that his ideas have often been misunderstood by scholars as being identical with those of the subsequent twentieth-century Indian Muslim reformers and of the Wahhabis of Arabia.[83] He reminds us that reformers associated with the school of Shah Wali Allah, with the Naqshbandi order or with the Nizami branch of the Chishtis, took a much more moderate stand than their successors would do in the twentieth century.[84]

It is only later, towards the end of the nineteenth century, that a systematic crusade was started against the practices of Indian Muslims that were regarded as 'blameworthy'. Sayyid Ahmad Barelwi (1786–1831) who created, with the help of his disciple Isma'il Shahid, a movement referred to as the Tarīqa-i-Muhammadiyya, is often believed to be a follower of the Wahhabi school of Saudi Arabia.[85] Although it has not been proved to this day that the Indian reformers mentioned above were indeed following that school, their ideas appear analogous and one can even notice the similarity between the name given by Muhammad Ibn 'Abd al-Wahhab to his movement and the title of Isma'il Shahid's work, both defined as *Ṣirāṭ al-mustaqīm* or 'the right path'.[86]

In fact, the debate of the former 'Indian Wahhabis' with their opponents is not primarily a controversy between Islam and Hinduism, but between rival interpretations of Islam, even between Sufis themselves, some reformers preaching a 'purified form' of Sufism rather than attempting to deny its value altogether. Subsequent movements will go still further in trying to define and delimit what Islam should be.

The Deobandi 'traditionalist' school founded in 1867 sought to teach the ulama what they considered to be the true form of religion through a network of madrasas. For them, Shi'ism and therefore Ismailism was heretical, as well as the popular devotional practices at dargas, but they did not reject Sufism altogether. They rather preached what they regarded as its 'purified' form. Much more radical, the Ahl-i Hadith rejected the whole of Sufism, as well as the consensus of the scholars, admitting no source of authority but the Qur'an and hadith.[87]

Actually, all these groups were drawn from the north-Indian Ashrafs, or members of the Muslim nobility. The active role of the ulama during that period corresponds to the decline of the Mughal empire. The ruler and the elites had lost their central position and the ulama emphasised a strict adherence to what they imagined to be a homogenous sharia by all members of the community, in all aspects of life.[88] In creating an image of the 'Other' where otherness was defined as *bidati* (lit. 'of innovation', hence heterodoxy), the Muslim reformists would thus inevitably provoke the response of Hindu revivalists.[89]

However, one must not forget that to begin with, the Hindu reformers were inspired by the British, both Orientalists and Anglicists. At first, their reaction was not against Islam, but against what they considered to be the 'Christian threat'. Orientalists had defined what they regarded as the 'genuine' traditions of the Hindus, while Anglicists had reviled en bloc their beliefs and practices. Confronted with the European and Christian world vision, the Hindus suddenly realised that they did not have one single or uniform religion. Hindus had never regarded themselves as sharing a common system, nor had they attempted to 'unify' their traditions.

In 1910 the 'categorising activities' of British administration reached a new peak when the following proposal was made for the 1911 census. Gait, the Census Commissioner sent a letter to the Provincial Census Superintendents suggesting that they modify the definition of the word 'Hindus'. Hindus were all those who worshipped the 'great Hindu gods', were allowed into Hindu (read Brahmanical) temples and did not cause ritual pollution. In this way the Untouchables and tribal people were excluded. Actually, the gap between these communities and the so-called 'twice-born' was considerable, in terms of customs, beliefs and practices. Dayanand Saraswati, who had played an episodic role at the court of the Jaipur ruler Sawai Jai Singh II, was to start a new chapter in the history of Indian religions by creating, in 1875, an organisation called Arya Samaj. A Brahmin by birth and a Shaiva Dasnami by his sectarian affiliation, Dayanand 'Rishi' – as he was later called – was eager to prove to the British that the 'original inhabitants of Hindoostan' did have, like the Christians, a higher form of religion. Humiliated by the critiques of the Anglicists, but inspired and guided by the Orientalists, the Hindu reformers sought to trace and to revive what they regarded as the original religion of Hindustan. Dayanand claimed that he had found it in the Vedas, the oldest Indo-Aryan scripture. His definition of the Vedic tradition as the only true revelation and as the ultimate authority, implied that all 'the rest' was 'false, illegitimate and filled with error'.[90] In this way, image worship, Puranic traditions, the privileges of Brahmins, as well as folk deities and rituals, etc., were denied any value. In his work entitled *Satyarth Prakash* (1875) the founder of the Arya Samaj also rejects all other world religions, including Buddhism, as false. Typical also is the fact that he preached in Sanskrit, addressing only members of the high castes – in the same way that the Islamic nineteenth-century reformers' teaching was exclusively meant for the Ashrafs. Therefore, the Arya Samaj was at first an elitist body, but its appeal to the masses was to initiate a second stage of reforms, as would be the case for the later Muslim movements which were gradually 'de-Ashrafised'. Dayanand's interpretation of the Vedas was, in fact, quite partial and personal. By 'Vedas' he meant rather the philosophy of the Upanishads which, in the eighth century, had been the base of the Vedanta system created by Shankaracharya. Instead, by prohibiting idol worship, which indeed was not prevalent in the Vedic period, he could demonstrate to the Europeans that the Hindus were not initially and basically idolaters. He adopted the Vedic rituals of *hom* (fire sacrifice) only in a modified form that excluded animal sacrifices. This arbitrary reinvention or reconstruction of the Vedic religion, which was later taken for granted and believed to be the real historical tradition by those who did not have direct access to the Sanskrit texts, was to have a deep impact on modern Hindu fundamentalist ideology.

The establishment of a new ritual, the *śuddhi* or 'purification' ceremony, was to play a major role in the development of the Arya Samaj, contributing, to a considerable extent, to the raising of the 'boundary wall' whose foundation stone had already been laid in the preceding years. Inspired by the conversion campaigns of Christian missionaries, and alarmed by what they thought was a threat to the original traditions of the Subcontinent – although the foreign preachers encountered only a limited success – the Arya Samajists thought first to 'reconvert' the Indian Christians by resorting to the *śuddhi* ritual. The same procedure was subsequently applied to the Muslims.

A tradition of 'conversion' or 're-conversion' to Hinduism was thus started, creating a precedent.[91]

At the turn of the new century the *śuddhi* programme was extended to the Sikhs and to some Untouchable groups; those who, for so many centuries, had been 'outside the pale' were now allowed, after having submitted themselves to the purification ceremony and abandoning certain non-Brahmanical customs (the consumption of cow flesh among others), to be on an equal footing with the high-caste communities. Through the activities of the Arya Samaj many Untouchables were thus invested with the sacred thread, once restricted to the *dvija*s ('twice-born'), and permitted to recite Vedic *mantra*s. At first, Brahmins and members of the higher castes strongly opposed the policy of *śuddhi* among Untouchables, but later some of them favoured this programme when it was applied with some success to upper caste Hindus who had been converted to Christianity and Islam. If the purification ritual was putting an end to caste discrimination, it was also reinforcing social cohesion among the Hindus and considerably increasing their number. Besides, the Aryasamajists were ready to make a few compromises, as for example, when they helped those who had stuck to idol worship to rebuild temples which had been demolished, even though Dayanand's hostility against image worship was very strong.[92]

Of considerable interest for our study, but hardly explored to this day, is the practice of *śuddhi* among members of the liminal communities. For instance, in the fifteenth century, a large group of Untouchables, Meghvals (Balais, Bhambis) of Rajasthan and Gujarat had become disciples of Ramdev Pir, that 'forgotten Ismaili missionary'.[93] Although they appeared outwardly as 'Gupti' Hindus, they had adopted various Islamic customs, such as the prohibition of eating pork which was otherwise widely consumed by non-Islamised Untouchables. After submitting many of them to *śuddhi*, the Aryasamajists told them to eat pork like the others. This detail reveals the way in which symbols can be manipulated in order to define or redefine identity. Similarly, it is alleged that the Nizari Ismaili Imam, Aga Khan III had invited some Gupti leaders to display openly their Islamic identity by partaking of beef which they had carefully avoided when they lived in the guise of 'orthodox' Hindu merchants. This particular point recalls the alliance struck in the fifteenth century between the Pathans and the Shekhawats who were the *murīd*s of Shaykh Burhan (mentioned in chapter

2): the former promised to abstain from killing cows, while the latter renounced the hunting of wild boar and eating its flesh.

In this way, influenced by Dayanand's movement, some Meghval religious reformers sought to modify a number of customs to which the Nizarpanthi followers of Ramdev Pir had adhered. For instance, near the holy lake of Pushkar, Swami Gokuldas performed his own version of the *śuddhi* ceremony. He told his followers to crawl under the body of a stone cow and made them swear not to eat its flesh any more.

While examining further the case of the Nizari Ismaili communities we will see one more example of the impact of the Arya Samaj on various liminal communities. But before doing so we must make a few additional remarks regarding the phenomena connected with proselytism, conversion and reconversion.

As a number of scholars have tried to demonstrate, proselytism was not only alien to the various indigenous religions, but the Muslim rulers themselves and even the Sufis had not developed an extensive programme of conversion.[94] If it is true that the Sunnis have not made any consequent attempts at changing the original religions of the local people, one should not forget that certain Sufi *ṭarīqas*, in particular the Suhrawardis, Qadiris and Naqshbandis, were on the other hand actively involved in converting the Ismailis (both Tayyibis and Nizaris) to Sunnism. Those who resisted generally chose to conceal themselves among the Hindus. The persuasive Ismailis themselves had developed highly effective methods of conversion into which their *dāʿī*s and local pirs were trained.

Coming back to the Aryasamajists, their rivals were not only Christians or Muslims. They had other opponents among 'orthodox' Hindus – mainly those who stuck to the Brahmanical *varṇāśrāma* dharma caste system, and had, through a series of religious assemblies (*dharm maṇḍals*) created the Sanatan Dharm movement. The idea of an 'eternal' (*sanātan*) dharma was shared by various reformist bodies and the Arya Samajists themselves sometimes referred to their Vedic or Arya Dharma as 'Sanātan Dharma', a detail which necessarily created confusion in the mind of those who read the various publications which appeared during that period. In contradistinction to the Aryas, the Sanatanis were the defenders of Brahmanical values and strong supporters of image worship. After they had admitted into their ranks various lower caste communities integrated through the same *śuddhi* ceremony, they eventually succeeded in outnumbering the Aryas, creating a different form of 'unified' Hinduism characterised by the cult of the great Brahmanical gods; they widely patronised the construction of temples where worship was performed with the help of Brahmin ritual specialists.

We will see that the bitter rivalry which opposed the Aryas and the Sanatanis in various parts of the Subcontinent was reflected in Gujarat when both reforming organisations sought to 'reconvert' the Kanbis or Patidars who had become the disciples of the Ismaili preacher Sayyid Imam Shah.

Towards the middle of the nineteenth century, a new chapter in the history of South-Asian religious communities started with the arrival of Aga Khan I, Hasan ʿAli Shah (1817–1881), in India. As a result of a series of controversies, disputes and court cases, the Nizari Ismailis of the Subcontinent gradually emerged as a distinct group. As has been said earlier, until their identity came to be defined and their original tradition disclosed, the various Nizari groups concealed themselves as separate castes or sects, bearing different names. The origin and nature of their religion had remained unknown to outsiders who were not aware of the historical and religious links existing between scattered communities referred to as Khojas, Shamsis, Maulais, Momins, Imamshahis, Athias, Nizarpanthis, Barmatis, Prahladpanthis (Bishnois), Jasnathis, Aipanthis, and so forth. In the course of time, as has been shown by various scholars, groups or sections of them had come closer to Sunni or Twelver Shiʿi Islam or to Hindu traditions.[95] While the Aga Khan was seeking to gather and unify these scattered communities, a party of Khojas known as the Barbhais refused to acknowledge his spiritual authority and argued that they were Sunni, like their pir, Sadr al-Din. We know that the diverse identities assumed by the Nizaris had their origin in the Shiʿa practice sanctioned by the Qurʾan of *taqiyya*, the precautionary concealment of beliefs. This long practice of *taqiyya* had surprising consequences: firstly, as has been already said, the absence of a clear group identity and secondly, the gradual identification of segments of the scattered Nizari communities with other religious groups. In October 1861 the Aga Khan took a historic decision. He published a paper in which he invited the Khojas to abandon *taqiyya*, which had become redundant with the advent of British power, and to acknowledge their identity as Shiʿi Imami Ismailis. The famous Aga

Khan Case of Bombay which followed in 1866 was a major event. The rigorous definition of what constituted a Khoja, given by Judge Arnould in support of the Imam's claims, induced some of them to secede and become either full-fledged Sunnis, Twelver Shiʿa or to leave Islam altogether. Although this phenomenon was initially restricted to the Khoja communities, the criteria of membership were gradually extended to Shamsis, Maulais and others, with similar consequences.

Efforts to integrate the Imamshahis who, in fact, shared the same history and development as the Nizaris, even if they had evolved in a somewhat different direction,[96] were only partly successful. At the beginning of the twentieth century, there was considerable controversy between the followers of the pir or *sajjāda-nishīn* of Pirana and those who had accepted the Aga Khan as their Imam. For instance, displeased with the changes that had been made at Pirana (mainly aimed at giving a more distinct identity to the Imamshahis, separating them from the mainstream Khojas and bringing them closer to the Hindus), a few Imamshahis of Bhavnagar belonging the Kachia caste decided to join the Nizari Khojas and accept the Aga Khan as Imam.[97] There was sharp controversy over their decision. Actually, at that time, following the Aga Khan or retaining one's allegiance to the religious leaders of Pirana was as much a question of doctrine as of authority. For the Khojas who accepted him as such, the Aga Khan was the Imam of the time, whereas the 'Piranapanthis' (Imamshahis), for whom the line of Imams had been interrupted, recognised various pirs, waiting for the arrival of the Imam Qa'im at the end of time. At first, the 'dissident' Imamshahis of Bhavnagar remained fully integrated in the Khoja *jamāt*, but later on, due to the pressure of their Imamshahi caste-fellows who did not recognise the same Imam, they had to form separate Gupti *jamāts* who owed allegiance to the Aga Khan. This phenomenon points to the persistence of caste identity which, for some groups, tends to remain stronger than religious affiliation.

The case of the Sayyids of Pirana, who also were persuaded by some Khoja devotees to join them, was probably different. Like other Nizari groups, they too had been concealing their Ismaili affiliation under the Sunni or Twelver Shiʿa guise – a fact which may have enabled them to come closer to the Islamised *jamāts*. Actually, the integration into the Khoja *jamāt* of Imamshahi Sayyids, Guptis, whether Shamsis or Imamshahis, and of newly converted members has been a long and complex process which has hardly been studied to this day.

As far as other liminal communities were concerned (Nizarpanthis, Bishnois, etc.), the author of this essay has attempted to show that after having severed their links from the parent body, they had gradually forgotten the nature of their original Ismaili tradition. Among them, those who remained members of these groups preserved most of their former beliefs and rituals while gradually identifying themselves with Hindu groups, whereas others, losing all their specific traits, with the exception of the reverence for the pir who had converted them, became integrated in Sunni and Twelver communities.[98] This process was basically the same as the later split of the Khoja community into Sunni, Twelver, Arya Samaji and Swaminarayani Khojas, although it may have occurred much earlier. As for the Khojas who had recognised the authority of the Aga Khan, they increased their numbers by joining all the Shamsis, Maulais and Imamshahis who chose to follow the living Imam. The shifting of identities was thus reflected in a dual mechanism of fusion and scission. It is this remarkable phenomenon that has been referred to in the title of this essay as 'crossing the threshold'. For most liminal communities, such a step had practically become a necessity, because the doorway on which they had stood for so many centuries was being gradually replaced by a partition wall.

The second important consequence of the Aga Khan court case was that for the first time in the modern history of the Subcontinent, the roots, doctrines and rituals of the local Nizari Ismailis were publicly disclosed. Interestingly enough, those who had chosen to leave the ranks of the Ismailis were the first to write extensive works on the history, literature and rituals of the South-Asian Nizaris. The most famous study is undoubtedly Nanjiani's *Khojā Vṛttānt* (1894) which, apart from providing rich information on the Khojas and Imamshahis, also throws light on communities like the Nizarpanthi worshippers of Ramdev Pir who are now perceived as Hindus. Nanjiani's understanding of this phenomenon and of the so-called acculturation of the Khojas, who drew inspiration from various indigenous beliefs and customs to create their own literature and ritual, certainly lacks in accuracy and is, at times, confusing; but in many respects his ideas simply reflect the current ideas of the colonial period.

To give an example, Nanjiani sees the Khojas who had not yet 'crossed the threshold' as 'oscillating between two religions'. Similarly, the Imamshahis, Matias or Momins (indigenous communities converted by Imamshah and his successors in Gujarat) had been portrayed by Dayaram (1777–1852), a Gujarati poet, in this picturesque way:

> The Momin swings in the middle,
> He is neither Hindu nor Turk.[99]

This situation did not fail to attract the attention of the leaders of the Arya Samaj who soon began to spread their ideas among the Momins. It is difficult to evaluate the exact number of those who joined the ranks of Dayanand Rishi's movement, but they may have been as many as the Gupti Khojas and Shamsis. Once they had joined the Arya Samaj, a few of them engaged in a campaign against the appeal of Aga Khan III, Sultan Muhammad Shah (1885–1957), to their caste-fellows. Curiously, one of them, Radhakrishnan, even joined forces with E.D. Kaba, a former Khoja, who had chosen to identify himself with the Sunni community. This alliance of two parties claiming to represent opposite, rival and even hostile traditions, is highly significant for the understanding of the issue connected with religious identities. In a sense, it is the first attempt to force the Khoja community into adhering to one of the major blocs which were emerging at that time.[100]

The life story of Narayan Ram Limbani 'Contractor' and of his companions exemplifies, as does the tragic fate of the Meos during Partition, the myriad personal dramas associated with the historical 'crossing of the threshold'. A Satpanthi Patidar of Kutch following the Imamshahi tradition in the Gupti style, Limbani went to Bombay in search of employment and came into professional contact with members of the upper castes. As a result of this encounter and of the curiosity aroused by the little that was known of his beliefs and practices, the young Contractor experienced an intense feeling of shame when his companions persuaded him that the *satpanth* was a 'debased' form of religion. Although, as a Gupti, he appeared to be a member of the Hindu community, his tradition was full of Muslim elements which the outsiders could by no means understand. Eventually, Contractor left the Imamshahi community to become a staunch Arya Samajist and devoted his life to 'reconverting' his caste-fellows to 'Hinduism'. His case is very much like that of E.D. Kaba, the Pirana Khoja who, after having embraced Twelver Shi'i Islam, denounced his former coreligionists.[101] Contractor, with the same sharp criticism, claimed to disclose in his main work entitled *Pīrānā Satpanthī nī pol,* as indicated by the title, 'The Real Secret of the Pirana Sect'. Adopting the point of view of a high-caste Hindu, he used the adjectives *ardhdagdh* (hybrid), *kabristānī* (funerary, an allusion to the practice of burial), and *kichḍiā* (hotch-potch) to describe his former *panth*. These words, one cannot fail to notice, echo those used by the British census reports and gazetteers to describe liminal communities.

However, in Gujarat also, the Arya Samaj lost ground, as it was opposed by the Sanatanis who defended a more 'orthodox' or rather 'Brahmanical' ideal. This contributed to an acceleration in the process of 're-Hinduisation' of those Imamshahi communities, as one of Contractor's companions, Ratan Si, had also joined the movement. In fact the Pirana Satpanthis who followed him went one step further by starting to build temples and to use images in worship.

Towards the end of the nineteenth century, therefore, it became extremely difficult to display a dual identity in the Subcontinent. Perceiving their traditions as 'degenerated forms of the Hindu religion', the reformers sought simply to eliminate them, forgetting that 'the sacred guardians of the doorway' had been, for centuries, a natural element of the native landscape.

At this stage, one should mention the interesting attempt made by the poet Ebrahim Varteji, a Khoja who had joined the Twelvers in his early years but finally chose to follow the Ismaili Imam. Varteji tried to 'revitalise' the *satpanth* and project it as a coherent system, not just as 'a mishmash of conflicting beliefs and practices'. In doing so he resorted to a typically Ismaili theory. Ismailism as the correct interpretation of Islam was the completion of previous revealed religious traditions, and in the context of South Asia, the culmination of Indian religions. By incorporating certain indigenous beliefs, the Ismaili faith sought to integrate them into the wider framework of its own doctrine by transforming some of its elements. Like some great Sufis, among whom one can quote Ibn ʿArabi, Rumi, ʿAbd al-Quddus Gangohi, Bullhe Shah, and so on, the Ismailis believed in the fundamental inner unity of all religions. In conformity with this vision, a number of Khoja publications of that period and, later on, some Imamshahi books, displayed a logo in which the Sanskrit mantra *Om* could also be read backwards as *ʿAli* in Arabic.[102]

But times had changed and it became more and more difficult for the non-Ismailis, or for those who had forsaken their Nizari affiliation, to understand the deep meaning of their original tradition. It is reported, for instance, that when Ebrahim Varteji tried to explain to Gandhi in 1918 about the close relations of the Ismailis with other Muslims, as well as Hindus, and that the Aga Khan was not just a Muslim but a universal Indian leader, the Mahatma remained silent for a few minutes before replying, 'I cannot say anything about these matters'. Although the fact is little known, in his childhood, Gandhi himself followed a liminal sect, the Pranami religion, to which his mother belonged. But it seems that he gradually drifted away from it and, at least outwardly, identified himself more and more with 'normative' Hindus, while retaining many of the Pranami teachings'.[103] His surprise may have been caused by the striking similarities that he was discovering between his mother's religion and Nizari Ismailism, rather than by his failure to understand the Imam's position.

Creating a 'Third Identity'

We may now conclude this chapter by re-examining the question of Sikhism in a more critical way that will enable us to shed some light on the process of identity development in the face of newly emerging orthodoxies. As members of another important liminal tradition, the Sikhs were submitted to the same historical pressure, but the consequences were to be drastically different.

We have seen that a considerable debate took place concerning the origin of the movement and its nature. Was it more Islamic or more Hindu? Although W.H. McLeod asserts that the influence of Islam (in particular its mystical dimension) on the *panth* founded by Guru Nanak has been minimal, evidence points to the contrary. While McLeod insists on this point, Bruce B. Lawrence discusses the whole issue in greater detail.[104] Sikh literature, hagiography and rituals are replete with Sufi and Shi'i elements which have been pointed out by various authors, although not fully and clearly exposed. Like McLeod, many contemporary Western scholars tend to denigrate such British views as reflected in Hughes' *Dictionary of Islam*, and to regard as negligible the Muslim influence on Sikhism. According to them, Guru Nanak's *panth* was simply an offshoot of the Sant Paramparā, and in particular a spiritual heir of Kabir. But even if it is true, one can argue that the

Islamic roots of some *nirgūṇ* Sant movements (like those of Kabir and Dadu) are far from having been fully explored. Be that as it may, it is clear that, under Sunni rule, the Sikhs were safe enough as members of one of the numerous indigenous *panth*s, but when perceived as Muslim 'heretics' they faced persecution. We have shown earlier their rapprochement with the Hindu social and religious world. In our opinion, this phenomenon has not been correctly understood.

Jones has remarked that 'heavily influenced by Islam, Sikhism's heritage of bloody struggle against Moghul persecution forcibly maintained Sikh ties with the Hindu community'.[105] Sikhism, according to him, was originally a Hindu tradition that has absorbed certain Muslim (Sufi) ideas; it could have drifted away further from its alleged roots but eventually had to remain close to them, mainly for political reasons. In surmising that Islam and Sunnism are one, Jones repeats the same mistake that has prevented scholars from looking at the 'syncretic' Sant Paramparā from a different perspective: the conflict which opposed the Sikhs to the Mughals is to be interpreted in the same way as their critique of legalistic, Sunni Islam. Similarly, the Sants' critique of the Muslims is constructed, in colonial and post-colonial communal discourse, as a 'Hindu' reaction. In fact, practically until the advent of the Arya Samaj, Hindu religious literature rarely included discussion of Islam.[106]

At this juncture, the Ismaili model may help us to view the issue in a totally different light. It is easy to see that South-Asian Nizari literature, although undoubtedly rooted in Muslim tradition, showed the most uncompromising attitude towards the narrow interpretation of Islam by qadis and mullahs. This critique, needless to say, was not levelled at Islam as such, but at one of its particular versions represented by 'legalistic' Sunnism. On the other hand, since Sunni rulers and theologians regarded them as 'heretics', in the face of persecution, the Nizaris, resorting to *taqiyya* as we have seen, often took refuge in the vast border-zone represented by the Hindu world. Satpanthi *ginān*s of the 'prophetic type' clearly point to the somewhat stifled political ambitions of the Nizaris. In many Khoja and crypto-Ismaili devotional texts of this type, the conquest of Delhi (the main seat of Sunni political power) has a highly symbolical meaning, although it is portrayed as a somewhat remote event that will take place only at the end of the present cosmic era or Kali Yuga.[107]

Therefore, the bitter rivalry that pitted the Sikhs against the Delhi rulers (as well as their critique of Sunni theologians) should not be perceived as reflecting an anti-Islamic attitude. Some authors have shown how Sikh culture, at the peak of its glory, and at the very time when it was proclaiming victory over the declining Mughal empire, was still pervaded with Persian/Mughal elements. If Ranjit Singh, who created an ephemeral Sikh kingdom in the Punjab, was referred to as 'maharaja', one must not forget that titles such as 'padshah', 'nawab' or 'sultan al-qawm' were widely used among Sikh military nobility.[108]

It must be stated that before the 'categorising activities' of the British had started to modify the social and religious fabric of colonial India, members of the various Sikh *panth*s did not care to know which elements were dominant in their tradition. Its liminality has been later underplayed, but it is clear that the Sikh gurus had preserved throughout a dual personality, as exemplified by the seventeenth-century guru Hari Krishan who was called Balmukund by the Hindus and Bala Pir by the Muslims.[109]

In the first census reports of Punjab, the Sikhs were listed as 'Hindus', but from 1868 onward 'Sikh' emerged as a separate category,[110] although it had not yet been clearly defined. Consequently, the figures registered by the census officers kept changing. In 1891, for the administrators of the British Raj, 'Sikh' meant exclusively a member of the Khalsa *panth* (the militant movement believed to have been founded by the tenth guru, Gobind Singh). Other followers of Nanak's religion could declare themselves as 'Nanakpanthis' or members of other Sikh branches. But in 1901, sect affiliation was not registered. Ten years later the census entered as a Sikh every person who claimed to be one. 'A new category, that of 'Sikh-Hindu' was also permitted. The same procedure was repeated in 1921, 'clearly implying that, although administrators are meant to be neat and precise, this particular tangle had proven to be too daunting to unravel'.[111] The judicial system established for all suits concerning inheritance, property and marriage, with its simplistic Hindu/Muslim dichotomy, was another trap. This can be illustrated by the debate that started in 1898, after the death of one Sardar Dayal Singh Majithia who had, under Hindu civil law, donated all his fortune to a trust. His widow contested the will, claiming that her husband was a Sikh and not a Hindu. 'Thus the Punjab High Court found itself faced with the question of determining whether Sikhs were or were not Hindus.' Eventually, the Court decided he was to be classified as Hindu.[112] The heated debate that ensued took place in the framework of local reform movements, among which the Arya Samaj played a prominent role, and eventually, it resulted in the creation of a new identity for the Sikhs.

Dayanand, the founder of Arya Samaj, was highly critical of Guru Nanak and of Sikhism; although he admitted that the founder of the *panth* had noble aims, he stressed his ignorance of Sanskrit and of the Vedas. According to him, Nanak's tradition was rooted in village culture and vernacular languages. The Sikh *panth* was, consequently, just one of the many local sects to be rejected. However, other Aryas who were of a different opinion had made followers among the Khatri and Arora trading castes.[113] In 1880, during a public lecture in Gujranwala, Bhai Basant Singh, a prominent Sikh leader, stated that 'the mission of Guru Nanak was simply to revive the Vedic religion of the ancient Rishis of Arya Varta.'[114] Soon, some Sikh leaders belonging to the Singh *sabhas* (representing the Khalsa reformist tendency), joined the Aryasamajists in their *śuddhi* (purification) movement. In 1885, both Sikhs and Aryas 'purified' a Muslim convert. When the Shuddhi Sabha was founded, it started to work actively from 1890 onward with the Arya Samaj and the Singh *sabhas*. One wonders what the ritual referred to as *śuddhi* could have meant for the Sikhs. It certainly remained ambiguous, and reflected the bias of some of their leaders for the Arya ideal. True, like the Muslims and contrary to the Brahmanical Hindus, they had a real tradition of conversion, with a ceremony that was nearly identical to that of the Nizari Ismailis. Members were integrated into the community through an initiation ritual including the partaking of *amṛt* (holy water) referred to by the same term in both traditions as *pāval/pāhul*.[115] However, the participation of the Sikhs in the *śuddhi* movement was theoretically aimed at preventing the Untouchable groups among them from converting to Christianity or Islam. In practice it had the strangest consequences, as in the case of a Sikh who converted to Islam and, through *śuddhi*, was allegedly 'taken back into the fold of Hinduism' after he had, for some time, 'lived like a good Hindu.'[116] One can conclude that in this particular context the word 'Hindu' had a caste rather than a religious connotation, the 'purified' Sikh being simply reintegrated into his former *jāti*. The new ambiguity, resulting from the earlier identity criteria of *jāt/panth*, was to disappear with the final crystallisation of the British legal and census categories, and with the new definitions given by various reform movements.

Following the 1898 court case, various Sikh leaders sought to re-define their religion. According to some of them Sikhism 'was merely an earlier version of the Arya Samaj' – a view which led to the conclusion: '*Sikh Hindū Hain*'(Sikhs are Hindus), whereas Sardar Kahan Singh declared in a famous tract: '*Ham Hindū Nahin*' (We are not Hindus). From this controversy was to emerge a new group of Khalsa Sikhs (those following the *panth* said to have been founded by the tenth and last guru Gobind Singh) demanding a separate identity. As Jones has stated: 'the search for identity within the Sikh community and between Sikhs and Hindus became embroiled in the Samaj campaign to purify and thus save outcastes from Christian conversion.'[117]

Soon, however, a number of Sikhs realised that they were basically different from the Arya Samajists, particularly when a group of Mazhabis (Untouchable Sikhs) gave up their religion to become Aryas. Besides, *śuddhi* was a concept that did not fit with the Sikh ethos. They had nothing to do with Arya or Sanatani proselytisation, since anybody could embrace Sikhism simply by taking *amṛt*. This reaction, and the Arya-Sikh debate, following the British 'categorising' policy of the 1890s, gradually induced the Sikhs to address more specifically the issue of their identity: were they simply another branch or sect of Hinduism, or did they have a distinctive faith of their own? Let us recall here that the question of Sikh identity could acquire some relevance only after the categories 'Hinduism' and 'Islam' came to be defined or redefined in a rigid way. For a long period the disciples of Guru Nanak distinguished themselves, like most other communities, by their specific religious traditions, as well as by their reverence for the founder of their *panth*. At that time, it would have been absurd to attach to them the labels 'Hindu', 'Muslim' or 'Sikh'.

Besides, the Sikhs did not constitute a uniform group. The modern tendency to identify all of them with the Khalsa *panth* makes us forget that all the followers of Guru Nanak and of his nine successors did not adhere exclusively to one tradition. They were variously referred to as Udasis, Jagyasis, Nanakpanthis, Sahajdharis, Kukas, Nirankaris, Sarvarias, and many others – even if some of these categories were overlapping, as for example in the case of Nanakpanthis who could be Udasis or Jagyasis and were called Sahajdharis (those who follow the slow, easy path) since the Singhs regarded them as potential adherents of the Khalsa.[118] A rapprochement which had occurred in the early nineteenth century between a number of Khalsa and Sahajdhari Sikhs resulted in the creation of a Sikh Sanatan movement. Claiming that its roots were much older than Guru Nanak, it sought to connect itself with the wider current of Indian religions referred to as 'Sanatan Dharm'. It was the Sanatan leadership that declared itself Hindu when the question of religious identity was raised through the judiciary and intellectual debates of that period. However, as Oberoi warns us, the term 'Hindu', in that context, should not be interpreted as it is today. It was more 'an ethno-territorial category which applied to people who inhabited the Subcontinent; on the other hand it was an umbrella word encompassing a body of indigenous religious beliefs, as distinct from exogenous religions like Islam and Christianity'.[119] However, the Singh Sabha's decision to dissociate itself from the Sanatan episteme (condemning the worship of popular deities as well as the cult of pirs) and to sever its links with the Arya Samaj, resulted in a new definition of Sikhism restricted to the Khalsa ideology, as a fully-fledged religion, totally distinct from Hinduism or Islam. This definition was reflected, as we have seen, in the assertion 'we are not Hindus'.

Another fact, which has been generally underestimated, deserves our attention. In the 1911 census, some Sikhs had still returned themselves as followers of Pir Sakhi Sarvar (mentioned above), a 'liminal' Sufi saint who flourished in Punjab.[120] In fact, many others also continued to worship Gugga Pir, another 'liminal' figure (dates unknown), who was very popular in North India, and was simultaneously worshipped as a snake god, a Rajput hero, a Muslim pir and a Sikh saint.[121] This means that in practice the Sikh community continued to be liminal, preserving Islamic as well as indigenous elements. Actually, if, at the end of the nineteenth century, some Sikhs could regard themselves as Hindus, or call themselves only Sikhs, never identifying themselves with Muslims, it does not mean, as been often taken for granted, that they were basically hostile to Islam as such. The Sikhs, we must insist, were certainly never close to the Sunni ethos, and one must recall that in the past, the words Musalman and Turk had been restricted to the followers of the Sunni forms of Islam, seldom referring to Sufis (even if they were Sunni) and to a lesser extent to Twelver Shiʿa, Ismailis or other Muslims. The disciples of Pir Sakhi Sarvar, perceived, as said earlier, as the 'brothers of the Sikhs', actually belonged to a Shi'i (maybe Ismaili) brand of Islam which, during the colonial period, came to be viewed as 'deviant' by the British as well as by Sunni reformers.

Towards the end of the nineteenth century the Sikh Sabhas started to oppose the multiple dimension of Sikh identity. They created a new 'great tradition' rooted in the Khalsa episteme and consigned all those who did not accept their standards to the margins of society: 'These marginalised groups finally turned their backs on Sikh tradition and went their own way. The older pluralist paradigm of Sikh faith was displaced forever and replaced by a highly uniform Sikh identity, the one we know today as modern Sikhism.'[122] On the other hand, as we shall see, the decision to submit the Sikhs to Hindu personal law would later have far-reaching consequences.

In this way, rather than choosing the label 'Hindu' or 'Muslim', refusing to 'cross the threshold', the Sikh reformers succeeded in transforming their *panth* into a distinctly separate faith, giving birth to a 'third identity'. But by defining their own boundaries, they eventually closed the doorway and in creating another orthodoxy, they contributed to the consolidation of the new boundary wall. Besides, their arbitrary classification as 'Hindus' according to Indian modern personal law was not to remain without consequences for the global issue of religious identity.

4

Nation and Religion (1920–2000)

'Why only two I do not know, for if nationality was based on religion, then there were many nations in India ...'

Jawaharlal Nehru*

From the beginning of the twentieth century, with the emergence of new definitions of the terms 'Hindu', 'Muslim' and 'Sikh', the former notions of *jāti* and *panth* were gradually marginalised. The wide spectrum of religious traditions which allowed a free flow of ideas through the open passage of the doorway, came to be reduced to two main, broad categories which posed as orthodox and looked at each other with hostility, each standing on one side of the boundary wall which they were trying to raise higher every day. Around 1920 the comparatively recent notions of 'religion' and 'nation' had become largely accepted as values superior to those of caste and sect. Religious and political discourse became more and more intertwined, playing a crucial role in this transformation, and eventually leading to the final drama of Partition.

In the last chapter of this essay we will examine how this process was gradually reinforced, leaving however pockets of resistance which continued to manifest themselves in various ways.

The Concept of a Hindu Nation: Who is Hindu?

The apparent faultline which revealed itself at that time came to be perceived as a phenomenon that had always existed since the advent of Islam in the Subcontinent. As we have seen, this perception resulted from the creation of 'orthodoxies' that sought to incorporate the myriad traditions which had flourished independently by fitting them into their mould, or to reject them altogether as 'heterodox'. Apart from having to choose between clear-cut allegiances the followers of different traditions were forced to transform some of their practices in order to make them fit into the new rigid framework.

First of all we will have to examine the movements that were instrumental in crystallising a 'Hindu' identity when the various issues connected with independence started to be raised during the last phase of colonial rule. For instance, once India was free, on what basis would the new independent country that consisted of so many religious communities, castes and regional and ethnic groups, be governed and administered? Neither the whole of the Subcontinent, nor even its largest portions, had been united into one single empire before the Mughals and the British; apart from being much smaller in size, pre-Mughal empires had never succeeded in surviving over a long period of time. In other words, there was no real historical model of what the modern thinkers would refer to as an 'Indian nation'.

Although Rishi Dayanand's Arya Samaj had established its own version of Hinduism based on Vedic ideals which, according to him, was the true, original religion and culture of all the inhabitants of Hindustan, he was not himself an exponent of Hindu nationalism. Besides, his movement had to face the strong opposition of all those who defended the Brahmanical caste-system enshrined in the *varṇāśrāma dharma.* During the 1891 census of Punjab, in order to dissociate themselves from 'idol-worshippers' (mainly represented by the Hindu Sanatanis), the Arya Samajists were told to return themselves as 'Aryas' and not as 'Hindus'. In 1911 the situation changed. The fact that they readily adopted the label 'Hindu' points to the emergence of an overall Hindu consciousness. Indeed, Sanatanis and Aryas were to minimise their differences and join their efforts in the activities of the Hindu Mahasabha. Founded in 1915, this political organisation which was to play a key role in the formation of Hindu nationalism, had its roots in the Bharat Dharmmandal of the Sanatanis and in the various Hindu Sabhas organised by the Arya Samajists during the first decade of the century. In 1909, Lala Lajpat Rai, a follower of Dayanand's movement, had already declared during the first Punjab Provincial Hindu Conference which took place at Lahore: 'There can be no doubt that Hindus are a "nation" in themselves because they represent a type of civilisation of their own'.[1] For Lal Chand, another Aryasamajist, patriotism should not be only geographical but communal. This declaration was meant to contradict openly the ideals of the Congress Party for which the Indian nation included all the communities living within the frontiers of the British-Indian realm.

But the final process of crystallisation took place only in the 1920s as a response to an imaginary Other. About ten years after separate electorates had been granted to the Muslims, some of them had mobilised themselves in 1919 to create the Khilafat movement (a protest against the part played by the British in the negotiations which led to the suppression of the caliphate.) In Kerala the movement had degenerated into violence. Actually, the cohesion of Muslims as one single community was grossly exaggerated. Not all of them subscribed to the Khilafat movement. Besides, different groups and currents continued to exist within Islam. But this event contributed to a sense of vulnerability among certain Hindus, in particular the Aryas and Sanatanis. Dr Moonje, one of the leaders of the Mahasabha, attributed the weakness of the Hindus to the fact that there were too many sects and traditions, too many castes which divided them. In contradistinction to this he perceived the Muslims as forming one, well-organised community sharing the same beliefs and ideals. This feeling, which Christophe Jaffrelot calls the 'inferiority complex of the majority', was instrumental in creating among the Hindus a new sense of unity and solidarity.[2] Since the idea of one single religious and social entity was entirely alien to the indigenous tradition, the leaders of the Hindu Mahasabha sought to organise the Hindus on the pattern of Muslims and Christians. For instance, the Birla family patronised the building of huge pan-Hindu temples without any regional or sectarian features, where all sorts of people could gather for worship, as they did in mosques and churches.

The final formulation of Hindu nationalism was due to a Maharashtrian Brahmim, Vinayak Damodar Savarkar, who later become one of the presidents of the Hindu Mahasabha. His famous work, published in 1923, *Hindutva, Who is a Hindu?*, was to serve as a model for all future Hindu nationalist and fundamentalist organisations. This new conception of 'Hinduness' (an approximate translation of the neologism *hindutva*) rested on an imaginary reconstruction of a Vedic Golden Age when people were supposed to be united under one nation. For Savarkar a Hindu was 'a person who regards the land of Bharatvasha from Indus to the seas as his fatherland as well as his holy land – that is, the cradle of his religion'. In this way the leader of the Mahasabha denied any patriotism to Muslims and Christians whom he wrongly suspected to be more faithful to their respective holy lands than to their native country. This definition, on the other hand, implied that all sectarian differences and caste discriminations should be left aside. Not only Untouchables, but Adivasis (tribal groups) were to be included in the great 'Hindu family'. However, the huge diversity that characterised all these groups was a large obstacle to the path of unity. That is why a number of symbols and concepts had to be selected as the 'markers' of this artificially forged Hindu identity.

In this way, festivals like Diwali and Rakhi, the great pilgrimage centres, worship of the cow, etc., were chosen as the main components of Hindutva, and people were encouraged to give up beliefs and practices which did not fit into that framework. In fact, nearly all the promoters of 'Hinduness' had been Brahmins, and Hindu nationalism was to remain deeply embedded in high caste ideology. As Jaffrelot has it, 'The Hindutva of Savarkar was conceived primarily as an ethnic community possessing a territory and sharing the same racial and cultural characteristics, three attributes which stemmed from the mythical reconstruction of the Vedic Golden Age'.[3] For these very reasons, Hindu nationalist ideology called for recognition of Sanskrit or Hindi as the national language and, consequently, the hegemony of a particular trend of South Asian culture and society represented by North Indian Brahmanical values which has constantly struggled for power, attempting to subdue rival currents, was recognised as the norm.

In 1925, deeply influenced by Savarkar's theories of Hindutva and initiated into politics by Moonje, Keshav Baliram Hedgewar, one of the leaders of the Mahasabha, founded the Rashtriya Swayamsevak Sangh (RSS), or Association of National Volunteers. After the decline of the Arya Samaj and the 'dilution' of Sanatani ideals the Hindu Mahasabha itself faded into the background and Hindu nationalist ideology came to be represented by the RSS. This movement, although basically pervaded by Brahmanical, north-Indian values, succeeded in attracting Sanskritised, low-caste and Untouchable groups, considerably broadening its base and projecting itself as the defender of threatened Hinduism. By emphasising martial values, it opposed Mahatma Gandhi's ideal of non-violence which was seen as a 'feminine' value and regarded as the cause of Hindu decline in the past. The RSS developed a para-military organisation whose aim was to transform the 'emasculated Hindus' (as compared with the allegedly aggressive Muslims) into manly warrior-ascetics, and sought to reinforce the sense of solidarity among frustrated middle-class youths.

Certain Hindu religious symbols were presented as national symbols which all communities were told to accept. Besides, the RSS attempted to create unity and cohesiveness among the Hindus by using the same arguments as the Arya Samaj and the Mahasabha. The image of the threatening Other, in particular, the Muslim, was supposed to rally a vast number of people who would otherwise have refused to unite. But, by doing this, the RSS went further than its predecessors. Instead of using politics to spread its ideas, it sought to go directly to the people and educate them through a network of schools where a new version of South-Asian history was taught. The period preceding the advent of Islam was presented as a Golden Age, an imagined Ram Rajya (Rama's rule) which was brutally interrupted by the coming of the Muslims. They were considered to be responsible for all the evils of society and for the division, weakness and submission of the Hindus. From the Muslim period onward, they argued, the whole history of the Subcontinent (Bharatvarsha) had been nothing but the constant assault by Muslims, who were accused of innumerable forced conversions and massacres, and the occasional resistance of some heroic Hindus. The character of some historical figures was reinterpreted so as to fit into this image. Wilfully ignoring the subtleties of history, the RSS ideologues transformed Prithvi Raj Chauhan, the last Hindu king of Delhi, Maharana Pratap, the ruler of Mewar, and the Sikh Guru Gobind Singh into national heroes who had fought for the independence of the Hindu nation. The irony is that in spite of all this, Savarkar himself, the first exponent of Hindutva, along with all the RSS leaders, remained carefully aloof from the battles which, in the 1920s, were fought for independence by other Hindus and Muslims.

In fact, the movement for a free India was mainly represented by the Congress Party and by its most charismatic figure Mahatma Gandhi. For him the ideal was a secular nation – secular in the sense that each religious community would be allowed to develop itself freely within the framework of a democratic state. And although Gandhi appeared to many as a kind of Hindu sadhu, using in the political battle symbols of Hindu asceticism, his original religion was of the 'inclusive' type, which recognised and respected the values of other faiths, as different paths to the same truth. Actually, as the Mahatma himself admits in his autobiography, and as has been said earlier, his mother was a devoted follower of the Pranami *sampradāy*,[4] a liminal sect that appears to have emerged in the seventeenth century as a separate branch of the Imamshahi Satpanth. However, while defending the principle of diversity, it seems that later on Gandhi implicitly recognised, and even encouraged to a certain extent, the idea of single, uniform religions called Hinduism and Islam, as he himself adopted a more sharply-defined Hindu identity.[5] By choosing to fight his battle for independence from within a religious tradition, and by appealing emotionally to the masses, he may have also unconsciously contributed to consolidating the notion of two separate religious blocs, even if he did not view them as hostile and made all possible efforts to reconcile them. This ambiguity was to be reflected in the attitude of some later Congress leaders.

The cases of other famous figures, such as Vivekananda also deserve to be mentioned. Often uncritically praised abroad as one of the great Hindu philosophers of modern times, the disciple of the famous Bengali saint Ramakrishna was, in fact, rather different from his spiritual master.

The latter was a semi-literate mystic who had experienced the vision of the profound unity of different religious traditions, including Islam and Christianity, while his disciple was an intellectual in search of something different. Vivekananda developed the concept of a Hindu *sanātan* dharma which he equated with the non-dualist philosophy of the Vedanta, having its original roots in the ancient Upanishads. For him, this was the 'true religion' which should be taught to the masses. In spite of his tolerance (he insisted that people should not be compelled to follow any doctrine or rites) he was deeply convinced that Vedantic Hinduism represented a universal truth. All other variants of Hinduism were, in his eyes, debased forms of religion. He even went abroad to preach his message and his travels to America are famous. In his speeches he declared Hinduism to be superior to all others religions of the world because it was non-violent. Vivekananda's version of neo-Hinduism may, at first sight, appear harmless, tolerant and purely 'spiritual'. Nonetheless, it contributed to reinforcing the idea that there existed 'one single, true Hinduism', radically different from other religions, which being deemed inferior, are seen as obstructive, if not hostile, forces.

Towards an Islamic Nation: Who is Muslim?

Although the great poet and philosopher, Muhammad Iqbal (1873–1938), regarded as one of the spiritual fathers of Pakistan, initially expounded an inner, Sufic vision of Islam based on human and spiritual values, he ended up perceiving Sunni Islam as the only genuine faith and eventually rejected Sufism as alien to the 'original' Muslim tradition. He was suspicious of Shi'i, Hindu and Christian traditions which he saw as inferior and sometimes false religions. Iqbal's idealistic approach to the issue of Indian Islam can be compared to that of Vivekananda, in the sense that – in spite of the importance he gave to humanism and tolerance, and his spiritual understanding of religion – unlike Ibn 'Arabi, Rumi and some South-Asian Sufis, such as 'Abd al-Quddus or Bullhe Shah, he did not encourage the diversity of traditions, nor did he believe in the fundamental oneness of all faiths. Iqbal favoured the formation of an Islamic state for Indian Muslims, where they would shape their own destiny according to the Islamic ideals defined by him. His appeal was to find a stronger expression in the famous 'two nations theory' which, as is well known, was carried to its final political consequence later by the changing ambitions of Muhammad 'Ali Jinnah.[6] We need not analyse this theory, which has been outlined at length in numerous publications, and will limit ourselves to showing its impact on the issue of religious identities.

Most Indo-Muslim separatists have been called 'modernists', insofar as they represented a 'progressive' trend within Muslim nationalist aspirations, which appeared to be totally at variance with the 'reformist' religious organisations such as the Deobandis and the scholars of the Jamiat al-ulama-i-Hind. The latter sought to 'purify' and unify Islam in a way that inevitably led to communalist tensions, but did not involve themselves in the nationalist debate. However, Mayaram has rightly warned us against any artificial use of the binary categories communalism/nationalism.[7] It would be more relevant to distinguish between Indian, Hindu and Muslim nationalism.[8] But, as far as the latter is concerned, distinctions should also be made between the later ideas of Jinnah, the ideals of Mawdudi (1903–1979), and the interesting role played by the Nizari Ismaili Imam, Sultan Muhammad Shah, Aga Khan III. He advised his Khoja followers to move away from the 'Hindu' symbols that pervaded their acculturated tradition, telling them to seek their primary roots in Shiʿi Islam and the old Ismaili ideals.[9] For instance, he stressed the priority of inner faith over rituals, and condemned those who kept their womenfolk in an inferior position, forcing them to stay at home or wear the veil – practices which the Ismailis thought contrary to the original tradition of the Prophet.[10] Actually, although the fact has been generally overlooked, the Aga Khan did not favour the idea of separate, irreconcilable religious blocs (he perceived himself as being 'between two cultures'), but rather attempted to defend the Muslims from their own excesses as well as from those of the Hindu fundamentalists.

In 1909 Sir Sultan Muhammad Shah had declared: 'The ideal for my country to which I look forward is that of an eventually united people of one nationality among whom religious differences, now so acute, will have the minor significance they have, for instance, in the United States between Christians and Jews'. However, he was aware of the difficulties to be faced in the near future. As he had explained in 1910:

> Then there is another fact, which makes the Muslim position more complicated. For all time to come Muslim interest is bound up with the progress of the sister communities and it is our duty and privilege to continue on the most cordial and fraternal terms with the vast Hindu population and also with many other small minorities, each sub-divided into castes and creeds, yet the welfare of every one depending upon the welfare of its neighbours. Again sentiment and love would always attach the Muslims of India to the welfare of their co-religionists outside India ... Now to coordinate all these interests and to harmonise conflicting elements and to reduce some of those sentiments to their legitimate places, and to concentrate more and more on the fundamental duties and interests without interfering in the legitimate sphere of the secondary ones is not an easy matter.[11]

The Aga Khan III thought that the development of the country, in particular in the fields of education and science, would be instrumental in maintaining this difficult balance. For him the Aligarh College had an important role to play. It was precisely 'to produce men morally and intellectually equipped for developing the resources of the country ...'[12] Later, but still before Partition, in 1932, he insisted that the realities of the communal problem which generated riots were 'simply a question of the level of civilization attained by the vast majority of the inhabitants of British India'. He believed 'that Hindu-Moslem differences existed and found occasional manifestation in pre-War days is not to be denied; but such conflicts were infrequent and altogether negligible in comparison with the many sanguinary conflicts of the last few years.'[13]

Attention should also be drawn to the fact that 'separateness' – whether in the political framework of a different nation ruled according to Islamic ideals or in the purely religious sphere where political considerations would be considered irrelevant – led to similar results.

In this way, the 'progressive' intellectuals of the Aligarh Anglo-Indian college, whose ideals appeared to be based on nineteenth-century liberalism and humanism, are as much responsible for the erection of the 'boundary wall' between Hindus and Muslims as are the separatists of the Muslim League, the partisans of a theocratic Muslim state represented by the Jama'at-i-Islami led by Mawdudi, or the various Islamic reforming bodies that sought to impose a unified, orthodox version of religion but were opposed to the creation of a separate nation. Sayyid Ahmad Khan (1817–1898), a key figure in this movement, had insisted on a specifically 'Indian', historically deep-rooted, Islam that would be as independent as possible from foreign models, although he defended at the same time the idea of one universal Muslim religion. In fact he was more a pedagogue than a reformer and his views were obviously not free from inner contradictions.

The ideas developed by the scholars of Aligarh were a typical product of the British period, and in particular of the Orientalist trend which relied on Muslim and Hindu intellectual elites. But these intellectuals, while opposing the orthodox stream, also fought 'syncretic' currents and non-Sunni traditions of Islam. They clung to pan-Islamic models and their self-image was that of 'being part of a community – a monolithic umma – that remained, or was normatively expected to remain, the same across spatial divisions and temporal boundaries'.[14] In so doing, they simply repeated the colonial stereotypes. The result, however, was that their understanding of Islam remained superficial, entirely influenced by the majority current and that 'its followers, whether converted or not, were cast in a specifically Muslim/Islamic mould. Regardless of economic status, caste, language, or regional affinity, their identity was understood, defined and described in strictly textual terms.'[15]

In this light, the role of the Tablighi Jama'at, the largest international movement for Islamic reform that was launched in Delhi, should be examined briefly. This 'transnational religious regime'[16] started to play a prominent part in South Asia from its very creation, at the beginning of the twentieth century. Founded by Muhammad Ilyas (1885–1844), it was systematised and globalised by his son M. Yusuf (1917–1965). It followed the Deobandi current of thought, with emphasis on the sharia and on the ulama as its interpreters, but contrary to it, it did not restrict itself to teaching 'true Islam' to the Ashraf elites through a network of madrasas. Its aim was to bring that Islam to the masses, teach them the correct performance of prayers, and instil in them virtues of piety and sacrifice. As for the Deobandis, Sufism was not rejected, but restricted to its most 'purified form'; the missionaries of the Tablighi Jama'at fought against the ideas of the Barelwi Sufis concerning worship at shrines, as they did against the popular practices of pilgrimages and vows at dargas.

Of particular relevance for our subject, is the interest various reformist organisations took in liminal communities.[17] The Deobandis and the missionaries of the Tabligh and Tanzim[18] movements sought to suppress local specificity in favour of universal practices and beliefs which, in their eyes, represented the only true form of Islam: 'centralised Islam has, thus, been superimposed over Sufi and subcontinental Islam', widening the gap between communities that could find less and less a common language in their everyday life.[19]

In this way, although the Muslim League, the Aligarh school, the Deobandis and the leaders of the Tablighi did not agree on various issues, often viewing each other with hostility and contempt, all of them contributed to the consolidation of clear-cut identities and to the construction of the boundary wall which, in 1947, was to be partly concretised by the creation of the two new states of India and Pakistan.

Partition and its Consequences: the Walled-up People

Could Partition have been avoided? The question has been raised time and again. The creation of a separate state for Muslims, later advocated by Jinnah, Mawdudi and other leaders, was opposed not only by Gandhi, Nehru and others, but also by prominent Muslims such as Abu'l Karim Azad and Zakir Husain, who was to become the first president of independent India. Could the balance of forces have turned in favour of the partisans of 'Indian' – and not Hindu or Muslim nationalism?

Those who postulate the existence of a 'faultline', which they view as having existed from the very beginning, conclude that Partition was inevitable; so do, for different reasons, those scholars who are aware of the role played by the nineteenth-century colonial constructs. Others, following Gandhi's ideal, claim that it could have been prevented and believe that the 1947 division of former British India into separate countries is at the root of current communal and national conflicts.

Be that as it may, one should not be blinded by the material presence of a borderline between the states now referred to as India and Pakistan. The formation of two sharply demarcated identities that crystallised at the beginning of the twentieth century, with or without the existence of separate nations, was already shaping the destiny of South Asians. When diversity came to be denied and forgotten in favour of two 'imagined communities', the fate of the populace was sealed, and the frontier was only a grosser, more visible symbol of the boundary wall that continued to be raised on both sides.

In fact, the formation of two states raised a number of issues. Which Muslims, settled in the territories ruled by India, would choose to join Pakistan and which Hindus, finding themselves in Pakistani territory, would cross over to India? Would there be any real choice?

Partition, naturally, was experienced as a major problem by the liminal communities – which exemplifies the importance of the issue debated in this essay. In their haste to build the new boundary extremists of both sides threatened to wall up 'the people of the threshold'. The forcible passage of the Meos to Pakistan and their return to India shows that 'crossing the threshold' could have tragic consequences.[20] Driven away from India by the Hindu extremists whenever they did not accept to abandon the Islamic elements of their tradition, the Meos were, however, not accepted as Muslims in Pakistan. Those who refused to leave India were killed or forced to become 'full-fledged' Hindus and the rest had to suffer discrimination by other Muslim groups in Pakistan before returning to India where, after many difficulties, they were given back their lands that had been appropriated by local Hindu communities.

The exodus of the Sindhi Lohanas from Pakistan to India took place along the same lines, but their story had a different end. For centuries this community had shared common cultural and religious values with the various groups who inhabited the same region of Sindh – Khojas,

Sunni communities and Khalsa Sikhs. Their liminality was of an even more complex nature than that of the Meos, as they worshipped simultaneously and with equal devotion, Hindu gods, Sufi pirs and Sikh gurus. We also know that a good number of the Lohana community had come under the influence of Nizari Ismailism. Sindh had ancient Buddhist, Jain and Nath traditions, and had been a flourishing centre of Ismailism, Sunni Sufism and Sikhism. Sindh, as a geographical and cultural region, was by itself a threshold. It was a doorway through which trade, arts and religions had flowed freely from west to east and from north to south. The Sindhi refugees still remember their initial difficulties in settling in a foreign land. These people, who claimed descent from the ancient warriors or Kshatriyas, had left their homeland in Pakistan and travelled to India, finding shelter in Rajasthan and Maharashtra, because they came to be labelled 'Hindus' according to the rigid, new categories. But the local upper-caste Hindus who considered them Untouchables did not take food or drink water from their hands and even, in some places, refused them access to the common water pumps. The Sindhis were viewed with suspicion because of their difference.

The trauma of exodus, which had meant for them nothing less than leaving their fatherland, generated a quest for identity among the Lohana elites. They decided eventually to 'cross the threshold', opting for a Hindu identity. The apparent re-Hinduisation of the Sindhis was, however, mainly reflected in the political sphere and was not really achieved in the domains of culture or religion.[21] Ultimately their integration into the Indian nation was due to the success of their commercial ventures.

Partition had split other liminal groups. The Khojas and the Maheshvari Meghvars (following the Barmati or Mahesh *panth*) of Gujarat and Sindh, for example, were now divided by the newly-defined border. So were the Sikhs, although the majority of those who were settled in Pakistani Punjab chose to 'cross over' to India. For all these people, including the Lohanas, access to the sacred places located across the border became difficult.

The Law and the State

In the context of a modern nation-state the old notions of dharma and sharia, as understood by the British when establishing their legal system in the Subcontinent, had to be reinterpreted or abolished altogether.

In India, Congress had succeeded in winning the majority and was trying to establish a secular state where equal rights and participation of religious and social minorities would be guaranteed. Indian nationalism differed in this respect from Hindu nationalism, but in spite of the former's claim to secularism, it did not succeed in freeing itself from earlier constructs: 'the tendency has remained strong to assume some kind of cultural or civilizational integration as the ultimate foundation of nationalism. And then it becomes difficult – even for a Nehru writing his *Discovery of India* – to resist the further slide toward assuming that unity, after all, has been primarily Hindu (and upper-caste, often north Indian Hindu at that'.[22] With few exceptions, leaders of the Indian nationalist movement belonged to the upper castes and originated from north India.

In free India separate personal laws were maintained under the pretext of respecting the diversity of the communities which were to be active participants in the democracy. But the system, which was inherited from colonial India, was to have contradictory effects: if it served to ensure the right to diversity, it also emphasised and legitimated the existence of blocs which it authenticated at the legal and juridical levels.

In order to apply personal law, Article 25 (2) of the Indian Constitution explains what was meant by the term 'Hindu'. It subsumed under this category all those who followed religions that originated on Indian soil: not only followers of Vedic or post-Vedic Brahmanical traditions and of various sects, but also those who practised folk and tribal religions, as well as Buddhists, Jains and Sikhs. The Orissa Religious Endowments Act of 1969 expressly states that 'The expression "Hindu Religion" shall include Jain, Buddhist and Sikh religions and the expressions "Hindu" and "Hindu public religious institutions and endowments" shall be construed accordingly'.[23]

One important point in this legal system is caste integration, and in particular the inclusion of the Untouchables. The term 'Scheduled Caste' was coined to refer to those communities to which special constitutional rights and protection were granted, mainly thanks to the action of Dr Ambedkar, although the Constitution (Scheduled Castes) Order of 1950, paragraph 3, unfortunately bears the imprint of Hindu nationalism: 'no person who professes a religion different from the Hindu religion shall be deemed to be Scheduled Castes'. When reservations (quotas) were granted to the Untouchables in universities and government jobs, the presidential order mentioned above deprived Christian and Muslim Untouchables from these advantages. From this point of view it meant that the Untouchables could be only Hindus and had to remain so. While for centuries the Brahmanical system had denied them the right to be called Hindus, the Indian constitution forced them into this category where they had to remain if they didn't want to lose the special rights which have been granted to them.

The broadest definition of the word 'Hindu' was to be incorporated in the Hindu Code Legislation of 1955–56 which includes the Hindu Marriage Act, Hindu Succession Act, Hindu Adoption and Maintenance Act, Hindu Minority and Guardianship Act, etc. The expression 'Hindu' in all these Acts is defined as including 'a person who, though not Hindu by religion, is nevertheless a person to whom this Act applies by the virtues of the provision contained in this section'[24] (Hindu Marriage Act 1955); and it is specified that the Act applies to all forms and developments of Hindu religion, including various sects, such as the Lingayats, the Brahmo and Arya Samaj, to any person who is a Buddhist, Jain or Sikh by religion, 'to any other person domiciled in the territories to which this Act extends who is not a Muslim, Christian, Parsi or Jew by religion, unless it is proved that any such person would not have been governed by the Hindu law or by any custom or usage as part of that law in respect of any of the matters dealt with herein if this Act has not been passed'.[25]

In this way the term 'Hindu' is defined negatively. The criterion for being a Hindu is solely the territory where the religion followed by them originated and not the native country of the believers. This codification does not aim only at making a uniform law for one category termed 'Hindu'; it is also directed towards unifying the Hindu community as such. Far from paving the way for the implementation of a uniform civil code for all Indian citizens, it goes much further than the British administration. It is actually a manipulation resulting in the creation of one great legal community, the boundaries of which are marked by the definition 'Hindu' contained in the statutes. For instance, all sorts of legal disabilities (not only for Untouchables but also for those who adopt children or divorce) are attached to those who convert to Islam or Christianity, while 'Hindus' adhering to Jainism, Buddhism or Sikhism would preserve the same rights. These discriminative measures, which place the followers of indigenous religions in a privileged position and dissuades its adherents from joining other 'non-Hindu' faiths, recalls Savarkar's definition of Hindutva. It has been rightly stated that 'although Christianity and Judaism have had roots on the Indian soil for about 2000 years, Islam for 1200 years and Zoroastrianism for 1000 years, these traditions remain forever "foreign" and their followers are excluded from the rest of the community'.[26] The consequences may be considerable in the near future if the constitution is not revised: 'The result of these developments, in any case, is politically unfortunate. The two major communities have unified their personal and family status laws, have removed internal differentiation as well as areas of overlapping and mediating customs. They now stand side by side as solidified blocs as far as legal regimes are concerned'.[27]

All this increasingly induced the liminal communities to 'cross the threshold' by identifying themselves, once and for all, with one particular community. During the colonial period, before India became a part of the British Empire, the Bombay colonial administrators had decided that the Khojas, whose way of life was similar to those of some Hindu merchants, would be submitted to their own customary laws; but eventually, those who followed the Aga Khan had to adhere to the uniform Muslim law like all Sunnis and Shiʿa.

The case of the Imamshahis deserves a separate mention as it created a paradox and, as a result of this paradox, a historical misunderstanding. Members of this separate branch of Nizari Ismailism had survived, by resorting to *taqiyya*, under the guise of Sunni Sufis, Twelver Shiʿa and Hindus. For example, some Sayyid descendants of Imam Shah appeared as Sunnis or Twelver Shiʿa, while the members of converted communities lived as Hindus or Muslims. After independence, although they were adherents of the same religious tradition, the Patidars were submitted to Hindu personal law, while the Sayyids had to follow Muslim law. The fact that the followers of the same religion were given a separate legal identity contributed to splitting the community, generating new tensions and conflicts within the sect. Personal law, as envisaged by the independent Indian state, did not have a place for liminal communities. Once again people were compelled to cross the threshold and join one of the artificially created blocs.

One additional remark must be made. Although the Bombay Public Trust Act of 1950 followed the legal definition of the term 'Hindu', it had reserved a place for charitable institutions which could not fit into any of these categories. 'A' was meant for the registration of Hindu charitable trusts (including as usual Jains, Buddhists and Sikhs), 'B' for Muslims, 'C' for Parsis, 'D' for Christians, Jews and 'others than 'A', 'B', or 'C'; the category 'E' which had been designed to accommodate 'Cosmopolitan' trusts could include 'non-religious' organisations, but also applied to 'shared' sacred places such as the Imamshahi shrines of Gujarat. This exception to the rule – which could have been a corrective – was unfortunately to prove fragile.

Although Pakistan had declared itself an Islamic state, it could not solve its legal problems more easily, as is shown by the successive attempts at defining legal and judicial rules which would apply to all its citizens. The leadership of the All-India Muslim League and early Pakistan saw politics as a secular and collective activity separate from religion which it considered a matter of private faith and ritual. Soon, however, the pressure for the establishment of a nation along purely traditional Islamic lines modified the situation. But this ideal proved extremely difficult to achieve since there was no political model of a Muslim state which could have applied to all Muslims, taking into account the difference between Sunni, Twelver Shiʿi and Ismaili concepts of sharia and *fiqh*. The first steps towards unification was, once more, the definition of 'orthodoxy' within Islam, leading to the rejection of some Muslim movements which were declared 'un-Islamic'.[28] Those who wished to select a particular form of Sunnism as a standard applicable to all, forgot too easily the active role – and the substantial personal involvement, for instance within the Muslim League, of some Shiʿi leaders, including the Aga Khan and Sayyid Ameer Ali – in defending the Islamic cause. In any case, it became gradually clear that no consensus could be reached, not because of sectarian disputes, but owing to the history of Islam which had, for centuries, maintained a tradition of diversity based on different interpretations of the Qurʾan.

Let us conclude this section by a final remark: far from solving the issue of 'differences', Partition contributed to reinforcing them, as religion became more and more an essentialised part of the political game. While the ideal of a Muslim Pakistani state remained purely theoretical, India failed to create a genuinely secular nation where religious identity would have had no relevance in legal and political matters.

Reinventing History and Traditions

In India the publications of the Gita Press, which started in 1926 with the monthly magazine *Kalyan*, reflect a phenomenon that can be referred to as the 'standardisation' or 'massification' of religion. Classical Sanskrit texts, their translations in Hindi, and medieval Hindi devotional literature were published by the Gita Press in great numbers after independence, as well as various didactic tracts. They aimed at projecting 'a new, yet conservative concept of Hinduism which is easily acceptable and accessible to the general public. *Hindū dharm*, as Hinduism is called, is said to be Vedic *sanātan dharm,* the 'eternal religion'. Its rules are simple to follow, so that whoever adheres to it is also authorised to preach it. 'An earlier concept of spiritual authority is superseded by a populist one, despite the fact that what is postulated does not sound technically populist, namely, the *vaidik sanātan dharm*. The vocabulary of tradition gains a new function: to serve as the foundation of a newly self-assured, yet religiously legitimised cultural identity'.[29] This type of publication is readily available at temporary or permanent bookstalls set up at fairs, outside temples and sometimes even in railway stations and bus stands. The promoters of the 'Gita mission', issued from a Sanatani Vaishnava trading class, do not only claim to bring religion to the masses, but demand that the state adopt *hindū dharm* as its leading principle. According to V.S. Agraval, the author of an article published in Kalyan in 1966, *dharm* is synonymous with culture. *Sampradāys* (sectarian traditions) are for the individual, and should not be considered lawful if they are contrary to the dharma as defined by one of the classical treatises, or *shastras*, the *Manusmṛti* (of which Manu is the alleged author) which lies within the responsibilities of the state. This concept of dharma, presenting itself as a 'catholic social norm' cannot accommodate non-Hindu creeds to which it remains alien insofar as it is based on the *varṇāśrāma* system of hierarchical castes. The popularity of this type of literature in Hindi (most readers of the Gita Press publications do not know Sanskrit and keep the Sanskrit text only for prestige) ended up in convincing the middle classes that there was indeed one single Hindu religion. Many modern religious or caste reformers followed this model. In this type of cheap vernacular literature, there was no room for deep analysis of history, society, philosophy or religion: everything was based on hackneyed concepts and hastily formulated conclusions. The Gita Press, like Vivekananda and various Hindu nationalist bodies, also contributed to the idea – now indiscriminately accepted by many people, including Westerners – that the *Bhagavad Gita* (a part of the *Mahabharata* epic) was the 'Bible' of the Hindus. Meanwhile, the RSS propagated similar ideas. Together with the *Gita*, the *Ramayana* (the other pan-Indian epic) was projected as the sacred text par excellence. For this para-military organisation, Rama, the avatar of Vishnu, the king and hero portrayed in the *Ramayana*, was to be imitated by all as a model of perfection. The ideal, in fact, would be to restore the former *Ramrajya*, Rama's kingdom in the sense of an ideal Hindu state which would have flourished in an alleged pre-Muslim Golden Age.

History and texts were manipulated in order to accommodate the new ideas. All that was not in conformity with them was said to be 'distortions' purposely made by the British scholars, who were accused of having a scanty knowledge of Sanskrit or of interpreting texts and events in their own way with the sole aim of glorifying their own civilisation. For example, as vegetarianism gained ground among the Sanskritising communities, becoming one of the cardinal virtues of Hinduism, the fact that, during the Vedic period animals, including bulls and cows, were regularly sacrificed as an offering to the gods, and the rest of their flesh consumed by devotees, became increasingly embarrassing. These facts, clearly and abundantly described in the Vedas, were denied and attributed to the 'demonic' distortions of the 'materialist' Westerners.[30] With the creation of a network of RSS schools, while learning the subjects common to other teaching institutions, the students who joined those educational institutions were systematically trained in the ideology of the Sangh. Revised history books claim to demonstrate the 'eternal antagonism' of Hinduism and Islam which are portrayed as uniform religious blocs, while the need for unity, as well as for organised and robust resistance, are stressed.

Let us now examine the consequences of all this on the Imamshahi sect of Gujarat and Maharashtra. The ideas connected with the *Sanātan*

Dharma that came to replace the declining model of the Arya Samaj deeply affected the life of the Pirana Satpanthi Patidars and of many other Guptis – that is to say, of the communities who had survived for centuries under Hindu guise. Whether previously affiliated or not to the Arya Samaj, an increasing number of them abandoned the sect to embrace the 'standardised' form of religion represented by the Sanatani episteme. They were encouraged by the Hindu nationalists, in particular by the leaders of the Vishva Hindu Parishad, a religious organisation of the Sangh Parivar which sought to 'unify' the Hindu religion. Adopting the Sanatani ideals meant performing image worship and consequently building new temples where idols of gods would be installed. In a few decades, between the 1930s and the 1980s, the landscape of the Satpanthi villages of Kutch, where the Imamshahi Patidars were the most numerous, underwent a spectacular transformation. 'Regular' Hindu temples were constructed everywhere, generally near the old *khāna*s meant for the traditional Satpanthi rituals. The alarming rate of these 'desertions' was a serious concern for the Imamshahi authorities of Pirana. At this stage, the *sajjādā-nishīn* who claimed to be the pir or main authority representing the hidden Imam, apparently resorted to the usual Shi'i custom of *taqiyya*. Understanding that the very existence of the Satpanth was threatened, the leader of the Gupti community, the head *kākā* or 'servant of God' according to the traditional Imamshahi terminology, who was also the *mujāvar* or custodian of the shrine in the Sufi idiom, undertook a series of Hinduising reforms. They were meant to help his disciples to remain faithful to their sect without incurring the criticism of their Sanatani caste-fellows. The Imamshahi Guptis could then assert their identity as 'orthodox' Hindus and even claim that their tradition had never been influenced by Islam. The newly built *khāna*s were made to resemble classical Hindu shrines and renamed Nishkalanki *mandir*s or temples to Vishnu's tenth avatar. No regular idols were installed, as this was contrary to the basic principles of the Satpanth, although behind the ritual table (*pāṭ*) the figures of the three main gods or the *Om* symbol were painted – but, according to the Brahmanical tradition, these could not be regarded as 'orthodox' idols, images meant for the cult being always tri-dimensional. Similarly the Pirana darga was to be renamed *samādhi* as the custom of burial which was reinterpreted as the *samādhi* of Shaiva ascetics. Then a number of learned Satpanthis were entrusted with the delicate task of rewriting their *gināns* by expurgating these devotional poems of their Islamic terminology and references and replacing them with Hindu equivalents. Earlier texts, as for instance those published by the deceased father of the present pir, were banned and the rewritten book openly circulated for sales and displayed at the Pirana bookstore.[31] There is reason to believe that these reforms are being made with the purpose of protecting the Pirana tradition in the present Gujarati context where the Hindu nationalist ideal is strong. In other words, that the changes 'officially' effected within the sect are due to *taqiyya*, rather than to a conscious wish to transform the tradition into a 'purely Hindu' one.[32] However, one should try to analyse the consequences of this 'revolution' from the point of view of religious identities. The present evolution of the Pirana sect that started in the 1980s once again confirms the fact that liminal traditions can hardly survive in contemporary South Asia. On the other hand, if the recent reforms are only a temporary move dictated by *taqiyya*, one cannot doubt that new generations, as we have been able to observe for ourselves during our field research among the Imamshahi Patidars of Kutch, readily follow the new trend which re-establishes their solidarity with their Sanatani caste-fellows and allows them to feel at ease in all Hindu milieus, whilst the youngest are even totally ignorant of the existence of an older 'syncretic' tradition tinged with Islamic elements.

The evolution of the Bishnoi or Prahladpanthi community, which functions simultaneously as a sect and as a caste, is another interesting example of the phenomenon which consists in a subtle 'reinvention' of tradition. After having 'crossed the threshold' a number of the followers of this liminal movement merged into the Sunni stream,[33] while others headed towards a rapid Hinduisation. But, as they cherished the memory of their spiritual teacher, it was hard to betray it openly. The reformers attempted to side-step the issue. Traditionally, the grave of their guru, Jambhoji or Jambeshvar Pir, which is the only object of worship, was covered with a green *chādar* (as is the case of the *mazār* of Nizarpanthi and Jasnathi saints). In the 1950s the darga (also referred to as *mukām*) was renamed *mandir*, and said to enshrine the *samādhi* or tomb of a Hindu ascetic. A painting representing the founder of the *panth* was hung on the wall behind the grave. 'Mukam', which had become the name of the village where the shrine stood was construed as a corruption of the term *muktidhām* (a sacred site where *mukti* or liberation is obtained). The leaders of the sect found a simple solution by which they hoped to please all the Bishnois without offending the memory of the pir. The green cloth was not removed but covered by a saffron one. In this way, outsiders visiting the shrine would be convinced of its Hindu identity. The presence of the hidden *chādar* was known only to the initiated members. We will come back to this interesting phenomenon which can be viewed as a metaphor.

Let us now examine the parallel evolution of Muslim 'normative' ideals. Apart from the activities of the reformist movements, such as the Tablighi Jama'at, the social and economic uplift of a number of middle-class Muslims, who went to the Arabian/Persian Gulf countries in search of employment before returning to their native villages and towns has been another factor of transformation. Apart from the considerable improvement of their financial situation, their ideas had changed. They did not only invest their money in various ways such as building houses, opening shops and enlarging their businesses, they also constructed mosques to show that they had become 'good' Muslims, often to the dismay of their elders for whom praying at home was generally deemed sufficient. Had their sons committed so many sins that they were obliged to expiate them through such grand projects? Those who came back from the Gulf had learned to underestimate their own regional values in favour of the 'universal' Muslim culture that was exclusively identified with the Arab model. Besides, the urban milieus were increasingly imbibing the discourses of the various reformist organisations who wished to gather all of them under the banner of one single 'normative' Islam.

It will not be out of place here to examine how this changed atmosphere affected the Imamshahis who had lived for centuries in the guise of Sunni or Twelver Muslims. This had, after all, been the case of the Sayyids who claimed to be the descendants of Imam Shah. For a long time the three main lines, Jalalshahis, Sayyidkhanis and Nurshahis, had evolved separately, each claiming the right to represent the main religious authority at Imam Shah's darga. The Jalalshahis, for instance, claimed to be Sunni, although some of them admitted the historical links that existed with Shi'i Ismailism and emphasised the particular nature of the Imamshahi Satpanth which, as a synthesis of Sufi and Hindu elements, would have been created to facilitate the conversion of local non-Muslim communities. Others among the Nurshahi Sayyids denied any connection with the Ismailis and asserted the Suhrawardi Sufi identity of Imam Shah who, like Muhammad Shah Bukhari, was a prominent Sufi settled in fifteenth-century Gujurat and was said to have been Rukn al-Din's *murīd*. A book was written to clarify this stand and prove the Sunni connection.[34] Needless to say these Sunni Nurshahi Sayyids did not perform any of the typical Satpanthi rituals and limited themselves to occasionally visiting the tomb of their ancestor Imam Shah (particularly on the *urs*, or anniversary of his death).

Meanwhile, a group of low-caste converts, referred to as Nurshahi Momins, who had been Gupti followers of Nur Shah, one of Imam Shah's descendents, were recently approached by Twelver Shi'i leaders from Lucknow. By emphasising the Shi'i elements (which were naturally present in their sacred literature owing to its Ismaili origin), they undertook to convince them that Twelver Shi'ism had always been the form of Islam followed by Nur Shah. Denying again any historical connection with the Ismailis, they explained that the 'syncretic' elements of their tradition were simply the remnants of a former 'strategy of conversion'.[35] Consequently, the whole community assumed full Twelver identity and gave up all their Satpanthi practices and beliefs, preserving only their reverence for the pir who converted them and whose darga they also visited on special occasions. Similarly we were told that some 'Hindu' Guptis fully assumed Sunni identity under the influence of the Tablighi Jama'at. They are also referred to as Momins.

As far as the Sayyidkhanis and some other Sayyids are concerned, we will see their evolution in the concluding part of this essay.

Dress Codes and Colour Symbols: Religion Standardised

The split of liminal communities into Hindus and Muslims did not only create communal and legal conflicts. In ordinary life newly emerging, clear-cut identities came to be expressed through a number of symbols that reinforced the estrangement between communities. This phenomenon also coincides with a more general and universal tendency to 'standardise' culture through the diffusion of popular books, newspapers and magazines, as well as through cinema and television.[36]

For centuries, costume had varied mainly along caste and regional lines. In Rajasthan most women, whether Hindu or Muslim, wore the typical *ghaghrā* (a full, pleated skirt), while in Bihar, the sari was preferred. As for Sindhi and Punjabi females, they were generally clad in *śalwār-kamīz* regardless of their religious affiliation. In the past, Rajput rulers had adopted the Mughal dress, in the same way as they had been inspired by Mughal styles of painting and architecture, and had found it convenient to use the Persian language. These were markers of a common culture encompassing regional, ethnic and religious differences. After Independence, Indians and Pakistanis came more and more to express their religious affiliation through a particular dress code. Muslim women exchanged their saris and *ghaghrā*s for *śalwār-kamīz*, traditional Hindu males stuck to *dhotī*s, while their Muslim brothers grew beards and wore typical skullcaps. Of course the Khalsa Sikhs had their unshorn hair and beards, wearing turbans and other insignia to distinguish themselves from the non-Khalsa Nanakpanthis who, according to the new orthodoxy, did not have the right to call themselves Sikhs.

The Hindu fundamentalist groups collectively designated as the Sangh Parivar are sometimes referred to as the 'Saffron brotherhood' or the 'Saffron brigade'. In political jargon 'saffronising' means painting something in the colours of Hindutva. The reason is that even outside the political context, the saffron colour has become one of the universal symbols of pan-Hinduism, while, across the 'boundary wall' everything that was connected with Islam was 'painted' green.[37] In a relatively short time the scenery was changed according to these symbolic colour patterns. Previously, the small street and village shrines, whether Hindu or Muslim, were so similar that it was impossible to distinguish between them from outside. They often consisted of a square whitewashed structure crowned by a dome. Gradually, the outer walls and gates of the dargas were painted green, while simultaneously, the number of green draperies (*chādar*s) offered to the tombs increased.[38] Temples generally remained white but displayed various symbols of red or saffron colours, namely in the form of flags.

In both countries, if dress codes and colour symbols have increasingly become markers of identity, attitudes and reactions also tend to be more and more stereotyped. The diversity of regional, caste and sectarian cultures is downplayed. Hindus, Muslims and Sikhs tend to behave as they are expected to behave. Some Hindus even believe that customs that are particular to their community are followed by all Hindus. They are often heard declaring 'We Hindus do this or that', when what they refer to is in fact a purely local or caste tradition. For instance, some of them regard Holi or Gangaur as typically pan-Hindu festivals, unaware of the fact that the former has never been celebrated in South India (except by the Marwari and Gujarati immigrants), and that the latter is totally unknown outside Rajasthan. Similarly, the image of the Other is constructed en bloc. For many Hindus a Muslim is a member of one single community speaking the same language and following uniform rituals,[39] while in the eyes of many Muslims, Hindus are perceived as 'polytheists' and 'idolaters'. They would be surprised to know that this view contradicts the monistic philosophy of classical yoga or Vedanta. Conversely, Hindus would be astonished to hear about the ideas and practices of the Shiʿa or the specific beliefs of the Ismailis. Without taking the trouble to verify this assertion (which the facts contradict every day), many middle-class Hindus think that Indian Muslims necessarily support Pakistan (for instance, during the popular cricket tests), whereas the Hindus living in Pakistan must be pro-Indian.

Misunderstandings or absurdities often arise from the compulsion of applying to each and everything the label 'Hindu' or 'Muslim'. The cover of a brochure published by the Indian Tourism Department a few years ago showed a photograph of the 'female dancer' of Mohenjo-Daro – a famous sculpture dating from the Indus Valley civilisation. Hindu nationalists were shocked by the fact that Indian (identified by them as Hindu) culture was represented by a female whose body was entirely naked. The booklet had, in fact, been a commercial success, although the nudity of the statue had certainly nothing to do with it. They immediately ordered the book to be withdrawn from circulation and the cover to be removed. It is a pity that the daily or weekly press did not echo the words of an author who at that time wrote for a hotel magazine.[40] He reminded his fellow countrymen that Hindu culture had never been characterised by puritanism. If the saffron brigade thought that female nudity was against the sacred principles of Hindutva, they should start the long and difficult undertaking of demolishing thousands of similarly shocking sculptures displayed in innumerable Hindu temples scattered all over the Subcontinent. History, when reconstructed, allows entire chapters to vanish into oblivion. Did the exponents of Hindutva remember that it was Tipu Sultan, a nineteenth-century Muslim ruler, and not a Hindu raja, who had requested the women of

Kerala to cover their naked breasts and legs? On the other hand, the custom of concealing one's face in public places or in front of strangers (adopted by so many north-Indian Hindu females to prove that they are Rajputs or belong to the high castes) is perceived by many as a universal Muslim practice. Few people know that the *purdah* system was never a part of the original Prophetic tradition and the majority of Muslims today, including the Ismailis, never resort to it.

Conclusion: The Metaphor of the Hidden Pir

In contemporary India and Pakistan, the general tendency is to align oneself along the newly defined categories. In Pakistan the Sunni model tends to impose itself as a norm with which other forms of Islam are more or less obliged to conform. As for India, as we have seen, 'Indian nationalism has become more and more an icon, with predominantly, though not invariably Hindu lineaments. The dividing line between national and Hindu communal assumptions and values became increasingly porous, to the great advantage of Hindutva political forces'.[1]

However, close observation of everyday life in rural as well as urban environments clearly reveals the existence of pockets of resistance that manifest themselves at various levels. To conclude this study, we will select a few examples that will serve to illustrate the phenomenon.

The first level is the regional one. In India the protest comes mainly from the non-Hindi speaking people who do not accept the standard of north-Indian culture (including social organisation and religion) as the norm. The inhabitants of Tamil Nadu, for instance, oppose the Dravidian episteme to the Aryan/Brahmanical model. The Tamils claim that belonging to the Dravidian group, their language has nothing in common with Sanskrit or with the north-Indian vernaculars (except, of course, through mutual influences); at any rate it is older than Hindi and has a classical literature of its own. This is why the Tamils have strongly opposed the decision of the Indian government to choose Hindi as the national language and have also carefully preserved their own customs, beliefs and religious practices.

At the social or 'caste' level, the protest movement can be illustrated by the attitude of some ex-Untouchables and Tribals who refuse to surrender to the ideology of Hindutva. While the VHP (Hindu Vishva

Parishad or World Hindu Committee – an outfit of the RSS) and its allies pursue their campaigns of *dharm paravartan* (conversion) among the Christian Adivasis, the absurdity of their claims are brought to the fore. In September 2000, Asaram Bapu claimed to have 'brought back to the fold of *sanātan dharm*', twenty thousand Minas of the Udaipur region. The terms that were used, such as *sanātan dharm* (eternal religion), *mul dharm* (original religion) or *Hindū dharm*, were unknown to the Tribals till the exponents of Hindutva convinced them that they had formerly adhered to Hinduism. In February 1999, when more than a hundred Catholic Adivasis were being 'reconverted' by the Sangh Parivar, a curious incident occurred. The *baiga* or priest of the community was told to recite the *Gayatri mantra*, and to sprinkle Ganges water before making oblations into the traditional Vedic fire-altar or *havan kuṇḍ*. At that time the tribal chief and his followers protested that before becoming Christians, they had never performed this type of ritual nor did they know a single word of Sanskrit. Eventually, they agreed to 'return to Hinduism', provided they could also perform their original tribal rites in their own language. Why did the Tribals insist on retaining their pagan customs instead of limiting themselves to the pan-Hindu rites, and did it mean that they had not abandoned their own animistic faith? To these questions, an RSS functionary answered: 'Whatever the process, it does not matter for us. We wanted to pull them away from Christianity'.[2] The author of another article that was published in the *Hindustan Times* declares clearly that Dalits (former Untouchables) and Tribals were never Hindus, being outside the *varṇāśrāma* order:

> The sudden aggressive mood and the claim that the Dalits are a part of Hindutva is the result of insecurity arising from the loosening of Brahmanical dominance: the interests of the Dalits and the Hindus are antagonistic to each other. The religion, beliefs, customs and ideals of the Dalits and Tribals have been the very anti-thesis to the inegalitarian, exploitative and repressive culture of the Hindus.

The author goes on to explain how the integration of these groups into the 'Hindu' family was done for political reasons. Initially, in the census, the Untouchables, like many other groups including a number of so-called 'syncretic' communities, were not registered as Hindus. As a result the Hindus were not much stronger numerically than the

Muslims. As Jones has shown, the reformists started at that time to play a numbers game between the two communities.[3] Another contemporary Dalit writer expresses his frustration in harsh words. The leaders defending the interests of the low-caste groups were silenced and their movements made secondary by the intelligentsia who succeeded in maintaining most of its upper-caste values.[4]

In spite of the efforts that have been made to 'close' the open doorways that allowed different religious traditions to meet or co-mingle, in between the newly erected boundary walls, a narrow space has been miraculously spared where patterns of composite culture and liminal movements can still survive. Both may become powerful means of resistance.

At the end of the nineteenth and at the beginning of the twentieth century, while Hindus and Muslims first opposed each other as two antagonistic blocs, some religious teachers gathered around them disciples of all castes. If the model followed by them appeared to be that of Kabir (often chosen as the paradigm of 'composite culture'), the context was entirely different. Sai Baba of Shirdi (d.1918), is probably the most famous of these modern sants. Although his original identity as a Hindu or a Muslim has never been clearly known, most of his disciples strive to continue his 'syncretic' tradition and readily call to mind the following facts. While sitting in a temple, their guru used to declare: '*Allah malik hai*' (Allah is the Lord), whereas the exclamation 'Rama is God' or 'Shiva is Allah' was uttered by him whenever he visited a mosque.[5]

Much less known and still mysterious in many respects, is the figure of Baba Diwana Shah to whom we have alluded briefly in a previous chapter. The Sufi saint who had attracted members of 'both communities',[6] is said to have settled in Rajasthan, at Kapasan in Mewar, around 1920, during a period of intense pre-Independence communal conflict. His Hindu, Brahman and Kumhar disciples continued his tradition, notwithstanding the disputes that arose over the management of the darga and the privilege of conducting certain rituals. On this very ground, Minoru Mio who has done an excellent preliminary study of the tradition[7] seems to question the popular image of the shrine of Kapasan (in size it is even bigger than the famous Ajmer darga) as a centre of communal harmony. If, he argues, the conflict is not purely or initially a communal one, it nevertheless originates from a fact which cannot be overlooked. Despite their common reverence for the pir, Hindu and Muslim disciples perceive their faith in a fundamentally different way. Even the Ashraf and non-Ashraf Muslims do not have the same approach to religion.

However, if in this case the conflict is not brought from 'outside' (by the intervention of Hindu or Muslim fundamentalists) it certainly emerges *a posteriori*. The Kapasan tradition takes shape in a period when the newly imposed binary categories still clash with older, traditional overlapping ones. As time passes and new generations appear, the 'boundary wall' is raised higher and higher, and perceptions keep shifting. However, the survival of the original tradition, namely the construction of a darga over the mortal remains of H.M. Kumawat, Baba Diwana Shah's main Hindu disciple, testifies that 'resistance' is still at work. Kumawat had expressed his wish to be buried according to the Muslim rites, and even if some prefer to call it a *samādhi*, his shrine is still a regular place of worship for Hindus and Muslims (except during the Urs festival attended, curiously, only by the former) where both *bhajan* singers and *qawwālīs* are invited to perform side by side.

From 1947 onward the Tablighi Jama'at intensified its action among the Meos of Rajasthan. For instance in 1950 their missionaries established a madrasa within the precincts of one of their shrines, the darga of Satchoka, a local pir worshipped by the members of this community.[8] They allow visitors to approach the tomb of the saint to pray, but forbid the Meos to organise the traditional *melā* held during the Urs, and do not allow devotees to make vows and offerings on the grave. Raymond Jamous tells us of his fascinating encounter with a Meo in a village located near the shrine of Satchoka. The man, who was a follower of the pir, clearly explained what was happening. For him, the action of the Tabligh was not only contrary to the customs of his community, but was threatening the very fundamentals of Islam, as he understood it. He believed in the essential role given by God to the prophets and to their legitimate heirs, the saints. According to him, Islam came to India with the mystics, thanks to whom people could become Muslims 'without losing their local or regional identity and without breaking their relationship with their Hindu brothers'.[9] Besides, the author observed that the Meos resumed all their former practices when the missionaries were absent.

A few years ago, a writer observing everyday life in Ajaysen and

Khadekri, two Mer villages located near Ajmer in Rajasthan, noted that the Merat, Khatat and Cheetah clans had not ceased to share most customs and festivals, regardless of their present religious identity.[10] For example, a Muslim Merat named Ala al-Din regularly went both to the local mosque and to the Ramdev temple, and had given Hindu names to his children. Some of their marriages were performed simultaneously with the traditional *pherās* (fire circumambulation) and the *nikāh* ceremony. Rawats and Merats celebrated Diwali and Holi with the same enthusiasm as ʿId or Shab-e-barat. Ala al-Din explained that if the majority of Hindu and Muslim Mers used to visit both temples and mosques, after their death all of them were buried according to the Islamic rite. In one of these villages the author of the article also met a Merat woman wearing the typical Rajasthani skirt and blouse favoured by Hindus who said she did not perform her prayers regularly, but declared herself to be a staunch Muslim.[11]

It is now time to revert to the two traditions which have been chosen as the focus of this study. As we have seen, although they share a common origin, history has thrown them in different, even at times, opposite, directions.

The evolution of the Nizari Ismailis of India and Pakistan and of the Imamshahis (currently referred to as Satpanthis) settled in Gujarat and Maharashtra is too complex a phenomenon to be analysed in detail here. An attempt has been made, in previous chapters, to throw some light on these little-known traditions. A few additional remarks will suffice here. The Ismailis of Pakistan and India have shown a remarkable ability to adapt themselves to the new historical circumstances and to a changed cultural environment – a feature which is typical of most communities who have had to struggle for long periods in order to survive, but which also has something to do with the nature of the tradition itself. Many former Guptis, for instance, have responded positively to the new historical pressures, and been able to shift their identity gradually, without abandoning their specific religious traditions. Diamond Rattansi[12] has shown that among the Ismaili Khojas of Pakistan, the nature of the Ismaili doctrine itself and the role of the Imam have been instrumental in achieving, in a smooth way, the delicate 'passage through the threshold'.

On the other hand, the Imamshahi branch, having started to follow its own way, probably from the late eighteenth century onward, is now experiencing an unprecedented crisis of identity, owing to the fact that they do not recognise one single religious authority. Caught between Hindu and Muslim 'orthodox forces', who literally drove them away from the 'threshold' where they had been standing for centuries, the Imamshahis, followers of the Satpanth, have evolved various responses to the crisis. As noted in the previous chapter, a number of 'Hindus', in particular the Patidars who form the majority of its members, have attempted to demonstrate to the representatives of Hindutva, in particular to the VHP, that their tradition was fundamentally a Hindu one. They are now trying to modify their rituals and literature in a direction that is opposite to that of the present Ismailis.

The leader of the Hindu-converted communities or Guptis now appears as a full-fledged Hindu *mahant* (superior), although he could, like the Nizari *dāʿī* Nasir al-Din in a famous *ginān* ascribed to Pir Hasan Kabir al-Din exclaim: '*Charitar hindū, andar musulmān*' (Outwardly Hindu, Muslim in his inner self).[13] In the previous chapter we have suggested that this may be a temporary measure of protection. Actually, many Satpanthis have remained true Guptis. They secretly continue to recite their *duʿā* (prayer) and to pay obeisance to their pir, who is himself careful not to appear in public in ordinary circumstances.[14] They may do so with the hope that better times will come. Apart from the Sayyids who have adopted a Muslim, Sunni or Twelver Shiʿi identity, a number of 'Hindu' Patidars, have organised their own resistance movement, supported by the followers of the Athia branch, a separate sect of Imamshahis who have been more successful in preserving their original traditions. In the course of this struggle, what may appear to uninformed observers as a series of communal conflicts reflected in heated religious debates and endless court cases, may well be the final outburst of a crisis that will reveal what is really at stake. In order to plead their case in front of puzzled lawyers who have been, up to now, largely used to thinking in terms of binary Hindu/Muslim categories, the protesting Imamshahis who had long denied any historical connection with the Ismaili tradition, now feel the urge to acknowledge their roots which lie in the Nizari acculturated tradition of the Subcontinent.

Myriads of other facts collected directly from the field would show that 'resistance' is a rather natural process in an artificially imposed world organised along uniform lines and simplistic dichotomies. The final example will give a temporary conclusion to this chapter.

Previously, we have seen that the Hinduised Bishnois concealed the green *chādar* covering the grave of their guru Jambha by putting over it an ochre drapery. As we know the Nizari origin of the sect, this can be symbolically understood as a form of *taqiyya*. In a broader and universal sense, *taqiyya* is the strategy through which a community, a tradition or its leaders, choose temporarily to conceal the elements of its identity which could endanger its survival in adverse historical circumstances. The secret tunnel or underground chamber is another symbol of resistance and of precautionary dissimulation, something like the catacombs where the first persecuted Christians allegedly had to hide before they could openly profess their faith.[15]

The story of Diggy Kalyanji will illustrate this phenomenon. The devotees who come back to this shrine, a famous pilgrimage centre located in Rajasthan, after an interval of twenty years or so, would hardly recognise it. Earlier, the sacred place was situated underground where an image of Hanuman, the monkey god, was standing beside the grave of a Muslim pir. The pilgrims worshipped both with equal devotion. Today, they have to ascend a small staircase to have access to the shrine which looks like a full-fledged Hindu temple. The Brahmin priests deny the existence of the underground chamber, or declare to those who have observed the presence of a locked staircase that it is just a 'cellar', built to store various discarded objects. For the new generations of Hindu devotees there has never been any pir in Diggy Kalyanji. They are far from suspecting that this highly popular pilgrimage centre is not just an 'ordinary' temple dedicated to Krishna. In Diggy itself the people dare not allude openly to the original structure, but a Muslim family living in a nearby town revealed to us some intriguing facts. A few months ago their son, who is a painter, was invited by the Brahmins of Diggy to put a fresh coat of paint on the walls and ceiling of the underground 'storeroom'. The artisan who went there, accompanied by the priest's son, saw to his amazement that just below the part of the temple which formed a rectangular enclosed space enshrining a Shiva lingam, lay an old Muslim tomb. When he inquired about this, the young Brahmin's son, who was on friendly terms with the Muslim artisan, told him the following story. A few years ago, when the Hindu trustees of Diggy Kalyanji thought of putting an end to the strange practice of worshipping the pir along with Hanuman, they locked the underground room and decided that people would no longer offer incense, roses or draperies to the grave. Unfortunately, the Sufi saint did not agree with the new resolution. The pir's wrath manifested itself when the electricity abruptly went off without any known physical cause. The whole city remained in the dark until the priests understood, and dashing without further delay to the underground room, asked the pir to forgive the offence. Afterwards the sacred chamber remained locked except for morning and evening offerings, a secret ritual that the Brahmins of Diggy Kalyanji have never discontinued to this day.

Nobody could tell us more about the mysterious saint whose cult continues in the utmost secrecy, but the hidden pir, like other similar phenomena mentioned here, can be understood as a metaphor. Do communal conflicts really point to the existence of a natural 'faultline' in the common ground shared by Hindus and Muslims, or are they rather the result of an artificially created division? If so, cracks have already appeared in the carefully erected boundary wall between what is supposed to be 'Islam' and 'Hinduism'.

Notes

Introduction

1. See Shail Mayaram, *Resisting Regimes: Myths, Memory and the Shaping of a Muslim Identity* (Delhi, 1997), p.37.

2. Peter Gottschalk, 'The Problem of Defining Islam in Arampur', ISIM Newsletter (August, 2001), p.23. In his fascinating study entitled *Beyond Hindu and Muslim: Multiple Identity in Narratives from Village India* (Oxford, 2000), the same author explores in depth the issue of religious identities, revealing the whole complexity of the subject.

3. Carl W. Ernst, *Eternal Garden: Mysticism, History, and Politics at a South Asian Sufi Center* (Albany, NY, 1992), pp.19–20. In his book entitled *Understanding the Muslim Mind* (Delhi, rev. ed., 2000), Rajmohan Gandhi, in spite of his initial assertion 'I hope that no one ... will infer from the title of this book, that its author believes in a single or uniform Muslim (or Hindu) mind' (p.x), goes on to state that 'Hindu-Muslim strife and coldness is an ancient tale that began in 712 AD when Muhammad bin Qasim, son-in-law of the Governor of Iraq, conquered Sind and declared it a Muslim state' (p.3). His biographies of twentieth century Muslim leaders – who were all upper class intellectuals constituting a minority – certainly reflect the diversity of their opinions. However, the author seems to take for granted that in order to understand the 'Muslim mind' it is not necessary to study the ideas and attitude of other Muslims belonging to different sects or layers of society, although they obviously belong to the majority. Similar – and somewhat contradictory opinions and cliches – are expressed in his *Revenge and Reconciliation: Understanding South Asian History* (Delhi, 1999).

4. For the concept of 'cultural fault-lines', see S. Joshi and B. Josh, *Struggle for Hegemony in India – 1920–1947: Culture Community and Power*, vol.3: 1941–1947 (Delhi, 1994).

5. Javeed Alam, 'Composite Culture and Communal Consciousness: The Itttehadul Muslimeen in Hyderabad', in Vasudha Dalmia and Heinrich von Stietencron, ed., *Representing Hinduism: the Construction of Religious Traditions and National Identity* (New Delhi, 1995), p.340.

6. Jackie Assayag, *Au confluent des deux rivières: Musulmans et Hindous dans le sud de l'Inde* (Paris, 1995), pp.215–216. The English version of this book has been published recently as *At the Confluence of Two Rivers: Muslims and Hindus in South India* (Delhi, 2003).

7. Sandria B. Freitag, 'Contesting in Public: Colonial Legacies and Contemporary Communalism', in David Ludden, ed., *Making India Hindu: Religion, Community, and the Politics of Democracy in India* (Delhi, 1996), p.220.

8. Shail Mayaram, 'Spirit Possession: Reframing Discourses of the Self and Other', *Puruśārtha*, 21 (2000), p.103.

9. Harjot Oberoi, *The Construction of Religious Boundaries* (Delhi, 1994), p.9.

10. Hugo G. Nut, 'Syncretism', in David Carrasco, ed., *Oxford Encyclopedia of Mesoamerican Cultures* (Oxford, 2001), pp.177–181.

11. Robert S. Carlsen, 'Transculturation', in Carrasco, ed., ibid., pp.257–260.

12. For these two formulations see Arnold Van Gennep, *Rites of Passage* (London, 1960), and Victor Turner, *Process, Performance and Pilgrimage* (New Delhi, 1991).

13. Mayaram, *Resisting Regimes*, p.38.

14. Ibid.

15. For this concept see Tazim Kassam, 'Syncretism on the Model of the Figure-Ground: A Study of Pir Shams' "Brahma Prakāśa"', in K.K. Young, ed., *Hermeneutical Paths to the Sacred Worlds of India* (Atlanta, 1994), pp.231–241.

16. Mayaram, *Resisting Regimes*, p.39.

17. Ibid., p.37.

Chapter 1: Who is Hindu, who is Muslim?

1. Azim Nanji, *The Nizārī Ismā'īlī Tradition in the Indo-Pakistan Subcontinent* (Delmar, NY, 1978), p.121, and Tazim R. Kassam, *Songs of Wisdom and Circles of Dance: Hymns of the Satpanth Ismā'īlī Muslim Saint, Pīr Shams* (New York, 1995), p.232.

2. Oberoi, *The Construction of Religious Boundaries*, p.3.

3. Ibid., p.4.

4. In order to simplify matters, the word 'Hindu' will be used throughout this essay to refer to original indigenous, South-Asian traditions – unless otherwise specified. This does not mean, however, that the author subscribes to the idea that there is one monolithic religion which can be called 'Hinduism'. I would rather agree with the declaration of the religious and social reformer from Kerala, Narayana Guru (1854–1928) when he said in an interview: 'There

is no such religion as Hinduism. It is a general term for those religions, except Christianity and Islam of foreign origin, which took shape in Hindustan itself.' See Sathya Bai Sivadas and P. Prabhakara Rao, *Narayana Guru: The Social Philosopher of Kerala* (Mumbai, 2002), p. 62.

5. Robert E. Frykenberg, 'The Emergence of Modern "Hinduism" as a Concept and as an Institution: A Reappraisal with Special Reference to South India', in Gunther D. Sontheimer and Hermann Kulke, ed., *Hinduism Reconsidered* (Delhi, 1991; repr. Delhi, 1998), pp.11–12; Heinrich von Stietencron, 'Hinduism: On the Proper use of a Deceptive Term', in Vasudha Dalmia and Heinrich von Stietencron, ed., *Representing Hinduism: the Construction of Religious Traditions and National Identity* (New Delhi, 1995), p.30.

6. This is explained in the *Manusmṛti*. See Margaret and James Stutley, *A Dictionary of Hinduism* (London, 1977), p.323.

7. Catherine Clémentin-Ojha, *Le Trident sur le palais: une cabale anti-Vishnouite dans un Royaume Hindou à l'époque coloniale* (Paris, 1999), p.266, n.58.

8. Ibid.

9. Stutley, *A Dictionary of Hinduism*, pp.69–77.

10. Romila Thapar, 'Syndicated Hinduism', in Sontheimer and Kulke, ed., *Hinduism Reconsidered*, p.58.

11. Except those three traditions, little is known of the religious or philosophical movements which opposed the Brahmins owing to the efforts which were made to erase all traces of them in the literature of that time.

12. There were more sub-divisions within the three main branches. The suffix *-yāna* literally means 'path' and has been often translated as 'vehicle'. The followers of Mahayana derogatorily referred to its rival tradition as 'the narrow path'. As far as the Jains are concerned, the situation is equally complex: Shvetambaras, for instance, were further divided into two sub-groups, one of them opposing temple and image worship.

13. Von Stietencron, 'Hinduism: On the Proper Use of a Deceptive Term', p.12.

14. Ernst, *Eternal Garden*, pp.20–21. The author shows that 'The practical political goals of nationalist historiography have politicised medieval texts in a manner that is foreign to their original political context.' Sources have been selected carefully among Muslim court histories and epic and Puranic traditions, leaving aside numerous other accounts which are still largely unexplored. Ernst suggests instead examining the medieval sources on their own terms, concluding that what emerges out of such an analysis would be 'not a nationalistic and religious concept of identity, but a variety of ethnic ones, based on common Indian and Islamic cosmologies'.

15. According to oral tradition, small communities of Jews and Christians

had already settled in South India from the first century CE.

16. Thapar, 'Syndicated Hinduism', p.63.

17. Ibid.

18. See P. Hardy, 'Modern European and Muslim Explanations of Conversion to Islam in South-Asia: A Preliminary Survey of the Literature', in Nehemia Levitzion, ed., *Conversions to Islam* (New York, 1979), pp.177–206.

19. For a discussion of this question see B.D. Chattopadhyaya, *Representing the Other? Sanskrit Sources and the Muslims 8th-14th Century* (Manohar, Delhi, 1998).

20. Louis Dumont, *Homo Hierarchicus: Le Système des castes et ses implications* (Paris, 1996).

21. See Azim Nanji, 'Shari'at, Custom and Legal Change', in Ewing, ed., *Shari'at and Ambiguity in South-Asian Islam* (Berkeley, 1988), p.66.

22. On these Shi'i kingdoms, see John N. Hollister, *The Shi'a of India* (London, 1953).

23. H.G. Keene, *History of India* (London, 1893), vol. 1, p. 43, and Murray Titus, *Indian Islam* (London, 1930), pp. 15, 31 and passim.

24. D.N. Maclean, *Religion and Society in Arab Sind* (Leiden, 1989).

25. James Tod, *Annals and Antiquities of Rajasthan, 1829–1832* (repr. Delhi, 1983).

26. Ernst, *Eternal Garden*, pp.20–21.

27. Field research conducted in that village led me, a few years ago, to the discovery of a Persian manuscript describing these events.

28. Harbans Mukhia, 'Medieval Indian History and the Communal Approach' in *Selected Writings on Communalism* (Delhi, 1991), p.21.

29. Ernst, *Eternal Garden*, p.21.

30. On the formation of Rajputs as a distinct caste claiming Kshatriya status, during the sixteenth century, see the interesting study of Dirk H.A. Kolff, *Naukar, Rajput and Sepoy: The Ethnohistory of the Military Labour Market in Hindustan, 1450–1850* (Cambridge, 1990), pp.181–192.

31. Thapar, 'Syndicated Hinduism', p.73.

32. See Romila Thapar's recently published book *Somnatha: The Many Voices of a History* (Delhi, 2004).

33. See Thapar, 'Syndicated Hinduism', p.64, and her *Somnatha*.

34. On the issues discussed here and on the destruction of mosques, see R.V. Somnani, *The History of Mewar* (Jaipur, 1976), p. 124, Richard M. Eaton, *Temple Desecration and Muslim States in Medieval India* (Delhi, 2004), p. 69, and Thapar, *Somnatha*, p. 225.

35. See R.M. Eaton's 'Temple Desecration and Indo-Muslim States', in David Gilmartin and Bruce B. Lawrence, ed., *Beyond Turk and Hindu: Rethinking Religious Identities in Islamicate South Asia* (Gainesville, Florida, 2000),

pp.246–281, and his more detailed monograph *Temple Desecration.*

36. Anncharlott Eschmann, 'Religion, Reaction and Change: The Role of Sects in Hinduism', in Sontheimer and Kulke, ed., *Hinduism Reconsidered*, p.111.

37. Ibid.

38. Daniel Gold, *The Lord as Guru: Hindi Sants in North Indian Tradition* (New York, 1987), p.49.

39. Eschmann, 'Religion, Reaction and Change', p.111.

40. Gold, *The Lord as Guru*, p.49.

41. For these rituals see my 'Deux rites tantriques dans une communauté d'intouchables au Rajasthan', *Revue d'histoire des religions*, 21 (1994), pp.443–462.

42. The first Tamil bhaktas, both Shaiva and Vaishnavas, all exponents of *sagūṇ bhakti* (devotion to a qualified God, involving image worship) flourish from the seventh century onwards. The *Bhagavad Gita* is a part of the *Mahabharata* epic, which is believed to have been composed between the fourth century BC and the fourth century CE. See Karine Schomer and W.H. McLeod, ed., *The Sants: Studies in a Devotional Tradition of India* (Delhi, 1987). For the roots of *bhakti* in the *Bhagavad Gita* and the South Indian tradition see, Susmita Pande, *Birth of Bhakti in Indian Religion and Art* (New Delhi, 1982).

43. See Sontheimer and Kulke, ed., *Hinduism Reconsidered*, and in particular the Introduction by Kulke, p.4.

44. Narendra K. Wagle, 'Hindu-Muslim Interactions in Medieval Maharashtra', in Sontheimer and Kulke, ed., *Hinduism Reconsidered*, p.55.

45. For instance, in the devotional compositions attributed to Jambha, the alleged founder of the Bishnoi *panth*, such as the fiftieth *sabad* of his Sabadvanis, the saint adds a third 'category', Jogi, which is distinct from the Hindu and Turk ones.

46. Wagle, 'Hindu-Muslim Interactions in Medieval Maharashtra', pp.57–58.

47. Linda Hess and Shukdev Singh, *The Bījak of Kabir* (Delhi, 1986), p.10.

48. David N. Lorenzen, *Praises to a Formless God: Nirguni Texts from North India* (Albany, NY, 1996), p.191.

49. Aziz Esmail, *The Poetics of Religious Experience: The Islamic Context* (London, 1998), pp.29–30.

50. Farhad Daftary, *A Short History of the Ismailis* (Edinburgh, 1998), pp.21–23.

51. Esmail, *The Poetics of Religious Experience*, p.47.

52. There are vague indications, for instance, of some kind of exchange or connection between Chishti saints and Nizari Ismailis during the medieval period. One can hardly expect to find clear references owing to the persecutions

which the latter had to face at that time. It is obvious that all those who would have openly admitted any link with them would have incurred the same severe reprobation. The best example concerns the way in which Badaoni, the 'orthodox' chronicler of Akbar's time, felt outraged by the participation of alleged heretics (apparently Ismailis) during the 'inter-religious debates' organised by the emperor at Fathepur Sikri. In his eyes it was a much greater offence than the presence of Jain, Hindu, Buddhist or Parsi religious leaders. I am indebted to Muzaffar Alam for this precious information.

53. See for example Aziz Ahmad, *An Intellectual History of Islam in India* (Edinburgh, 1969), and Simon Digby, 'Qalandars and Related Groups: Elements of Social Deviance in the Religious Life of the Delhi Sultanate of the Thirteenth and Fourteenth Centuries', in Y. Friedmann, ed., *Islam in Asia, Vol. 1: South Asia* (Jerusalem, 1984), pp.60–108.

54. Nanji, *The Nizārī Ismāʿīlī Tradition in the Indo-Pakistan Subcontinent*, pp.68, 75.

55. Daftary, *A Short History of the Ismailis*, p.40.

56. On this issue see my *Conversions and Shifting Identities: Ramdev Pir and the Ismailis in Rajasthan* (Delhi, 1997).

57. This is the case of Aziz Ahmad, *An Intellectual History of Islam in India*, pp.24–25.

58. See Zawahir Moir, 'Historical and Religious Debates Amongst Indian Ismailis, 1840–1920', in Mariola Offredi, ed., *The Banyan Tree* (Delhi, 2001), pp.133–135, and Amrita Shodhan, passim, quoted above, and J. Masselos, quoted above, pp.111–114.

Chapter 2: 'There is no Hindu, there is no Musulman'

1. Denis Matringe, 'Kṛṣṇaite and Nāth Elements in the Poetry of the Eighteenth-century Panjabi Sūfī Bullhe Sāh', in R.S. McGregor, ed., *Devotional Literature in South Asia* (Cambridge, 1992), p.190.

2. Khan, *Conversions and Shifting Identities*, p.21.

3. Recently, however, inscriptions have been found which testify to the presence of Ismailis, not only in Gujarat but also in medieval Rajasthan, confirming our idea that a number of local sects in that region are 'lost branches' of Ismailism; see Mehrdad Shokoohy, *Bhadreshvar: The Oldest Islamic Monuments in India* (Leiden, 1988), p.18.

4. Very few authors have written on South Asian Ismailism. Let us mention here Nanjiani, Ivanow, Nanji, Shackle and Moir, Mallison, Asani, Boivin, Esmail and Kassam. It is only recently that scholars have started to show more interest in the subject, gradually discovering its importance.

5. For the Rajasthani ex-Nizari communities, see Khan, *Conversions and*

Shifting Identities. For the Imamshahis, see Wladimir Ivanow, 'The Sect of Imamshah in Gujarat', *Journal of the Bombay Branch of the Royal Asiatic Society*, NS, 12 (1936), pp.19–70, and D.S. Khan and Zawahir Moir, 'Coexistence and Communalism: The Shrine of Pirana in Gujarat', *South Asia*, 22, Special Issue (1999), pp.133–154. Mohandev Thontiya, a student in Karachi, is currently preparing a thesis on the Barmati *panth* (a Sindh and Kutch based sect), whose Nizari origin he openly acknowledges. We thank him for sending us valuable information on the subject, along with some original *ginān*s of the tradition.

6. The concept of 'traces' is used here in the sense proposed by the historian Carlo Ginzburg in his *Clues, Myths and the Historical Method* (Baltimore, MD, 1989). Whatever cannot be proved or found out in written documents can be sometimes traced through the 'conjectural method'. To claim that such a method is unscientific would amount to denying the achievements of palaeontology, criminology, medical science, etc. We have resorted to this method in our *Conversions and Shifting Identities*.

7. Numerous other examples could be given, where the shrine of a Muslim saint protects the entrance of a Hindu/Jain sacred place or fortress; let us mention just a few: Angar Shah's darga at the entrance of the Jain Shatrunjaya temple complex at Palitana in Gujarat; the darga of a nineteenth-century *shahīd* who helped the Hindu Maharaja of Jodhpur (Rajasthan) to defend his fort against the attack of his enemy, the ruler of Jaipur, who was his co-religionist; the tomb of the Muslim warrior-saint, Vavar, which guards the temple to Ayyappa at Sabarimalai, and so on.

8. Shail Mayaram, 'Spirit Possession: Reframing Discourses of the Self and Other', pp.101–131.

9. Ibid., p.110.

10. During my field research among Punjabis I was told that many Sikhs, particularly in the rural milieus, regarded some Sufi pirs, such as Guga, as a saint belonging to the Sikh tradition.

11. See Desiderio Pinto, *Piri-Muridi Relationship: A Study of the Nizamuddin Dargah* (Delhi, 1995). In a Sunni Sufi context, a certain master-disciple relationship can be established, it seems, without any necessity of formal conversion in the cases where the devotee is not already a Muslim.

12. Wagle, 'Hindu-Muslim Interactions in Medieval Maharashtra', p.62.

13. Ibid.

14. Chirag is the name for an oil lamp kept in Muslim shrines. It can also be used as the title for a saint such as the famous Sufi, Nizamuddin Chishti, who was referred to as 'Chirag Delhi'.

15. See D.S. Khan, 'Saix Burhān Cistī: le culte d'un saint musulman chez les Rajput Shekhāvat', in Annie Montaut, ed., *Le Rajasthan, ses dieux, ses héros,*

ses hommes (Paris, 2000).

16. Minoru Mio, 'Faith, Identity and Communal Discourse: Some Ethnological Considerations on the Conflicts over the Administration of a Sufi Saint's Mausoleum in Rajasthan', in Steering Committee of the Research Project Institutions, Networks and Forces of Changes in Contemporary South Asia, ed., *Rituals as Popular Culture: Towards Historico-Anthropological Understanding of Modern Indian Society* (Tokyo, 1999), pp.1–58.

17. Ibid., p.29.

18. Raja Mukal Singh's younger son was named Shekha because he was born by the grace of Shaykh Burhan and adopted certain Muslim customs to please his allies, but his elder brother became a Muslim fakir as the result of the same vow made by their father. Similarly, we have heard of a Hindu Brahmin family who promised to the Sufi saint of Ajmer that they would become Muslims if he blessed them with a son: when their wish was granted they all converted to Islam and, as a consequence, became outcastes.

19. It could be of some interest to mention in passing a Rajasthani rural tradition. On the eve of the Holi spring festival (Dulendi) the villagers temporarily change their roles: the Brahmin, for example, dresses and behaves like an Untouchable sweeper, while the leather-worker will act the part of a respectable Baniya (high-caste merchant). This interplay between the Self and the Other speaks once more of the 'fragility' of assumed caste, gender and ritual categories which, in order to maintain the social and cosmic order, have to be delineated and preserved in ordinary life, but must, in other circumstances, be transgressed precisely to prevent the 'chaos' which could result from too much rigidity.

20. The Imamshahis are a Nizari community who seceded from the Nizari Ismailis and now comprise several groups, residing mainly in Gujarat and Maharashtra, claiming allegiance to Sunnism, Twelver Shiʿism or Hindusim. See Daftary, *A Short History*, pp.181–182.

21. The present controversy around the sacred place of Pirana is strikingly similar to that analysed by Yoginder Sikand in his article, 'Another Ayodhya in the Making? The Baba Budhangiri Dargah Controversy in South India', *Journal of Muslim Minority Affairs*, 20, 2 (2000), pp.209–225. It has also resulted in court cases related to the administration of the shrine.

22. Sayid Athar Abbas Rizvi, *A History of Sufism in India* (Delhi, 1978, repr. 1986), vol.1, pp.336–344.

23. Ibid., pp.337, 341.

24. Better known is the work by the Mughal emperor Awrangzib's brother Dara Shikoh, condemned for heresy by the ulama in 1659. In his *Majmaʿ ul-baḥrain* (lit. 'The Mingling of the Two Oceans') he attempts to show the similarities that exist between the traditions of Vedanta and of Hatha yoga

with Sufism. See ibid., p.417.

25. Matringe, 'Kṛṣṇaite and Nāth Elements in the Poetry of the Eighteenth-century Panjabi Sūfī Bullhe Sāh', in McGregor, ed., *Devotional Literature in South Asia*, pp.191, 193, and passim.

26. Ibid., p.196.

27. Gold, *The Lord as Guru*, pp.208–209.

28. Eleanor Zelliot, 'Eknath's Bharuds: the Sant as a Link between Cultures', in Schomer and McLeod, ed., *The Sants: Studies in a Devotional Tradition of India* (Delhi, 1987), p.96. Interestingly, a legendary Muslim saint of Karnataka, Dada Hayat, is also viewed as an incarnation of Guru Dattatraya. See Sikand, 'Another Ayodhya in the Making?' According to the author, the 'Hindu identity' of the saint would have been 'fabricated' by the Sufis to make his teaching acceptable to non-Muslims. We will argue that there was no need to do this, since, as has been shown, numerous Sufi pirs are readily worshipped by Hindus who do not feel the necessity of giving them a 'Hindu' identity to legitimise this cult. Instead, one should examine in more detail the 'Hindu' legends relating to Dada Hayat as Dattatraya. In the local tradition of the Baba Budhangiri *darga*, this deity was equated with Kalki, the tenth avatar of Vishnu, whereas in the Shaiva tradition connected with the same figure, he is the combined incarnation of Vishnu, Shiva and Brahma and the first guru of the Dasnami sect. Another interesting example is that of the Brahmin Cand Bodhale, who appears at first sight like an 'ordinary' Hindu saint, but who had received the teaching of a Sufi pir. One could think that he had imbibed a certain amount of Muslim mysticism, simply borrowing Sufi ideas to enrich his own vision without shifting his identity (in the same way that some Sufis had resorted to indigenous concepts and terminologies). This would be true if we could disregard the following fact: it is recorded (rightly or wrongly) that the Brahmin saint actually became a full-fledged Sufi, a member of the Qadiri order known in that *ṭarīqa* as 'Caṇdsaheb Qadiri'. Furthermore, he is believed to have been the spiritual teacher of the celebrated Marathi mystic, Sayyid Shaykh Muhammad Qadiri. See Wagle, 'Hindu-Muslim Interactions in Medieval Maharashtra', pp.56, 64.

29. Rizvi, *A History of Sufism in India*, vol. 1, pp.349–351.

30. Mohammad Ishaq Khan, *Kashmir's Transition to Islam: The Role of Muslim Rishis (Fifteenth to Eighteenth Century)* (Delhi, 1994), pp.68–69. The other version is that it was Nuruddin Rishi who incorporated Shaiva and other indigenous ideas into this religious message.

31. See Véronique Bouillier, *Ascetes et rois* (Paris, 1998), where the author suggests, rightly in our opinion, that the saint was initially a Muslim mystic.

32. Matringe, 'Kṛṣṇaite and Nāth Elements in the Poetry of the Eighteenth-century Panjabi Sūfī Bullhe Sāh', p.189.

33. Kassam, 'Syncretism on the Model of the Figure-Ground'. The figure-ground can be seen as two figures (two faces) facing each other or as one figure only, representing a chalice. To those who perceive the latter as a 'reality' the duality of the faces is a mere illusion. Our Janus Bifrons, instead, always remains a 'composite' figure, being one and two at the same time.

34. Ibid.,241.

35. D.N. Maclean, *Religion and Society in Arab Sind*, p.152.

36. See Nathabhai Gohil, *Āgāmvāṇīs* (Ahmedabad, 1994), p.107.

37. Struck by the fact that the Satpanthi literature contained numerous elements drawn from various indigenous traditions, Nanjiani (*Khoja Vṛttant*, Ahmedabad, 1892; repr. 1918, pp.118–119),wrongly surmises that the Nizari pirs borrowed certain beliefs from the Mahamargis: for instance the myth of the four *pāṭh*s (ritual tables) and four sacrifices during the four successive *yugas*, and the soteriological role played by a particular sacred figure during each of these eras to save five, then seven, then ten and twelve crores (one crore corresponds to ten million) of devotees If each of these elements or characters, taken separately, has an indigenous origin, their combination and particular configuration is typical of Ismailism in general, at least from the Fatimid period onwards. See, for instance, Farhad Daftary, *The Ismāʿīlīs: Their History and Doctrines* (Cambridge, 1990), pp.139, 394. In fact, the Mahamargis, adopted 'en bloc' the whole structure which I have referred to as 'Ismailized Hindu pattern' in my *Conversions and Shifting Identities*, pp.48–51 and 147–148.

38. Among them, the Punjabi saint Ratan Nath/ Haji Ratan, traditionally connected with Goga Dev/Gugga Pir, Balmik/Bala Shah worshipped by the Untouchable Chuhras (Banghis) of Punjab, Darya Nath/Darya Shah (also Jhulelal/Khwaja Khizr) of Sindh, Lal Das/Lal Pir of Mewat (eastern Rajasthan), Nuruddin/ Nand Rishi of Kashmir and Changadev/Rajabag Sarvar of Karnataka.

39. These Gujarati texts are mentioned in Moir, 'Historical and Religious Debates Amongst Indian Ismailis, 1840–1920'. See also Samira Sheikh, 'Devotee or Renegade:Infanticide and the Muslim Taint, 1300–1467', unpublished paper. On these crypto-Ismailis, see my *Conversions and Shifting Identities*.

40. See Moir, 'Historical and Religious Debates amongst Indian Ismailis, 1840–1920', p.132.

41. Ibid., p.138.

42. For the persecution of unnamed 'heretics' (probably mainly Ismailis) see Hollister, *The Shiʿa of India*, pp.344–345, 349–350, quoting British histories referring to Sunni sources. Some Gujarati texts, as well as oral traditions of the Sindh-Kutchi Barmati Meghvars, also allude to the concealment, persecution and conversion to Sunnism of various Gujarati dynasties, such as the Jadejas, Sammas and Sumras. I am indebted to Samira Sheikh and Mohan Devraj

Thontiya for this valuable information.

43. This is a challenging task, as both written documents and legends inevitably select the facts and interpret them according to what is supposed to be, at a particular time and for a particular person, their correct, 'orthodox' version.

44. Various authors listed in the bibliography have written on these traditions. They are also mentioned in my *Conversions and Shifting Identities*, passim. The Jasnathi and Ai *panths*, the Pranami Sampraday, the Daryashahi *panth*, the sect of Lalbegis, and the Nagesh Sampraday are but a few; their links with Ismaili Islam have never been explored.

45. This has been noted in the numerous works devoted to the Sant tradition. See for example, Schomer and Mcleod, ed., *The Sants*.

46. See the articles and books by Asani, Kassam, Nanji, Mallison, Shackle and Moir, listed in the Bibliography.

47. See for example, Kassam, *Songs of Wisdom and Circles of Dance*, and my *Conversions and Shifting Identities*.

48. Charlotte Vaudeville, *Kabir* (Oxford, 1974), vol. 1, p.89, who follows the Hindi author Dvivedi.

49. Iconography of Guru Nanak from the eighteenth and nineteenth century shows him in different garb, with or without a sect mark, which also varies in colour, on his forehead. This could be profitably compared to the various 'metamorphoses' undergone by the pictorial representations of the Nizari saint Imamshah, in the Pirana tradition: he appears as a typical Muslim pir, as a 'syncretic' saint (namely, a Sufi reading the four Vedas) or, more recently, with a red tilak (Hindu sect mark) on his forehead. One should add the interesting and original analysis done by Yoginder Sikand in his 'Sikh-Muslim Harmony: The Contribution of Khwaja Hasan Nizami', available through the internet. The author of this paper goes through the various perceptions of Nanak's religious identity and mentions, among others, the theory according to which the Sikh guru had turned Muslim. The focus of the article is however on the approach proposed by Nizami who identifies the guru's religion with Sufi Islam.

50. See my *Conversions and Shifting Identities*, pp.235–266. Another analogy between Nizari Ismailism and Sikhism is the use of the term Gurmukhi to refer to the sacred/secret script of the *panth*: according to Abualy Alibhai, 'On the Origin of the Khojki Script', Proceedings of the S.O.S. Khojki Conference 1990, p.47, the Khojki alphabet used by the Nizari Khojas was earlier referred to as Gurmukhi. Oral Sikh and Nizari traditions also point to that link. According to a Sikh oral source, Guru Nanak regarded himself as a *murīd* of the Ismaili Pir Shams and regularly visited his shrine at Multan. The Gujarati writer Varteji reproduces a Nizari *ginān* where it is said that both Ramdev and Nanak were appointed as preachers by Pir Shams. See E.J. Varteji, *Ismaīlī*

āftāb sāhitya śrenī (n.p., 1930).

51. Esmail, *The Poetics of Religious Experience*, p.40.

52. Legends about miracle competitions between Ismaili pirs and Sunni Sufis are no less common than those between the latter and Nath yogis or other Hindu gurus; these competitions are also frequent between Sikh gurus and Sufis, between 'liminal' saints such as Jambha or Ramdev and their various sectarian rivals. For the former, see Zawahir Moir, 'The Life and Legend of Pir Shams as Reflected in the Ismaili Ginans: A Critical Review', in Françoise Mallison, ed., *Constructions hagiographiques dans le monde indien: entre mythe et histoire* (Paris, 2001), pp.365–384.

Chapter 3: Creating Orthodoxies

*Epigram from India Office Ms.1728, fol.239–240

1. Joshi and Josh. *Struggle for Hegemony in India, 1920–1947,* vol. 3: 1941–1947.

2. Quoted by Rizvi, *A History of Sufism in India*, vol. 2, p.411.

3. This episode is mentioned in one Jānam Patrī quoted by Thomas Patrick Hughes, *A Dictionary of Islam* (London, 1887; repr. Delhi 1996; Ottawa, 1996), pp.588–589.

4. Ibid. A variant of the same story is told about the Sindhi saint Jhulelal/Darya Shah whose body disappeared miraculously in the Indus. The quarrelling followers were advised by a heavenly voice to build two shrines side by side at this place, one for Hindus, another for Muslims. Ratan Nath/Ratan Haji (twelfth century) who also appeared to be endowed with a 'dual personality' as a Sufi and as a Jogi, is said to have created, by his magic powers, a boy who became his disciple and was named Kayanath/Qaim al-Din: 'When Kayanath died, both Musalmans and Hindus claimed his body; but it disappeared, only the cloths remaining. Hindus built a *samādhi* for him and Musalmans a tomb'. Ratan's disciple is, so to say, buried twice, one as Kayanath, according to the custom of the Nath Jogis, the other according to the Islamic ritual as Qaim al-Din. Vatayo Fakir (sixteenth/seventeenth-century?), who has become a legendary figure of Sindh and an inexhaustible source of witty anecdotes, is said to have been the victim of a somewhat similar dispute. After having removed the cloth which covered his body, people found that the head was missing. Apparently the Hindus had immersed it in the river (as do the members of the high castes with the bodies of dead children, mutilated people, and persons having died of some infectious disease and who should not be burnt), and later on, when the head was found the Muslims buried it and built a tomb over it. The Sindhi saint Jhulelal/Daryashah's spiritual body (his physical body is said to have been immersed in the Indus) is symbolised in two separate

but analogous monuments, the first being called *darga*, the second *mandir* (temple); characteristically, the latter does not enshrine any idol, containing only a burning lamp.

5. Shastras is a term that refers to classical texts in Sanskrit, including the Upanishads, Brahamanas, Aranyakas, and Manusmṛti, etc.

6. Guru Nanak's Muslim, and more precisely, Ismaili connection, 'lies buried', so to say, in the memory of some ex-Lohana Khojas and also in the Ahmadiyya tradition. The orthodox Sikh tradition is curiously silent about their founder's funeral monument. It is known only by a few. In an interview given with a Sufi pir, Makhdoom Syed Chan Pir, in London, about Sikh-Muslim relations, Yoginder Sikand mentions some fascinating details given by the pir who describes the place where Guru Nanak died. As it is revelant to our discussion on 'dividing the Divine', we quote here his reply to one of Sikand's questions: 'This happened at a place called Kartarpur, which is now in Pakistan, not far from Lahore. The shrine complex in Kartarpur still remains a major centre of pilgrimage, and is presently administered by the Awqaf board. It has two sections, one containing a Sikh-style *samādh* shrine, and the other a Muslim style *mazār*. Many local Muslims, and occasionally pilgrims from India still come to the shrine, to ask for Baba Nanak Sahibs' blessings.' I am grateful to Yoginder Sikand who sent me this interview by mail and permitted me to quote it.

7. It seems that earlier, after their conversion, some Ismaili groups in the Subcontinent retained the custom of cremating their dead. To this day, a few Imamshahis have kept the strange custom of burning the dead bodies with the exception of one finger which they bury and over which they erect a grave. A similar custom exists among Pranamis, a liminal tradition that appears as another offshoot of the Nizari, possibly Imamshahi, *satpanth*. To the present day some followers of the sect cremate their dead and later on go to Panna, the main centre of the Pranamis, to build a *mazār* enshrining the sacred, unburnt bones.

8. Rizvi, *A History of Sufism in India*, vol. 1, pp.50, 375, suggests a Sufi origin for these legends. He recalls the story of the ninth-century mystic, Maʿrūf, who is claimed by Jews, Christians and Muslims alike. According to the Muslims, he was one of them since, ultimately, only his brothers were able to lift the bier. The Shaykh himself, as a true Sufi, may have disapproved of the dispute as well as its resolution. Not because he would have denied that his roots and his path were Islamic, but for the same reason which caused ʿAbd al-Quddus to exclaim, 'I am neither Hindu nor Muslim'.

9. M.N. Srinivas, *Religion and Society among the Coorgs of South India* (Oxford, 1952).

10. This issue is exposed, among others, in A. Eschmann, H. Kulke, G.C.

Tripathi, ed., *The Cult of Jagannath and the Regional Tradition of Orissa* (Delhi, 1986), pp.xiii–xv. On the other hand, as Eschmann, Kulke and Tripathi warn us, a careful study of local traditions shows that 'Sanskrit has never been the only medium through which Sanskritisation developed and that its agents were not always Brahmins'. Similarly, the role of regional variants of the Dharmashastra law books and the regional languages may have been of considerable importance.

11. The emergence of 'left-handed' Tantrism (Vāmmārg), where the values most sacred to the high caste were literally mocked in the course of ritual performances, can be regarded as a reaction to the Brahmanical *varṇāśrāma* dharma, the traditional hierarchy of castes. But, although Tantrism had given prominence to low caste values, this did not prevent the upper caste participating in the rituals. Communities such as the Charans and the Naths, traditionally connected with goddess worship, cults including animal sacrifices (which had been banned in the Brahmanical world probably owing to the influence of various ascetic movements), consumption of alcohol and drugs, ritual possession, Vammargi and Aghori practices, were linked to Tantrism. At the court of Rajput rulers, competition between ritual specialists of various status, Brahmins, Charans and Naths, ended with a Pyrrhic victory for the latter. Charans and Naths could retain their position only at the cost of Sanskritising themselves.

12. The twelfth-century Tamil philosopher Ramanuja was inspired by the popular Vaishnava saints who preceded him and spread devotion among the masses. Among 'the twelve Alvars', as they were known, one was an Untouchable and one was a woman. However, Ramanuja broke away from their tradition by reverting to a form of religion that was closer to the Brahmanical texts. See, Susmita Pande, *Medieval Bhakti Movement* (Meerut, 1989), pp.1–34.

13. Legend has it that Kabir was in reality the abandoned child of a Brahmin woman adopted by a poor Muslim weaver.

14. A fifteenth-century saint who was an exponent of 'non-qualified' devotion. His tradition was later modified to be in conformity with the Brahmanical model.

15. According to a Tamil tradition, a Shaiva saint induced the king of Madurai to have eight thousand Jains impaled, whom he accused of having defiled a Shiva temple. The episode is reported by Dennis Hudson in his 'Violent and Fanatical Devotion among the Nayanars: A Study of the Periya Puranam of Cekkilar', in A. Hiltebeitel, ed., *Criminal Gods and Demon Devotees* (Delhi, 1990), p.391.

16. Imtiaz Ahmad, *Caste and Social Stratification among Muslims in India* (2nd edn, Delhi, 1978), p.35, n.12.

17. An excellent example is given by the religious 'competition' which

opposed in the fourteenth century the de facto sultan Ala al-Din Khilji to the Sufi saint Nizam al-Din, the 'spiritual' sultan of Delhi. 'Ironically, both ruler and saint argued that they were the protectors and strengtheners of the Sharī'a. The latter, however, caricatured the outward, ritualistic understanding of the Holy Law, an interpretation taught by the 'ulamā' in the madrasas and mosques constructed by the Sultan', and further, 'the moral claims of the Sultan and the Sufi saint to be the protectors and guides of the Muslim community were sustained by contradictory interpretations of Islam, the discordance reflecting the social and doctrinal complexities which existed within the Muslim community during the thirteenth and fourteenth centuries'. See Sunil Kumar, 'Assertions of Authority: A Study of the Discursive Statements of Two Sultans of Delhi', in Muzaffar Alam, Françoise 'Nalini' Delvoye, Marc Gaborieau, ed., *The Making of Indo-Persian Culture: Indian and French Studies* (New Delhi, 2000), pp.40, 57, 61.

18. Digby, 'Qalandars and Related Groups', p.69.

19. Ibid.

20. Ibid., p.91., and for the idea of the 'concealed wali' see n.65.

21. He was also perceived as the Nath yogi Bhartṛhari, see S.F.D. Ansari, *Sufi Saints and State Power: The Pirs of Sind, 1843–1947* (Cambridge, 1992), p.19. In a similar way, Nur al-Din/Nand Rishi could become the patron saint of predominantly Sunni Kashmir when he was appropriated by the Kubrawiyya order. Rizvi has shown that his ideas considerably differed from the doctrines of that *ṭarīqa*, although Ishaq Khan has attempted to legitimise Nur al-Din as a 'regular' and 'orthodox' Sufi. See Rizvi, *A History of Sufism in India*, vol. 1, p.350 and I. Khan, *Kashmir's Transition to Islam*, p.167 and passim. Let us also mention the fascinating Ratan Nath/Ratan Haji (see n.4 above), who 'continues' his dual existence as a Nath yogi, patron of an important monastery in Nepal, and as saint of the same Kubrawiyya *silsila*.

22. See Wladimir Ivanow, 'Satpanth', in *Collectanea* (Leiden, 1948), vol.1, p.10, and Ali S. Asani, 'The *ginān* Literature of the Ismailis of Indo-Pakistan', in D.L. Eck and F. Mallison, ed., *Devotion Divine* (Groningen, 1991), p.3.

23. The author of this work visited Pir Dadu's darga in January 2001. Not surprisingly, the caretakers were not aware of any Ismaili connection of the shrine.

24. See n.19.

25. Khan, *Conversions and Shifting Identities*, and H.A. Rose, *A Glossary of the Tribes and Castes of the Punjab and Northwest Frontier Provinces* (Delhi, 1919; repr. 1990), vol. 3, pp.402–403.

26. Aziz Ahmad, *An Intellectual History of Islam in India*, pp.24–26.

27. Esmail, *The Poetics of Religious Experience*, p.29–30.

28. Ansar Zahid Khan, *History and Culture of Sind* (Karachi, 1980),

pp.276,279.

29. In her unpublished paper, 'Devotee or Renegade', Samira Sheikh has mentioned the battles fought by the Gujarati Sunni sultans against the part-Hindu, part-Muslim 'heretic' (probably Nizari) 'tribes' such as the Sumras and Sammas, followed by their defeat and conversion to Sunnism. I thank her for permitting me to quote some fragments.

30. Rizvi, *A History of Sufism in India*, vol. 1, p.302.

31. F.E. Keay, *Kabir and his Followers* (New Delhi, 1931; repr. 1995), pp.95–97. The author has included some photographs showing the two twin shrines and the dividing wall.

32. *Dasondh* or *dasvandh* is still customary among the Sikhs although the word is now applied to voluntary donations, namely for the *langar*. One also finds it in the Nizarpanthi, Barmati, Bishnoi, Jasnathi and Aipanthi traditions, but it is not observed in the Hindu sects which have not come under the influence of Ismailism. The institution and term *dasondh/dasvandh* can therefore be regarded as 'traces' of Nizari influence.

33. The miracle consisted in diverting the Ganges. On this see my 'Diverting the Ganges – Nizari Ismaili Methods of Conversion', in R. Robinson and S. Clarke, ed., *Religious Conversion in India* (Delhi, 2003), pp. 29–30.

34. Khan, *Conversions and Shifting Identities*, p.112–113 where the author has traced the alleged descendants of Pir Shams settled in Rajathan who now claim a Suhrawardi and Naqshbandi affiliation.

35. E.A. Mann, 'Religion, Money and Status: Competition for Resources at the Shrine of Shah Jamal, Aligarh', in Christian W. Troll, ed., *Muslim Shrines in India: Their Character, History and Significance* (Delhi, 1989), pp.158–159.

36. Khwaja Nizami, *Fatimi daʿwat-e-Islam* (Delhi, 1338/1919), p.229.

37. Currently identified with the Vaishnava current, the Dadu *panth* may, at first sight, appear to have been an original indigenous sect connected with the *bhakti* movement. However, according to M. Boehm-Tettelbach, a scholar who has done extensive research on this *panth*, within the precincts of the shrine, in a locked underground hall, are stored an impressive number of old manuscripts, some of which contain interesting Islamic references, among others, quotations of Ibn ʿArabi. It is not surprising, of course, to find evidence of his influence on Dadu, who, like Kabir, Nanak and other similar sants, appear as the spiritual heir of the great Sufi. A detailed examination of the manuscripts of this hidden library would probably reveal more details.

38. Rizvi, *A History of Sufism in India*, vol. 2, pp.388–405.

39. Hughes, *A Dictionary of Islam*, p.583.

40. Rizvi, *A History of Sufism in India*, vol. 2, pp.388–405.

41. Catherine Clémentin-Ojha, *Le trident sur le palais*, p.351. From a very long period onward the Amber-Jaipur rulers had been devotees of Vishnu.

To the devotion of Sitarama (a form of Rama) which was connected with the Galta Ramanandi (Shrivaishnava) Sampraday, Jai Singh had added the cult of a form of Krishna, Govindadeva.

42. Ibid., pp.351–352.

43. Monika Horstmann, 'The Temple of Govindadevaji: A Symbol of Hindu Kingship?', in N.K. Singhi and R. Joshi, ed., *Religion, Ritual and Royalty* (Jaipur, 1999), pp.119–131, p.129. The ideal of Kalki as the fighter of *mlecchas* is illustrated in a Sanskrit text entitled *Kalki Purana*. On this see my article, 'The coming of Nikalank Avatar: A Messianic Theme in Some Sectarian Traditions of North-Western India', *Journal of Indian Philosophy*, 25 (1997), pp.401–426. Religious debates took a new turn when the Gaudiya Vaishnava tradition (founded by the sixteenth-century Bengali saint Chaitanya) made its entry, among others, into the Jaipur kingdom. The specific religious policy of Jai Singh II after the decline of the Mughal empire can be reconstructed on the basis of a number of official documents dating from his reign. According to V.S. Bhatnagar, during the same period a letter was sent by the ruler of Jaipur to request Chhatrasal, a rule of Bundela (modern Madhya Pradesh) who was affiliated with the liminal Pranami sect, to give up what was not in conformity with the Vedas and Puranas. In yet another document, which is of particular interest to us, Jai Singh recommends to the Brahmins that gurus from the lower castes (Shudras and Untouchables) should not initiate the twice-born (*dvijas*) disciples belonging to the upper *varṇas*. This is an allusion to a practice that was prevalent in a number of non-Brahmanical sects, such as the Nath Sampraday, the Mahapanth of Ramdev, the sect of Jasnathis and of Aipanthis, the Kabir and Dadu *panths*.

44. 'Attempt at Revivalism or Reassertion of Vedic and Sastriya Traditions through Open Debate in the 18th Century', unpublished paper presented at the Second International Seminar on Rajasthan, IRS, Jaipur, 1991.

45. Horstmann, 'The Temple of Govindadevaji', p.129.

46. The term '*tilaka*' refers here to the sect mark that many Hindus bear on their forehead. The main distinction is between Vaishnava and Shaiva marks, therefore this alludes clearly to the fact that the dispute was between these two broad affiliations.

47. Clémentin-Ojha, *Le Trident sur le palais*, pp.353–357.

48. Ibid., p.359.

49. Lynn Zastoupil and Martin Moir, ed., *The Great Indian Education Debate: Documents Relating to the Orientalist-Anglicist Controversy, 1781–1843* (Richmond, 1999), p.2.

50. In this way not only were traditional studies encouraged with the local population, but the British themselves, as some other Europeans, took an active interest in South-Asian culture, learning Sanskrit, Arabic and Persian

and later vernacular languages, studying the literature, art and architecture of the Subcontinent. As far as the latter is concerned, the British were surprised at first by the indifference of the local elites; many old temples had fallen into ruins or had disappeared, covered by thick jungle.

51. A fragment from a petition sent by the students of the Sanskrit College of Calcutta in 1835 may serve to illustrate this phenomenon. Hearing that the British were going to withdraw their financial support to this institution, the young Bengali Brahmins reacted by writing a letter to the government. According to the petitioners, Sanskrit 'is the fountain from whence all other dialects commonly current in this Country derived their origin', that this language led to the 'path of truth', and nobody could respect the opinion of a person who did not know Sanskrit, 'the study of which among Brahmins is the only means of their support', a support which even the Muslim rulers had never thought of withdrawing. From this petition and from other documents related to the education policy of the British, one can infer that non-Islamic culture was entirely identified with the Brahmanic/Sanskrit ethos and with North Indian civilisation. Similarly, the admiration vowed by Hastings and others to the Islamic heritage was restricted to classical Sunni learning, as testified by the foundation of a madrasa in 1780. Ibid., p.5.

52. Ibid.

53. Oberoi, *The Construction of Religious Boundaries*, p. 9.

54. Mayaram, *Resisting Regimes*, p.37. As Mayaram has it, this project 'initiated Indian society into an enumerative world'.

55. Denzil Ibbetson, *Panjab Castes: Races and Tribes of the People of Panjab* (1906; repr. Delhi, 1981), p.iv.

56. Ibid., p.v.

57. Oberoi, *The Construction of Religious Boundaries*, p.9.

58. For all the following references see Rose, *A Glossary of the Tribes and Castes of the Punjab and Northwest Frontier Provinces*, vols. 2 and 3, pp.84, 160, 380–381, 541–543. Gohil Nathabhai, in his *Āgāmvāṇīs*, p.120, writes that the founder of the Pranami sect, Prannath (seventeenth century) who was a Gujarati Lohana, was referred to by his followers as Nishkalank. In fact this is the name of Vishnu's tenth incarnation Kalki, represented as the Ismaili Imam. Prannath's prophetic poems are similar to those of the Satpanthis, Nizarpanthis and other sects formerly connected with Nizari Ismailism. See our 'The Prannathis of Rajasthan: Bhakti and Irfan', in L.A. Babb, V. Joshi and M.W. Meister, ed., *Multiple Histories: Culture and Society in the Study of Rajasthan* (Jaipur, New Delhi, 2002,), pp.209–231 and 'The Mahdi of Panna: A Short History of the Pranamis', Part 1, *Indian Journal of Secularism*, 6 (2003), pp.61–93, Part 2 ibid., 7 (2003), pp.46–66. The same views have been expressed earlier by Khwaja Nizami in his *Fatimi daʿwat-e-Islam*, and by Sadruddin Dargawala

in his *Tavariqe Pir* (Navsari, 1935), vol.2, p.63.c58. Rose also examines some old records of the Khokkhars, a Rajput community converted to Islam, and writes that 'It is curious to find Hindu and Muhammedan names mixed up in this history without apparent sense of incongruity', although he admits having found the same configuration among the Muslim Meos of Gurgaon (near Delhi) who are said to 'profess a happy combination of Hinduism and Islam'. The sect of Laldasis, of which many Meos are the followers together with Hindu merchants and carpenters, is credited with a similar 'confusion': although the worship consists mainly in repeating the name of Ram, Lal Das, the founder of the *panth*, was regarded as a pir; like a true Muslim he had banned image worship, but on the other hand he did not perform his ablutions, nor the five daily prayers.

59. Oberoi, *The Construction of Religious Boundaries*, p.10.

60. See Rose, *A Glossary of the Tribes and Castes of the Punjab and North-west Frontier Provinces*, vol. 3, p.384 mentioning the popular couplet: 'The Sikhs and the Sarais are both brothers, Baba Nanak made them his sons'.

61. Ibid., vol. 3, pp.402–403.

62. Ibid., vol. 2, pp.182–214.

63. Khan, *Conversions and Shifting Identities*, passim. Mohan Devraj Thontiya has also collected an impressive amount of data related to the hagiography of the Barmati or Mahesh *panth* where he clearly establishes its historical connection with the Nizari Ismialis. I thank him for having given me access to this valuable material.

64. They are mentioned in the Bombay Gazetteers originally published in 1901. See James M. Campbell, ed., *Muslim and Parsi Castes of Gujarat*, pp.66–68, and also, same ed., *Hindu Castes and Tribes of Gujarat* (Gurgaon, 1901; repr. 1990), vol.1, pp.153, 167–172.

65. Quoted from Oberoi, *The Construction of Religious Boundaries*, p.9.

66. Ahmad, *An Intellectual History of Islam in India*, pp.25–26. It is a fact that a small number of Nizari Khojas and Imamshahi Satpanthis became Swami Narayan's followers towards the end of the nineteenth century. An intriguing Imamshahi legend reported by some of my informants at Pirana has it that the founder of this sect was originally a Satpanthi tithe collector who decided to run away with the money and to found his own separate sect. This could be mere legend, but there is obviously some kind of Nizari influence on the Swami Narayan movement, which may simply be due to the fact that a good number of followers were Nizaris who, breaking away from their former tradition, may have brought some of its elements into the new sect.

67. On this process of identity fragmentation of the former South-Asian Nizari communities, see my *Conversion and Shifting Identities*, pp.97–126 and passim.

68. Ibid., pp.10–11. On the influence of the census on religious identities see the excellent study by Kenneth W. Jones, 'Religious Identity and the Indian Census', in Gerald N. Barrier, ed., *The Census in British India* (Delhi, 1981), pp.73–102.

69. Ibid., p.92.

70. This valuable information is taken from Shafique Virani's unpublished paper, 'Vive l'Avatar: Quelques Hindous Musulmans de l'Inde', presented at Inde médiévale et moderne: textes et contextes, Ecole Pratique des Hautes Études, Sorbonne University, Paris, on 8 February, 2000. According to Virani, for these Guptis the term 'Hindu' refers to a culture and a way of life, whereas 'Muslim' indicates only religious affiliation.

71. The Anglicists, who despised 'all things Indian', would rather have imposed a single code modelled on the British system, which would have, at least in the legal sphere, unified the Empire at the cost of entirely 'westernising' it.

72. The above material is quoted from Conrad Dieter, 'The Personal Law Question and Hindu Nationalism', in Dalmia and von Stietencron, ed., *Representing Hinduism*, pp.306–337.

73. Amrita Shodhan, 'Legal Formulation of the Question of Community: Defining the Khoja Collective', in *Indian Social Science Review*, 1 (1999), pp.142–143.

74. Moir, 'Historical and Religious Debates Amongst Indian Ismailis 1840–1920', pp.131–153, and Shodhan, ibid., p.145.

75. Ibid., pp.138–139.

76. Ibid., pp.141, 145.

77. Ibid., pp.146–147.

78. See Khan and Moir, 'Coexistence and Communalism', passim.

79. Moir, 'Historical and Religious Debates amongst Indian Ismailis 1840–1920', pp.131–153.

80. D. Conrad, 'The Personal Law Question and Hindu Nationalism', in Dalmia and von Stietencron, ed., *Representing Hinduism*, p.310.

81. Dharma, as we have seen in the first chapter, can be translated neither by the word 'law' nor by the term 'religion' as it corresponds to a specific concept which has no equivalent in the Western world. Similarly, sharia cannot be said to coincide with any European idea of one legal or ritual system as is demonstrated by the numerous examples where mutual accusations of being 'contrary to the sharia' are bandied by rival groups.

82. Mushirul Hasan, 'The Myth of Unity: Colonial and National Narratives', in Ludden ed., *Making India Hindu*, pp.185–210.

83. For this and subsequent references to Shah Wali Allah we have quoted Marc Gaborieau, 'A Nineteenth-century Indian "Wahhabi" Tract against the

Cult of Muslim Saint', in Troll, ed., *Muslim Shrines in India: Their Character, History and Significance*, pp.198–200. The argument proposed by Aziz Ahmad is baseless. According to this author, tomb worship was one of the major evils denounced by Wali Allah, as a blameworthy practice inspired by 'Hindu idolatry'. But one should not forget that pilgrimages to saints' graves was a much older custom, prevalent in many other countries not influenced by Hinduism, from Turkey, to Iran and North Africa.

84. Shah Wali Allah's synthesis was inspired by three principles: a return to Islam in the light of hadith studies, reconciliation of the schools of law and theology, and a concern for social problems. But although he criticises unscrupulous Sufis and the excessive practice of pilgrimages to famous tombs, he remained committed to Sufism and saints.

85. One should recall briefly here that the founder of Wahhabism and his successors, in their jihad against what they considered to be wrong practices, went so far as to damage the mausoleum of al-Husayn at Karbala and that of the famous Hujrah containing the tomb of the Prophet, until the sultan of Turkey launched a campaign to uproot the movement whose leader he executed in 1818. See Hughes, *Dictionary of Islam*, pp.660–661.

86. Marc Gaborieau, 'Les Débats sur l'acculturation chez les musulmans indiens au début du XIXe siècle', *Alterité et Identité – Islam et Christianisme en Inde, Puruśārtha* 19, pp.221–238. Let us recall here that the Ismailis also referred to their tradition as *Sirāṭ al-mustaqīm*, which was translated as *satpanth* in Indian vernaculars.

87. See Gaborieau, ibid., pp.207–208, and Mayaram, *Resisting Regimes*, pp.231–233. Both movements were opposed by various schools, such as the modernist current of Sayyid Ahmad Khan (1817–1898) which tried to find a link with Western rationalism through the doctrines of Muslim medieval philosophy, and the Barelwis, another division of the Sunni ulama led by Ahmad Riza Khan Barelwi (1856–1921), who advocated worship at shrines and believed in the mediation of saints. But they were challenged by the reformists who emerged as the leading force of that time.

88. According to Gaborieau, ibid., a tract entitled *al-Balagh al-mubin*, issued by the Ahl-i Hadith and probably wrongly attributed to Shah Wali Allah (it seems to be the work of later so-called 'Wahhabi' reformists), exemplifies the way in which Islam as an orthodoxy was invented: 'objectionable practices' of Muslims are listed (mainly worship of dead and living saints) and condemned as *shirk* (polytheism) and *bid'a* (innovation). An interesting fact is that these practices are compared to those of the Jews, Christians and 'deviant' Muslims, and of course the religious customs of the so-called heathens. Besides, one powerful argument is that true Muslims should not worship saints because it makes them resemble the Hindus among whom they live. Based on the

concept of resemblance and imitation (*mushāba* and *tashabbuh*); *pīr parastī* (worship of the *pirs*) was equated with *but parastī* (idol worship). By accepting this simile the reformists were laying the foundation of the boundary wall dividing Muslims from the other groups broadly classified as Hindu.

89. Mayaram, *Resisting Regimes*, p.243.

90. K. Jones, 'The Arya Samaj in British India, 1875–1947', in Robert D. Baird, ed., *Religion in Modern India* (Delhi, 1981; repr. 1988), p.27.

91. It has been demonstrated that this purification ceremony was invented on the basis of older Brahmanical rites of expiation intended to reintegrate into the caste those who had violated the sacred dharma. For all these references see Catherine Clémentin-Ojha, 'La Śuddhi de l'Arya Samaj ou l'invention d'un rituel de (re)conversion à l'hindouisme', in *Archives de Science Sociale des Religions*, 87 (1994), pp.99–114, and Christophe Jaffrelot, 'Les (re)conversions à l'hindouisme (1885–1990): politisation et diffusion d'une "invention de la tradition"', *Archives de Science sociale des Religions*, 87 (1994), pp.73–98.

92. By educating the people and promoting uniform religious and domestic ceremonies Dayanand and his followers contributed to the change in society of that time. For example, the Arya Samaj established a specific marriage ritual which was eventually to be adopted by most North Indians. Nowadays many are convinced that, regardless of caste, sect and region, the Hindus have always shared the same rituals, without realising that they owe this unification mainly to the Arya Samaj.

93. Following Nanjiani's *Khojā Vṛttant*, an Imamshahi source, published at Ahmedabad in 1892, Tajjdin Mumtaz Ali, in his 'Ramdeo Pir, A Forgotten Ismaili Saint', *Sindh Review*, 32 (1995), pp.24–29, also supports the theory that Ramdev, worshipped nowadays as a folk-deity mainly in Rajasthan, Sindh and Gujarat, was actually a fourteenth/fifteenth-century Ismaili *dā'ī* preaching in Uchh-Multan.

94. Jaffrelot, 'Les (re)conversions à l'hindouisme (1885–1990)', and Catherine Clémentin-Ojha and Marc Gaborieau, 'La Montée du prosélytisme dans le sous-continent indien: introduction', *Archives de Sciences Sociale des Religions*, 87 (1994), pp.13–33.

95. See for example Nanji, *The Nizari Ismaili Tradition in the Indo-Pakistan Subcontinent*, and J.C. Masselos, 'The Khojas of Bombay: The Defining of Formal Membership Criteria during the Nineteenth Century', in Imtiaz Ahmad, ed., *Caste and Social Stratification among Muslims in India* (Delhi, 1978), pp.97–116.

96. Some elements point to the fact that the Pirana Satpanthis may have broken away from the parent body as late as the end of the eighteenth century or even the nineteenth century. One document given by one of our informants from Pirana, Mr. Samsad Ali, even mentions that tithes were sent to the Imam

in Iran until the arrival of Aga Khan I. I am grateful to Zawahir Moir who generously shared with me her recent findings concerning the history of the Imamshahi communities. We are both preparing an extensive study dedicated to that group.

97. I owe this information and the following remarks on the Kachias to Shafique Virani; see n.64 above.

98. See my *Conversions* and *Shifting Identities*.

99. Quoted by M.R. Majumdar, *Cultural History of Gujarat* (Bombay, 1965), p.255, n.90.

100. Moir, in her 'Historical and Religious Debates amongst Indian Ismailis 1840–1920', throws considerable light on these issues.

101. See ibid., p.142.

102. Ibid.

103. Ibid. For the Pranami sect, see n. 56 above.

104. See 'The Sant Movement and North Indian Sufis', Schomer and McLeod, ed., *The Sants*, pp.359–373.

105. Kenneth W Jones. 'Ham Hindū nahīn: Arya-Sikh Relations, 1877–1905', *Journal of Asian Studies*, 32 (1973), p.457.

106. Ernst, *Eternal Garden*, p.30, for instance: ' … The Sanskrit tradition has never taken official notice of the existence of Islam'.

107. For a comparison between Hindu, Nizari and crypto-Ismaili 'prophetical' poems, see my 'The Coming of Nikalank Avatar', and, with Z. Moir, 'The Lord will Marry the Virgin Earth: Songs of the Time to come', *Journal of Indian Philosophy*, 28 (2000), pp.99–115.

108. See A.S. Melikian-Chirvani, 'Ranjit Singh and the Image of the Past', in Susan Stronge, ed., *The Arts of the Sikh Kingdoms* (Delhi, 1999), pp.61–67.

109. On the possible influence of Nizari Ismailism on Sikhism, see my *Conversions and Shifting Identities*, pp.242–254, and my 'The Coming of Nikalank Avatar', pp.421–423. Kalki, Vishnu's tenth incarnation, also typically called Nikalank in Sikh prophecy, is seen, for instance, in the Dasam Granth drawing a double-edged sword. This can be interpreted as the *khaṇḍā* of Sikh baptism, but also as 'Ali's *dhu'l-fiqār* with which it is identified in an oral Sikh tradition. See Surindar Singh Kohli, *Sikh Predictions (Based on all Relevant Texts)* (Delhi, 1998), pp.21, 76. For 'Ali's sword, in a Sikh oral tradition, see V.S. Naipaul, *India: A Million Mutinies Now* (1990; repr. London, 1997), pp.438–439.

110. Jones, 'Religious Identities and the Indian Census', in Barrier, ed., *The Census in British India*, p.79.

111. W.H. McLeod, *Who is a Sikh? The Problem of Sikh Identity* (New York, 1989; repr. Oxford, 1992), pp.86–87.

112. Ibid., p.84 and Jones, 'Ham Hindū nahīn: Arya-Sikh Relations, 1877–1905', p.467.

113. Mcleod, *Who is a Sikh?*, p. 82.
114. Jones, 'Ham Hindū nahīn: Arya-Sikh Relations, 1877–1905', p.459.
115. The Hindi/Gujarati syllable '*va*' becomes '*ha*' or '*hu*' in Punjabi like the name Lav which becomes Lahu.
116. Jones, 'Ham Hindū nahīn: Arya-Sikh Relations, 1877–1905', p.464.
117. All the above remarks, as the following discussion, are drawn from Jones, ibid., pp.467–468.
118. Oberoi, *The Construction of Religious Boundaries*, p.420.
119. Ibid., p.396.
120. See Rose, *Glossary*, 1990, vol.3, pp.435–437.
121. See *Conversions*, pp.232–233.
122. Ibid.

Chapter 4: Nation and Religion (1920–2000)

*Epigram from Jawaharlal Nehru, *The Discovery of India* (1946), pp.341–342)

1. Christophe Jaffrelot, *The Hindu Nationalist Movement in India* (Delhi, 1996), pp.18–19.
2. This analysis and the following remarks are drawn from Jaffrelot, Ibid.
3. Ibid., p.27.
4. See Pyarelal, *Mahatma Gandhi* (Ahmedabad, 1965), vol. 1, pp.113–114. On the Pranami sect and its connection with the Nizari, possibly Imamshahi, tradition, see also our 'The Prannathis of Rajasthan: Bhakti and Irfan', in L.A. Babb, V. Joshi, M. Meister, ed., *Multiple Histories: Culture and Society in the Study of Rajasthan* (Jaipur, 2002), and our 'The Mahdi of Panna'.
5. Moir, 'Historical Debates', p. 150.
6. See Vajpeyi, 'Muslim Fundamentalism in India' in Vajpeyi and Malik, ed., *Religious and Ethnic Minority Politics*, pp.53–55, and Gandhi, *Revenge and Reconciliation*, p.147.
7. Mayaram, *Resisting Regimes*, p.221.
8. Sumit Sarkar, 'Indian Nationalism and the Politics of Hindutva', in Ludden, ed., *Making India Hindu*, p.273.
9. See Shackle and Moir, *Ismaili Hymns*, p.10 and Diamond Rattansi, 'Islamization and the Khojah Isma'ili Community in Pakistan', (unpublished Ph.D. dissertation, McGill University, Montreal, 1987)., p.157.
10. See *Aga Khan III: Selected Speeches and Writings of Sir Sultan Muhammad Shah*, with an introduction by K.K. Aziz (London, 1988). The issue has been examined by Michel Boivin, 'The Reform of Islam in Ismaili Shi'ism from 1885 to 1957', in Françoise 'Nalini' Delvoye, ed., *Confluences of Cultures:*

French Contributions to Indo-Persian Studies (New Delhi and Tehran, 1994), p.199.

11. Aga Khan III, *Selected Speeched and Writings*, vol. 1, pp.288, 320–321, 325 and vol. 2, p. 903.

12. Ibid.

13. Ibid.

14. For these insights and for the following quotations, see Mushirul Hasan, 'The Myth of Unity', p.196.

15. Ibid.

16. See Mayaram, *Resisting Regimes*, pp.221, 243, and passim. We have drawn from the same source this brief discussion on the Islamic movements, as well as all the references to the role they played among the Meos of Rajasthan. See also, Yoginder Sikand, *The Origins and Development of the Tablighi-jama'at (1920–2000): A Cross-country Comparative Study* (Delhi, 2002).

17. From the point of view of a centrally-defined norm of Islam, the Meos, as a number of other communities, appeared as 'half Hindus' and Muslims in name only. Therefore, they constituted the privileged target of the action of both Hindu *śuddhi* and Muslim Tabligh cadres. See Mayaram, *Resisting Regimes*, pp.66, 236, 242.

18. The Tanzim (consolidation) movement, which emerged in the mid-1920s, was a Muslim response to the attempts at uniting and mobilising Hindus along militant lines.

19. Mayaram, *Resisting Regimes*, pp.66, 236, 242.

20. Ibid., pp.188, 197, 203 where Mayaram describes the tragedy experienced by the Meos who were not accepted by the local Arya Samajis and other similar Hindu organisations, and were also rejected by the Muslim Pakistani communities.

21. This is visible in their customs, as well as in their various publications. Besides, some Sindhi Lohanas or Baibhandis, as they prefer to call themselves, insist on the value of the Sindhi variant of the Persian-Urdu script which they still try to teach to the young generations who tend to stick to the Nagari or other local Indian scripts. See for example *Aseen Sindhi*, a monthly magazine published in Bombay.

22. Sarkar, 'Indian Nationalism and the Politics of Hindutva', p.275.

23. Dalmia and von Stietencron, *Representing Hinduism*, pp.20–21.

24. For this quotation and the following ones, see Conrad, 'The Personal Law Question and Hindu Nationalism', p.323.

25. Ibid.

26. Dalmia and Stietencron, *Representing Hinduism*, p.21.

27. Conrad, 'The Personal Law Question and Hindu Nationalism', p.327.

28. For instance, the Ahmadiyya movement. See Charles H. Kennedy, 'To-

wards the Definition of a Muslim in an Islamic State: The Case of Ahmadiyya in Pakistan', in Vajpeyi and Malik, ed., *Religious and Ethnic Minority Politics in South Asia* (London and Delhi, 1989), pp.71–108.

29. Monika Horstmann, 'Towards a Universal Dharma: Kalyan and the Tracts of the Gita Press', in Dalmia and von Stietencron, ed., *Representing Hinduism*, pp.294–305.

30. The type of superficial, mass culture which was spreading did not encourage the readers of such publications to question or verify those assertions which they took for granted like all the rest. A few words should be said about the 'fashionable' new theory regarding the Aryan origin of the Harappeans, the ancient inhabitants of the Indus Valley. This theory, which does not hold ground from many points of view, including linguistics and archaeology, nonetheless enjoys huge popularity among middle-class Hindus.

31. The task of rewriting the Ginanic literature of the Imamshahis has not been completed to this day. The author of this essay incidentally met in Kutch one of the writers entrusted with the 'amendment' of the Satpanthi sacred literature. It is interesting to note here that the Hindu terms and names meant to replace the Muslim Ismaili ones had already been used to a great extent in the Nizari tradition of South Asia – a phenomenon for which the literature, as the whole tradition, could be termed precisely 'liminal' as we have seen in the previous chapters.

32. See Khan and Moir, *Coexistence and Communalism.*

33. As my field research has shown, among those 'lost' Prahladpanthi communities which are not referred to as Bishnois, the Silawats of Roll (a village near Nagaur in Rajasthan) have come under the influence of the local Suhrawardi Sufis.

34. The author, Abuali Bapu Miya, is a Sayyid from Petlad, Gujarat. The book, published in 1933, is written in the Urdu language but transcribed in the Gujarati script.

35. This information is taken from the field inquiry we conducted at Pirana in January 2000. In view of our common project, Zawahir Moir has undertaken a detailed study of Imamshahi history based on original sources which has remained largely unexplored to this day. I thank her for helping me to clarify the complex issues related to the evolution of the various lines of Imam Shah's descendants.

36. In contemporary India, although they are supposed to be secular, the media tend to reproduce this simplistic and dualistic vision. Popular TV serials on the *Mahabharata* and the *Ramayana* convey the same message of uniformity and mediocrity, as similar productions do for an image of oversimplified and standardised Islam in Pakistan. On this topic see Angelika Malinar, 'The Bhagavadgita in the Mahabharata TV serial: Domestic Drama

and Dharmic Solutions', in Dalmia and von Stietencron, ed., *Representing Hinduism*, pp.442–467.

37. The politicization of religion, which had begun before Partition, also helped to consolidate the image of separate antagonistic blocs. In many cases the clever manipulation of religious symbols not only alienates one community from the other but engenders violent conflicts and leads to communal violence. The cow movement and the dispute over religious sites are but a few examples. In spite of the efforts of secular parties, India and Pakistan have been shaken by continuous – although not regular – waves of Hindu and Muslim extremism.

38. However, in everyday practice, red, yellow or pink chadars are still sold in the shops that are located in the vicinity of most dargas.

39. The author of this essay remembers the reaction of a Hindu ophthalmologist who, hearing the name of his patient, automatically gave him something to read in Urdu. To his great surprise, the man answered that although he was a Muslim, he knew only the Nagari alphabet used for Hindi.

40. It is unfortunate that the author of this essay does not remember the name of the writer or the title of the publication. Another author, the Indian novelist Shashi Tharoor, makes similar remarks in his article entitled 'After the Dust has Settled', published in *The Hindu* (15 April, 2001, p.iii).

Conclusion: The Metaphor of the Hidden Pir

1. Sarkar, 'Indian Nationalism and the Politics of Hindutva', p.276.
2. See 'Āsārām "Bāpu" ke sannidhyā men huā pun dharmantaran', *Dainik Bhaskar* (4 September 2000), p.18; Ajaz Ashraf, 'Whose Hinduism is it, Anyway?', *Hindustan Times* (24 January 1999); and for the next quotation Rao Y. Chinna, 'Dalits and Tribals are not Hindus', *Hindustan Times* (20 January 2000), p.13.
3. See the interesting facts mentioned by Jones, 'Religious Identities and the Indian Census', pp.88–89.
4. Baburao Bagul, quoted by Sarkar, 'Indian Nationalism and the Politics of Hindutva', p.275.
5. S.P. Ruhela, *Sri Shirdi Sai Baba, the Universal Master* (New Delhi, 1994), pp.29–30.
6. We are purposely using here the language of the media when referring to Muslims and Hindus.
7. Minoru Mio, 'Faith, Identity and Communal Discourse', *passim*.
8. Raymond Jamous, '"Faire", "défaire" et "refaire" les saints: Les *pir* chez les Meo (Inde du Nord)', *Terrain*, 24 (March 1995), pp.43–56.
9. Ibid. p.49.

10. Paul Sumita, 'Where Muslims perform Diwali "puja"', *Sunday Times of India* (10 September, 1995), p.11.

11. Ibid.

12. Rattansi, 'Islamization and the Khojah Isma'ili Community in Pakistan'.

13. Nanjiani Sachedina, *Khojā Vṛttāṇt* (Ahmedabad, 1892), p.149.

14. The author of this work has met some Gupti women at Pirana belonging to the same Kachia community studied by Virani (see n.64 of ch.3), who secretly continue to perform the old Imamshahi rituals and recite the former version of the *du'ā*. They have, however, maintained their allegiance to the present pir of Pirana.

15. In the legends connected with some 'liminal' shrines the allusion to a secret tunnel can be understood as a metaphor pointing to the existence of a secret tradition. See my *Conversions and Shifting Identities*, p.95, n.8 and Sikand, *Another Ayodhya in the Making?*, pp.216–217.

16. D.S. Khan. 'The Graves of History or the Metaphor of the Hidden Pir', in Varsha Joshi, ed. *Culture, Communities and Change* (Jaipur and New Delhi, 2002), pp.154–172.

Glossary

'Abd al-Quddus Gangohi: a fifteenth/sixteenth-century Chishti Sufi poet.

'Abu'l Karim Azad (1888–1958): a prominent Muslim leader who supported a universalist view of Islam.

Advaita Vedanta: 'non-dualism', a school of thought said to have been founded by the eighth/ninth-century philosopher Shankara.

Adivasi: The tribes who claim to be the oldest inhabitants of the Subcontinent.

Aghori: Shaiva ascetics who used to practice penance in cremation grounds.

Ahmad Sirhindi: a sixteenth-century Sunni scholar and Sufi.

Ahmadiyya: a messianic sect of Islam founded by Ghulam Ahmad in the nineteenth century.

Aipanth(i): a fifteenth-century sect found mainly in Gujarat and Rajasthan. Its founder, known as Ai Mata, is said to have been a disciple of the Nizari Ismaili missionary Pir Shams.

Ajlaf: a Muslim who is a member of the converted community.

Ajmer: city of Rajasthan where Khwaja Mu'in al-Din Chishti's shrine is located.

Akbar (r.1542–1605): the third emperor of the Mughal dynasty who founded his own syncretic sect.

Alakh: name of the formless God in Nath tradition.

Aligarh: city in modern Uttar Pradesh, the seat of a famous Islamic University.

Ala al-Din Khilji: a fourteenth-century sultan of Delhi.

amṛt (see pāval, pāhul): lit. 'nectar of immortality', consecrated water.

Amarnath: a famous pilgrimage centre located in the mountains in the present-day state of Jammu-Kashmir.

Ambedkar: one of the main authors of the Indian Constitution who was by caste an Untouchable Mahar of Maharashtra.

Arya (n): 'noble', a name that initially referred to the population who settled in the Subcontinent from 1500 BC onwards and brought the Veda tradition. A member of the Arya Samaj.

Arya Dharma: the religion preached by the Arya Samaj, supposed to be the original tradition of the Vedas.

Arya Samaj: a Hindu reformist organisation founded by the Brahmin Dayanand Saraswati in 1875.

Ashraf: a Muslim who is supposed to be the descendant of Mughals, Pathans, or Sayyids and Shaykhs from Arabia.

Awrangzib (r.1658–1707): the sixth emperor of the Mughal dynasty.

Ayyappa: a Dravidian god whose main shrine is located in Sabarimalai, Kerala.

Bala Pir: one of the names of the eighth Sikh Guru, Har Krishan.

Balmik: Valmik or Balmik was the presumed author of the Sanskrit *Ramayana*; it is also one of the Hindu names assumed by the Nizari missionary Bala Shah who converted the Untouchables in the region of Dera Ghazi Khan (Punjab).

Banya: a member of the Hindu merchant community.

Barelwi: a division of the Sunni ulama founded by Ahmad Riza Khan Barelwi (1856–1921). Also the name of Sayyid Ahmad (1786–1831), the founder of the so-called Wahhabi school of India.

Bar Shah: A Sufi pir who has his shrine in Karnataka.

baraka: prosperity or blessing. In popular Sufism the power through which the pir is able to grant a boon to a devotee.

Bhagavad Gita: 'The Song of the Lord'. Spoken by Krishna, this is a section of the *Mahabharata* epic (fourth century BC, fourth century AD) outlining, among others, the theory of *bhakti*, as the path of devotion to a personal God.

Bhairava: a fierce aspect of the god Shiva. Also Bheru or Bhairon.

bhajan: devotional composition.

bhakta: devotee, follower of the *bhakti* movement.

bhakti: the path of devotion. First outlined in the *Bhagavad Gita*, it gave rise to various religious movements throughout the Subcontinent.

Bhambi(s): also Balai and Meghval, and Untouchable community of North India whose traditional occupation is weaving and removal of dead cattle.

Bharatvarsha: a name for the Subcontinent in ancient Indian literature.

Bharatya Janata Party (BJP): the nationalist party of India that was created by the RSS (Rashtriya Swayamsevak Sangh).

bid'a(ti): 'objectionable innovation' according to those who claim to represent the 'orthodox' viewpoint in Islam.

Bishnoi: member of a caste and a sect founded by Jambha, also known as Jambhoji or Jambeshvar Pir, in the fifteenth century.

Brahma: A Hindu deity, considered one of the Trimurti, and in charge of creative power; not to be confused with Brahman or Brahmin.

Brahman: the ultimate reality, from which everything comes, in which it rests and into which it will eventually go.

Brahmanas: philosophical commentaries on the Vedas.

Brahmin: The first of the four *varṇa*s, the principal group from which priests are drawn.

Bullhe Shah: an eighteenth century Sufi poet of Punjab.

chādar: ornate cloth or drapery covering the grave of a Muslim saint or martyr.

Chand Bhodale: a Maharathi Brahmin who, according to tradition was initiated by a Muslim saint and had a famous Sufi as his main disciple.

Chishti: one of the main Sufi *ṭarīqa*s of South Asia.

Chittor: a famous city and fortress of Rajasthan, eventually conquered by Akbar in the sixteenth century.

Dadu: a sixteenth-century saint, by caste a cotton-carder. He preached in Rajasthan where his main shrine is located. Not to be confused with a famous Ismaili missionary of the same period and name.

Dadu *panth*: the sect created after Dadu.

dāʿī: a Muslim missionary. Refers generally to Ismailis and at times to Twelver Shiʿa.

Dalit: a member of one of the former Untouchable communities.

Dara Shukoh: one of the brothers of the Mughal emperor Awrangzib.

darbār: the royal court, also royal assembly.

darga: Muslim shrine containing the grave or relics of a saint or martyr or holy relics.

Darya Nath/Shah (Jhulelal): a 'syncretic' saint mainly revered by the Sindhi Lohanas.

Dayanand Saraswati (Dayanand Rishi): nineteenth-century founder of the Hindu reformist movement of Arya Samaj.

Dasnami: one of the ten Shaiva orders of ascetics said to have been founded by Shankara.

dasondh: a tithe associated with the South-Asian Nizari and crypto-Ismaili traditions.

Dattatreya: a combined avatar of Vishnu, Shiva and Brahma. The Hindu name of a mysterious Sufi pir associated with a syncretic tradition of Gujarat, Maharashtra and Karnataka.

Davalmalak: a fifteenth-century Marathi Sufi worshipped mainly by Hindus.

Deobandi: an Islamic reformist movement founded in 1867 and associated with the Barelwis.

dharamśālā: originally a pilgrim resthouse. A synonym for *gurudvārā* in Sikh tradition and of *jamāʿat-khāna* among the Ismaili Imamshahis.

Dharm Paravartan: campaign of re-conversion initiated by the Vishva Hindu Parishad.

dharma (*dharm*): a word encompassing various meanings, such as cosmic or religious law, religion etc. (lit. 'intrinsic quality of the self', or 'that which sustains one's existence').

Dharmashastra: Hindu treatise on dharma.

Diggy Kalyanji: famous pilgrimage centre in Rajasthan.

Diwana Shah: a late nineteenth-century Sufi saint who has his tomb at Kapasan, in Rajasthan.

Draupadi: the wife of the five Pandava brothers in the Mahabharata; she is worshipped as a goddess in some popular traditions.

Dravidian: a culture and a group of languages mainly connected with South India.

dvīja: 'twice-born', a member of one of the four high *varṇas*.

Eknath: a sixteenth-century Marathi saint and poet.

fiqh: Islamic jurisprudence. The science which deals with the observance of rituals, the Five Pillars and social legislation.

Gentoo: 'heathen', a term used by the British to refer to those who followed the indigenous religions of South Asia.

ginān: literature of the Nizari Ismailis of South Asia; the same word also refers to the religious texts of the Barmati *panth*.

Gobind Singh: the tenth and last guru of the Sikhs.

Goga Dev/Gugga Pir: a 'syncretic' saint/deity worshipped mainly in Punjab and Rajasthan.

Gorakhnath: one of the alleged founders of the *Nath panth*, his guru was Matsyendranath.

Gupti: 'secret', generally refers to the covert Nizari Ismailis who concealed their faith under Hindu guise.

Gurudvārā: a more recent synonym of *dharamśālā* in Sikh tradition.

Guru Granth: also referred to as Guru Granth Sahib and Adi Granth, the holy scripture of the Sikhs, a collection of religious hymns composed by Sikh gurus, and Hindu and Muslim saints.

Hanuman: the monkey god, a character of the Ramayana epic.

Harijan: 'God's people', used by Mahatma Gandhi to refer to the Untouchables.

Hinglaj Mata: a Tantric goddess who has her main shrine at Las Bela (Baluchistan).

Hindu Mahasabha: a national confederation founded in 1915 to represent Hindu nationalist ideals.

Hindutva: 'Hinduness', supposed to have a wider meaning than the term 'Hindu', including the social and cultural spheres.

Imamshahi: a branch of the Nizaris who revere the fifteenth-century Ismaili missionary Imam Shah whose main shrine is located at Pirana, in Gujarat. Also referred to as Piranapanthis and Satpanthis.

Jagyasi: refers to some of the followers of Guru Nanak who did not adhere to the Khalsa *panth*, chiefly among the Sindhi Lohanas.

Jai Singh II: the eighteenth-century ruler of Amber who founded Jaipur in 1727.

Jambha/Jambeshvar Pir: the fifteenth-century founder of the Bishnoi or Prahlad *panth*.

Jamaʿat-i-Islami: a Muslim organisation founded by Mawdudi.

Jamiat al-ulama-i-Hind: an association of Indian ulama founded in 1919.

Jasnath, Jasnathi: a fifteenth-century saint, founder of the Jasnathi *panth* in Rajasthan.

jāt, jāti: as distinct from *varṇa*, it is a group of endogamous sub-castes.

Jogi: synonym of yogi, generally refers to a member of one of the Nath orders.

Julaha: a caste of Muslim weavers.

Kabir: a famous fifteenth-century saint and poet born in Benares.

Kabir *panth*: the sect founded in the name of Kabir.

Kalki Purana: an undated minor Purana (not one of the 18 main Puranas) describing the event of Vishnu's tenth avatar or 'descent'.

Kanbi (Patidar/Patel): an agricultural community found mainly in Gujarat.

khānaqāh: the Persian name for a traditional Sufi meeting place. In the Arabic-speaking world the term used is *zāwiya*.

Katu Shyam: a popular pilgrimage centre in Rajasthan.

Khalsa: the dominant movement within Sikhism said to have been initiated by the tenth guru.

Khatri: a merchant community claiming a warrior status. The Sikh gurus originated from that caste to which many Shamsis, or followers of the Nizari Pir Shams, also belonged.

Khilāfat movement: a movement to protest against the abolition of the Caliphate.

Khoja: the word initially refers to a section of the Lohana community converted in the fifteenth century, or earlier, by the Nizari Pir Sadr al-Din. At present the term often refers to all the Nizari Ismaili communities of South Asia, as well as to members of the original caste who adopted other religious identities.

Kshatrya: one of the four *varṇa*s.

Kumbha: a fifteenth-century ruler of Mewar.

Lal Das: a Meo saint (1540–1648) worshipped with a dual Hindu-Muslim identity; his followers are referred to as Laldasis.

Lal Shahbaz Qalandar: a thirteen-century Muslim saint described as a Suhrawardi Sufi in Sunni sources; according to the South-Indian Nizari tradition (both Khoja and Imamshahi), he was an Ismaili missionary.

Las Bela: a pilgrimage centre in Baluchistan where Hinglaj Devi's shrine is located.

Lohana: a Sindhi community.

Mahamarg: one of the numerous synonyms of Nizarpanth, the sect connected with Ramdev Pir.

Maharana Pratap: a sixteenth-century ruler of Mewar who rejected the Mughal alliance.

Mahmud Ghazni: the famous eleventh-century Muslim conqueror who ruled in Afghanistan.

malāḥida: 'heretics' according to Sunnis and Twelver Sh'ia and often applied to the Ismailis.

Malāmatiyya: lit. 'men of blame', used to describe a dervish who tries to conceal his spiritual achievement by behaving in an offensive manner.

Mapilla: a Muslim community of Kerala, descendants of Arab traders who intermarried with the local population.

Man Singh I: a sixteenth-century Rajput ruler of Rajasthan who was Akbar's commander-in-chief.

mandir: Hindu temple.

mantra: mystical or magical formula.

Maratha: a community of Maharashtra; also means originating from Maharashtra.

mārg: 'way', often synonym of *panth.*

Matia Kanbis: section of the Kanbi community affiliated to the Imamshahi *satpanth*. Today they are referred to as Satpanthi Patidars.

Mawdudi, Abu'l A'la (d.1979): the founder of Jama'at-i-Islami, he favoured the creation of a separate Muslim state.

mazār: a Muslim tomb.

melā: a public fair.

Meo: a Muslim community found mainly in eastern Rajasthan. Many of them are Laldasis.

Mer: a Rajasthani community with a liminal identity, comprising various sections, namely the Rawats who consider themselves as Hindu and the Merats who are regarded as Muslims.

Mira Bai: sixteenth-century female Hindu saint who composed famous devotional songs in praise of the god Krishna.

mlechha: lit. 'barbarian', traditionally refers to the non-Brahmanical castes and tribes, as well as to the Muslims and to various foreign communities.

Muhammad Ali (1878–1931): a Muslim leader of pre-Independence India.

Muhammad Ali Jinnah (1876–1948): although he was initially against partition he eventually became the father of the Pakistani nation.

Muhammad Iqbal (1876–1938): a famous Muslim poet and thinker.

Mu'in al-Din Chishti: the celebrated Sufi saint whose tomb is at Ajmer (in Rajasthan).

mukām: lit. 'place of rest', often refers to a Muslim place of burial. It is the name of the village where Jambha's tomb is located, near Bikaner (in Rajasthan).

murīd: disciple of a Muslim saint. The word frequently referred to the followers of the Nizari Satpanth.

murshid: Muslim spiritual teacher, often referred to as pir in the South-Asian tradition.

Muslim League: a Muslim political party founded in 1906.

murti: form. The image or deity used as a focus in Hindu worship.

Nanak: the fifteenth-century founder of the Sikh *panth*, the first of the ten gurus.

Nanakpanth: the sect created by Nanak. The word currently refers to the non-Khalsa Sikhs. They are also referred to as Nanakshahis.

Naqshbandiyya: a prominent Sufi order founded in Bukhara in the fourteenth century.

Narhar: a pilgrimage centre in Rajasthan where a *chillā* of Shaykh Farid Shakarganj is located.

Nāth: a religious movement of ascetics and householders divided into many orders and said to have been founded by Gorakhnath.

Nikalank or Nishkalanki: the name of Vishnu's tenth incarnation in the Nizari Ismaili tradition, where he is identified with the Imam.

nirgūṇ: lit. 'non-qualified', *nirgūṇ bhakti* is the devotion to a formless God.

Nizam al-Din: Nizam al-Din Awliya was a fourteenth-century Sufi Chishti saint whose tomb is in Delhi.

Nizar *panth*: one of the sects of Nizari origin connected with Ramdev Pir.

Nizari: a branch of the Ismailis recognising the Aga Khan as their Imam.

Nur al-Din (Nand) Rishi: a fourteenth-century Kashmiri Muslim saint.

pāhul (*pāval*): consecrated water, also *amṛt* or *ami*. The former term, typical of Nizari Ismailism, is not found in purely Hindu traditions.

Palitana: a city in Saurasthra (Gujarat) where the holy mountain of Shatrunjaya is located. It is a famous Jain piligrimage centre.

Pandit: a title by which Brahmins are known.

panth: literally 'path', often synonymous with *marg*, 'way'.

paramparā: tradition, also lineage.

parchā: miracle.

Pathan: an Afghan noble, name of an *ashraf* caste.

Patidars: synonym of Kanbi and Patel.

pir: often synonym of shaykh, *murshid*; in Nizari tradition it refers to the main *dāʿī* appointed by the Imam of the time.

Pir Hasan Kabir al-Din: A fifteenth-century Nizari missionary, said to be one of the sons of Pir Sadr al-Din.

Pir Nasir al-Din: a Nizari missionary.

Pir Sadr al-Din: a fifteenth-century Nizari pir, one of the descendant of Pir Shams, father of Hasan Kabir al-Din.

Pir Shams Sabzwari: one of the most famous Nizari pirs who has his tomb in Multan.

Pirana: a village near Ahmedabad (Gujarat) where the main seat of the Imamshahi Satpanthi sect is located.

Pranami or Parnami: a 'syncretic' sect founded by Prannath in Gujarat and whose main seat is located in Madhya Pradesh. Also called Chajju *panth*.

Prithviraj Chauhan: a twelfth-century Rajput ruler who fought with Muhammad Ghori.

pūjā: generally refers to worship in the Hindu tradition.

Purana: Hindu sacred texts.

purdah: the seclusion of women from the sight of strangers in various Hindu and Muslim communities including the custom of veiling the face.

Pushtimarg: a Vaishnava sect founded by Vallabha in the sixteenth century.

Qadiriyya: a prominent Sufi order.

Qalandar: a wandering dervish.

rāfiḍī: one of the words meaning 'heretic' in Sunni heresiography.

Raidas: a fifteenth-century Untouchable saint of the Chamar community.

Rajabag Sarvar: a saint of Karnataka endowed with a dual Hindu-Muslim identity.

Rajput: a caste claiming Kshatrya origin.

Ram (Rama): an incarnation of the god Vishnu, hero of the *Ramayana* epic.

Ramakrishna: a famous nineteenth-century Bengali mystic who believed in the unity of all religions.

Ramananda: a fifteenth-century saint of northern India.

Ramanuja: a twelfth-century Tamil Vaishnava saint.

Ramayana: Hindu epic that relates the story of Rama and Sita.

Ramdev Pir: an obscure Nizari missionary who made conversions in Rajasthan and Gujarat, namely among the Untouchable Meghvals.

Ram Singh II: the nineteenth-century Maharaja of Jaipur who declared that the Vaishnavas were heretics.

Rashtriya Swayamsevak Sangh (RSS): a nationalist para-military organisation founded in 1925 by Hedgewar.

Ratan Nath/Ratan Haji: a saint endowed with a dual identity, connected with Goga.

Sabarimalai: a famous pilgrimage centre of Kerala dedicated to the Dravidian god Ayyappa and his ally the Muslim pirate Vavar.

Sabhā: assembly.

Saffron (Brigade): also Sangh Parivar. Refers to the Hindu nationalist organisations as a whole.

sagūṇ: lit. 'qualified'. *Sagūṇ bhakti* or devotion to a qualified god is generally associated with the use of images in worship.

Sahajdhari: one of the terms used by the followers of the Khalsa *panth* to refer to those who follow the message of Guru Nanak but have not adhered to the Khalsa.

Sajadda Nishin: also Gaddi Nishin, lit. 'one who sits on the carpet'. Refers to the main pir of a Muslim shrine who generally claims descent from the saint to whom it is dedicated.

Sakhi Sarwar: a Punjabi saint, generally regarded as a Sufi. His followers, the Sultanis, are connected with the Sikh tradition.

samādhi: a deep state of yogic meditation, also refers to a Hindu funeral monument.

sampradāy: tradition, also refers to a sect.

sanātan: lit. 'eternal'.

Sanātan dharma: the concept of an 'eternal' Hindu religion associated with a Brahmanical movement founded in the late nineteenth century.

Sanātan movement (Sikh): an early nineteenth-century Sikh movement that sought a rapprochement between the followers of the Khalsa and the Sahajdharis.

Sangh (Parivar): Hindu fundamentalist groups, sometimes referred to as the 'Saffron Brigade'.

Sanskritisation: the process through which communities seek to identify themselves with the Brahmanical tradition.

Sant: a medieval saint supposed to be a non-sectarian adept of *nirgūṇ bhakti*.

Sant Mat (*Sant Paramparā*): the Sant movement.

Sat Dharm /Satya Dharma: lit. 'the true law' or 'the true religion': the term was used by rival sects, including Ismailis, to refer to their own tradition.

Sat *panth*: a synonym of Sat Dharm, one of the names used to designate the Nizari community. It still refers to its Imamshahi branch.

Satpanthi: a follower of the Sat *panth*.

Savarkar: one of the presidents of the Hindu Mahasabha, author of the famous book *Hindutva: Who is a Hindu?* published in 1923.

Sayyid Ahmed Khan (1817–1898): a Muslim reformer and advocate of Hindu-

Muslim unity.

Shaivism: The religion of Hindus who are devoted to Shiva.

Scheduled Caste: the official name used by the Indian government to refer to the former-Untouchable communities who are entitled to certain privileges.

Scheduled Tribe: a tribal or *adivasi* community to whom certain privileges are granted, as for the Scheduled Castes.

Sehwan: a place of pilgrimage in Sindh where Lal Shahbaz Qalandar's tomb is situated.

Shah Wali Allah: a Muslim scholar and reformer (1703–1762) associated with the Naqshbandi order.

Shaykh (as a community): a clan found in various Muslim *jāti*s, the name of various Muslim castes.

Shaykh Burhan: A fifteenth-century Sufi said to belong to the Chishti lineage, he is the patron saint of the Hindu Shekhawat Rajputs.

Shankara: the eight-century philosopher who is regarded as the first exponent of of the Advaita Vedanta.

Shastra: a Brahmanical treatise.

Shekhawati: a region of Rajasthan.

shirk: the sin of 'association' of something with God, or ascribing partners to God. Often used by Muslims to mean 'paganism'.

śiṣya: disciple.

Shivaji: a famous Maratha leader (1627–1680) who fought against the Mughal power.

Shramana: ascetics or monks belonging to non-Brahmanical orders.

śuddhi: purification ritual initiated by the Arya Samaj.

Shudra: one of the four divisions of Hindu society, or *varṇa*s, corresponding mainly to the non-Untouchable artisan castes.

Sikandar Lodi: a fifteenth-century ruler of Delhi.

silsila: Sufi lineage, or initiatic chain of transmission.

ṣirāṭ al-mustaqīm: lit. 'the right path', refers to the Wahhabi movement but also to various Islamic traditions including Ismailism.

Suhrawardi: one of the main Sufi orders.

Sultan Muhammad Shah: Aga Khan III, forty-eighth Imam of the Nizari Ismailis.

Swami Narayan: a nineteenth-century Hindu reformer who converted a number of Khojas and Imamshahis.

Tabligh/Tablighi Jama'at: a Sunni missionary organisation founded by M. Mohammad Ilyas (1885–1944).

Tanzim movement: a Muslim missionary organisation.

taqiyya: precautionary dissimulation in the Shi'i tradition.

ṭarīqa: lit. 'path', a Sufi order.

Tayyibi (Ismaili): a branch of Ismailism represented mainly by the Bohras in South Asia.

tilaka: Hindu sect mark painted on the forehead.

Udasi: a sect of the Sikhs, followers of Shri Chand who was one of Nanak's sons.

Untouchables: hereditary Hindu caste held to defile members of higher castes on contact.

Upanishads: later commentaries to the Vedas said to have inspired the Vedanta school of thought.

Vaishnava (Vishnuite): The religion of Hindus who are devotees of the god Vishnu.

varṇa: lit. 'colour'. The four socio-religious categories described in the ancient Brahmanical treatises, often wrongly translated as 'caste'.

varṇāśrama dharma: the Brahmanical religious law which recognises the traditional hierarchy of castes.

Vatayo Fakir: Sindhi saint endowed with a dual identity.

Veda: lit. 'knowledge', also refers to the oldest scripture of the Aryas.

Vedanta: philosophical school founded by Shankara.

vīr (*bīr*): hero, also refers to a deity, often Bhairava or Hanuman.

Vishnu: a Hindu god; together with Brahma and Shiva forms the Trimurti (three deities that control the functions of creation, preservation and destruction).

Vishva Hindu Parishad (VHP): a Hindu reformist organisation founded in 1964 to reconcile the sadhus of rival orders and fight against conversions.

Vivekananda: Ramakrishna's disciple.

Wahhabi (Wahhabism): a Sunni sect founded in Arabia by 'Abd al-Wahhab (d.1787). Said to have influenced some Indian Muslim revivalists.

Bibliography

Ahmad, Aziz. *An Intellectual History of Islam in India*. Edinburgh, 1969.

Ahmad, Imtiaz ed., *Caste and Social Stratification among Muslims in India*. 2nd ed. Delhi, 1978.

—*Ritual and Religion among Muslims in India*. Delhi, 1984.

Alam, Javeed. 'Composite Culture and Communal Consciousness: The Ittehadul Muslimeen in Hyderabad', in Dalmia and von Stietencron, ed., *Representing Hinduism*, pp.338–348.

Alam, Muzaffar, Françoise 'Nalini' Delvoye, and Marc Gaborieau, ed. *The Making of Indo-Persian Culture: Indian and French Studies*. New Delhi, 2000.

Ansari, Sarah F.D. *Sufi Saints and State Power: The Pirs of Sind, 1843–1947*. Cambridge, 1992.

Asani, Ali S. *Ecstasy and Enlightenment: The Ismaili Devotional Literature of South Asia*. London, 2002.

—'The Khojahs of Indo-Pakistan: the Quest for an Islamic Identity', *Journal of the Institute of Muslim Minority Affairs*, 1 (1987), pp.31–41.

—'The *ginān* Literature of the Ismailis of Indo-Pakistan', in D.L. Eck and F. Mallison, ed., *Devotion Divine*, Groningen, 1991, pp.1–18.

'Asha', Dayal Kotumal Dhameja. *Saints of Sind*. Sindhunagar, 1996.

Assayag, Jackie and Tarabout, Gilles, ed. 'Altérité et identité – Islam et Christianisme en Inde', *Puruśārtha*, 19, Paris, 1997.

—*Au confluent des deux rivières – Musulmans et Hindous dans le Sud de l'Inde*. Paris, 1995.

Aziz, K.K., ed. *Aga Khan III: Selected Speeches and Writings of Sir Sultan Muhammad Shah*. London, 1997–1998.

Baird, Robert D., ed. *Religion in Modern India*. Delhi, 1981; repr. 1988.

Barrier, Gerald N., ed. *The Census in British India*. Delhi, 1981.

Bhatnagar, V.S. 'Attempt at Revivalism or Reassertion of Vedic and Shastriya Traditions through Open Debate in the Eighteenth Century', unpublished paper, 2nd International Seminar on Rajasthan, December 1992.

Boivin, Michel. 'The Reform of Islam in Ismaili Shi'ism from 1885 to 1957', in

Delvoye, ed., *Confluences of Cultures,* 1994, pp.197–216.
Bouillier, Véronique. *Ascetes et rois.* Paris, 1998.
Briggs, G.W. *Gorakhnāth and the Kānphaṭā Jogīs.* Delhi, 1938; repr. 1990.
Carlsen, Robert S. 'Transculturation', in David Carrasco, ed., *Oxford Encyclopedia of Mesoamerican Cultures.* Oxford, 2001, pp.257–260.
Champion, Catherine. 'Entre la caste et la secte: un *kissā* du répertoire des Bhartrhari Jogī musulmans de la région de Gorakhpur (Uttar Pradaesh)', in *Puruśārtha,* 17, Paris, 1994, pp.25–41.
Chattopadhyaya, B.D. *Representing the Other? Sanskrit Sources and the Muslims 8th–14th century.* Delhi, 1998.
Clémentin-Ojha, Catherine. *Le Trident sur le palais: une cabale anti-Vishnouite dans un Royaume Hindou à l'époque coloniale.* Paris, 1999.
—'La *śuddhi* de l'Arya Samāj ou l'invention d'un rituel de (re)conversion a l'hindouisme', *Archives de Science Sociale des Religions,* 87 (July-September, 1994), 87, pp.99–114.
Clémentin-Ojha, Catherine and Marc Gaborieau. 'La montée du prosélytisme dans le sous-continent indien: introduction', *Archives de Science Sociale des Religions,* 87 (1994), pp.13–33.
Conrad, Dieter. 'The Personal Law Question and Hindu Nationalism', in Dalmia and von Stietencron, ed., *Representing Hinduism,* pp.306–337.
Daftary, Farhad. *A Short History of The Ismailis.* Edinburgh, 1998.
—*The Ismā'īlīs: Their History and Doctrines.* Cambridge, 1990.
Dalmia, Vasudha and Heinrich von Stietencron, ed. *Representing Hinduism - The Construction of Religious Traditions and National Identity.* New Delhi, 1995.
Dargawala, Sadruddin. *Tavariqe Pir.* Navsari, 1935.
Das, Veena. 'Counter-concepts and the Creation of Cultural Identity: Hindus in the Militant Sikh Discourse', in Dalmia and von Stietencron, ed., *Representing Hinduism,* pp.358–368.
Delvoye, Françoise 'Nalini', ed. *Confluences of Cultures: French Contributions to Indo-Persian Studies.* New Delhi and Tehran, 1994.
Digby, Simon. 'Qalandars and Related Groups: Elements of Social Deviance in the Relgious Life of the Delhi Sultanate of the Thirteenth and Fourteenth Centuries', in Friedmann, ed., *Islam in Asia - vol. 1: South Asia,* pp.60–108.
Dumont, Louis. *Homo Hierarchicus - Le Système des castes et ses implications.* Paris, 1996.
Eaton, Richard, M. 'Temple Desecration and Indo-Muslim States', in David Gilmartin and Bruce B. Lawrence, ed., *Beyond Turk and Hindu - Rethinking Religious Identities in Islamicate South Asia* (Gainesville, Florida, 2000), pp.246–281.

—*Temple Desecration and Muslim States in Medieval India*. Delhi, 2004.
Ernst, Carl W. *Eternal Garden: Mysticism, History, and Politics at a South Asian Sufi Center*. Albany, NY, 1992.
Eschmann, Anncharlott. 'Religion, Reaction and Change: The Role of Sects in Hinduism', in Sontheimer and Kulke, ed., *Hinduism Reconsidered*, pp.108–120.
Eschmann, Anncharlott, Hermann Kulke, and G.C. Tripathi, ed. *The Cult of Jagannath and the Regional Tradition of Orissa*. Delhi, 1986.
Esmail, Aziz. *The Poetics of Religious Experience - The Islamic Context*. London, 1998.
—*A Scent of Sandalwood: Indo-Ismaili Religious Lyrics (Ginans)*. Richmond, 2002.
Ewing, Katherine P., ed. *Shariʿat and Ambiguity in South-Asian Islam*. Berkeley, 1988.
Freitag, Sandria B. 'Contesting in Public: Colonial Legacies and Contemporary Communalism', in Ludden, ed., *Making India Hindu - Religion, Community and the Politics of Democracy in India*. Delhi, 1996, pp.211–234.
Friedmann, Yohanan. 'Islamic Thought in Relation to the Indian Context', in *Puruśārtha*, 9, Paris, 1986, *Islam et Sociéte en Asie du Sud*, pp.79–91.
—ed. *Islam in Asia - vol. 1: South Asia*. Jerusalem, 1984.
Frykenberg, Robert E. 'The Emergence of Modern "Hinduism" as a Concept and as an Institution: A Reappraisal with Special Reference to South India', in Sontheimer and Kulke, ed., *Hinduism Reconsidered*, pp.29–50.
Gaborieau, Marc. 'A Nineteenth-century Indian "wahhabi" Tract against the Cult of Muslim Saint', in Troll, ed., *Muslim Shrines in India: Their Character, History and Significance*, pp.198–239.
—'Les débats sur l'acculturation chez les Musulmans indiens au début du XIXe siècle', in Assayag and Tarabout, ed., *Altérité et Identité - Islam et Christianisme en Inde, Puruśārtha*, 19, Paris, 1997, pp.221–238.
—'Typologie des spécialistes religieux chez les Musulmans du sous-continent indien - Les limites de l'islamisation', *Archives de Science Sociale des Religions*, 55 (January–March, 1983), pp.29–51.
Gandhi, Rajmohan. *Understanding the Muslim Mind*. Delhi, 2000.
—*Revenge and Reconciliation*. Delhi, 1999.
Gilmartin, David and Bruce B. Lawrence, ed., *Beyond Turk and Hindu - Rethinking Religious Identities in Islamicate South Asia*. Gainesville, FL, 2000.
Ginzburg, Carlo. *Clues, Myths and the Historical Method*. Baltimore, MD, 1989.
Gohil, Nathabai. *Āgāmvāṇīs*. Ahmedabad, 1994.
Gold, Daniel. *The Lord as Guru - Hindi Sants in North Indian Tradition*.

New York, 1987.
Gottschalk, Peter. *Beyond Hindu and Muslim: Multiple Identity in Narratives from Village India*. New Delhi, 2001.
—'The Problem of Defining Islam in Arampur', *ISIM Newsletter* (August, 2001).
Hardy, P. 'Modern European and Muslim Explanations of Conversion to Islam in South-Asia: A Preliminary Survey of the Literature', in Nehemia Levtzion, ed., *Conversions to Islam*. New York, 1979, pp.177–206.
Hedayetullah, Muhammad. *Kabir, The Apostle of Hindu-Muslim Unity*. Delhi, 1977; repr. 1989.
Hollister, John N. *The Shi'a of India*. London, 1953.
Horstmann, Monika. 'Towards a Universal Dharma: *Kalyān* and the Tracts of the Gita Press', in Dalmia and von Stietencron, ed., *Representing Hinduism*, 1995, pp.294–305.
—'The Temple of Govindadevaji: A Symbol of Hindu Kingship?', in N.K. Singhi and R. Joshi, ed., *Religion, Ritual and Royalty*, Jaipur, 1999, pp.119–131.
Hudson, Dennis. 'Violent and Fanatical Devotion among the Nayanars: A Study of the *Periya Puranam* of Cekkilar', in A, Hiltebeitel, ed., *Criminal Gods and Demon Devotees*. Delhi, 1990.
Hughes, Thomas Patrick. *A Dictionary of Islam*. London, 1887; repr. Delhi, 1996; Ottawa, 1996.
Husain, Yusuf. *L'Inde mystique au moyen-age*. Paris, 1929.
Ibbetson, Denzil. *Panjab Castes – Races, Castes and Tribes of the People of Panjab*. Simla, 1916; repr. Delhi, 1981.
Ivanow, Wladimir. 'Satpanth', in *Collectanea*, vol. 1. Leiden, 1948.
—'The Sect of Imam Shah in Gujrat', *Journal of the Bombay Branch of the Royal Asiatic Society*, NS, 12 (1936), pp.19–70.
Jaffrelot, Christophe. *The Hindu Nationalist Movement in India*. Delhi, 1996.
—'Les (re)conversions à l'hindouisme (1885–1990): politisation et diffusion d'une "invention de la tradition"', *Archives de Science Sociale des Religions*, 87 (1994), pp.73–98.
Jambheshwar. *Sabadvānī kī Jambhsāgar*. Rishikesh, 1966.
Jamous, Raymond. '"Faire", "défaire" et "refaire" les saints: Les *pir* chez les Meo (Inde du Nord)', *Terrain*, 24 (1995), pp.43–56.
Jones, Kenneth W. 'Religious Identity and the Indian Census', in Barrier, ed., *The Census in British India*, pp.73–102.
—*Arya Dharm: Hindu Consciousness in 19th-century Punjab*. Berkeley, 1976.
—'*Ham Hindū nahīn*: Arya-Sikh Relations, 1877–1905', *Journal of Asian Studies*, 32:3 (1973), pp.457–475.

Joshi, S. and B. Josh. *Struggle for Hegemony in India – 1920–1947 – Culture Community and Power. vol. 3: 1941–1947.* Delhi, 1994.

Jotwani, Motilal. *Sindhi Literature and Society.* New Delhi, 1979.

Kabir. *The Bījak*, trans. Linda Hess and Sukhdev Singh, essays and notes by L. Hess. Delhi, 1986.

Kassam, Tazim R. 'Syncretism on the Model of the Figure-Ground: A Study of Pir Shams' "Brahma Prakāsa"', in K.K. Young, ed., *Hermeneutical Paths to the Sacred Worlds of India – Essays in Honour of Robert W. Stevenson.* Atlanta, GA, 1994, pp.231–241.

—*Songs of Wisdom and Circles of Dance: Hymns of the Satpanth Ismā'īlī Muslim Saint, Pīr Shams.* Albany, NY, 1995.

Keane, H.G. *History of India.* Vol.1. London, 1893.

Keay, F.E. *Kabir and his Followers.* New Delhi, 1931; repr. 1995.

Kennedy, Charles H. 'Towards the Definition of a Muslim in an Islamic State: The Case of Ahmadiyya in Pakistan', in Vajpeyi and Malik, ed., *Religious and Ethnic Minority Politics in South Asia*, pp.71–108.

Khan, Ansar Zahid. *History and Culture of Sind.* Karachi, 1980.

Khan, Dominique-Sila. 'Deux rites tantriques dans une communauté d'intouchables au Rajasthan', *Revue d'histoire des religions* 211 (1994), pp.443–462.

—*Conversions and Shifting Identities – Ramdev Pir and the Ismailis in Rajasthan.* Delhi,1997.

—'The Coming of Nikalank Avatar: A Messianic Theme in Some Sectarian Traditions of North-Western India', *Journal of Indian Philosophy*, 25 (1997) pp.401–426.

—'Conversations between Guru Hasan Kabiruddin and Jogi Kanipha: Tantra Revisited by the Isma'ili Preachers', in David Gordon White, ed., *Tantra in Practice*, Princeton, 2000, pp.285–295.

—'Karsan Das – Un héros vivant: L'identité Paṭīdār et la secte des Satpanthī au Gujarat', in V. Bouillier and C. Le Blanc, ed., *Usage des héros: Traditions narratives et affirmations identitaires dans le monde indien* (forthcoming).

—'Saix Burhān Cisti: le culte d'un saint musulman chez les Rajput Qekhāvat', in Annie Montaut, ed., *Le Rajasthan, ses dieux, ses héros, ses hommes.* Paris, 2000.

—'The Prannathis of Rajasthan: *Bhakti* and *Irfan*', in L.A. Babb, V. Joshi, and M. Meister, ed., *Multiple Histories – Culture and Society in the Study of Rajastahn.* Jaipur, 2002, pp.209–231.

—'The Mahdi of Panna: A Short History of the Pranamis', *Journal of Secular Studies*, Part I, 6:4 (2003), pp.61–93; Part II, 7:1 (2003), pp.46–66.

—'Diverting the Ganges – Nizari Isma'ili Methods of Conversion', in R. Robinson and S. Clarke, ed., *Religious Conversion in India.* Delhi, 2003, pp. 29–55.

—'The Graves of History or the Metaphor of the Hidden Pit', in Joshi Varsha, ed. *Culture, Communities and Change*. Jaipur and New Delhi, 2002.

—'Liminality and Legality: A Contemporary Debate among the Imamshahis of Gujarat', in Ahmad Imtiaz and Helmut Reifeld, ed. *Lived Islam in South Asia*. Delhi, 2004.

Khan, Dominique-Sila and Moir, Zawahir. 'The Lord will Marry the Virgin Earth: Songs of the Time to Come', *Journal of Indian Philosophy*, 28 (2000), pp.99–115.

—'Coexistence and Communalism: the Shrine of Pirana in Gujarat', *South Asia*, 22, Special Issue (1999), pp.133–154.

Khan, Mohammad Ishaq. *Kashmir's Transition to Islam – The Role of Muslim Rishis (Fifteenth to Eighteenth Century)*. Delhi, 1994.

Kohli, Surindar Singh. *Sikh Predictions (Based on all relevant texts)*. Delhi, 1998.

Kolff, Dirk H.A. *Naukar, Rajput and Sepoy – the Ethnohistory of the Military Labour Market in Hindustan, 1450–1850*. Cambridge, 1990.

Kumar, Sunil. 'Assertions of Authority: A Study of the Discursive Statements of Two Sultans of Delhi', in Alam, Delvoye, and Gaborieau, ed., *The Making of Indo-Persian Culture*, pp.37–65.

Lawrence, Bruce B. 'The Sant Movement and North Indian Sufis', in Schomer and Mcleod, ed., *The Sants*, pp.359–376.

Lorenzen, David N. *Praises to a Formless God – Nirguni Texts from North India*. Albany, NY, 1996.

Ludden, David, ed. *Making India Hindu – Religion, Community and the Politics of Democracy in India*. Delhi,1996.

Maclean, D.N. *Religion and Society in Arab Sind*. Leiden, 1989.

McDonough, Sheila. 'The Spirit of Jamia Millia Islamia as Exemplified in the Writings of S. Abid Husain', in Baird, ed., *Religion in Modern India*, pp.144–165.

McGregor, R.S., ed. *Devotional Literature in South Asia*. Cambridge, 1988.

McLeod, W.H. *Who is a Sikh? The Problem of Sikh Identity*. New York, 1989; repr. Oxford, 1992.

Majumdar, M.R. *Cultural History of Gujarat*. Bombay, 1965.

Malkani, K.R. *The Sindh Story*. Delhi, 1984; repr. 1997.

Malinar, Angelika. 'The *Bhagavadgita* in the *Mahabharata* TV Serial: Domestic Drama and Dharmic solutions', in Dalmia and von Stietencron, ed., *Representing Hinduism*, pp.442–467.

Mallison, Françoise. 'Hinduism as Seen by the Nizārī Isma'ili Missionaries of Western India: The Evidence of the *ginān*', in Sontheimer and Kulke, ed., *Hinduism Reconsidered*, pp.93–104.

—'Muslim Devotional Literature in Gujarati: Islam and *bhakti*', in McGregor, ed., *Devotional Literature in South Asia - Current Research, 1985–1988*, pp.89–100.

Mann, E.A. 'Religion, Money and Status: Competition for Resources at the Shrine of Shah Jamal, Aligarh', in Christian W. Troll, ed., *Muslim Shrines in India - Their Character, History and Significance*. Delhi, 1989.

Masselos, James C. 'The Khojas of Bombay: The Defining of Formal Membership Criteria during the Nineteenth Century', in Ahmad, ed., *Caste and Social Stratification*, pp.97–116.

Matringe, Denis. 'Kṛṣṇaite and Nāth Elements in the Poetry of the Eighteenth-century Panjabi Sūfī Bullhe Sāh', in McGregor, ed., *Devotional Literature in South Asia*, 1988, pp.190–206.

Mayaram, Shail. *Resisting Regimes: Myth, Memory and the Shaping of a Muslim Identity*. Delhi, 1997.

—'Spirit Possession - Reframing Discourses of the Self and Other', *Puruśārtha*, 21 (2000), pp.101–131.

Melikian-Chirvani, A.S. 'Ranjit Singh and the Image of the Past', in Susan Stronge, ed., *The Arts of the Sikh Kingdoms*. Delhi, 1999, pp.61–67.

Mill, James. *The History of British India*. London, 1817.

Mio, Minoru. 'Faith, Identity and Communal Discourse: Some Ethnological Considerations on the Conflicts over the Administration of a Sufi Saint's Mausoleum in Rajasthan', in Steering Committee of the Research Project Institutions, Networks and Forces of Changes in Contemporary South Asia, ed., *Rituals as Popular Culture:Towards Historico-Anthropological Understanding of Modern Indian Society*. Tokyo, 1999, pp. 1–58.

Moir, Zawahir. 'Historical and Religious Debates amongst Indian Ismailis 1840–1920', in Mariola Offredi, ed., *The Banyan Tree*. Delhi, 2001, pp.131–153.

—'The Life and Legends of Pir Shams as Reflected in the Ismaili Ginans: A Critical Review', in Françoise Mallison, ed., *Constructions hagiographiques dans le monde indien - entre mythe et histoire*. Paris, 2001, pp.365–384.

Mukhia, Harbans. 'Medieval Indian History and the Communal Approach', in *Selected Writings on Communalism*. Delhi, 1991, p.21.

Mushirul, Hasan. 'The Myth of Unity: Colonial and National Narratives', in Ludden, ed., *Making India Hindu*, pp.185–210.

Naipaul, V.S. *India - A Million Mutinies Now*. 1990; repr. London, 1997, pp.438–439.

Nanji, Azim. *The Nizārī Ismā'īlī Tradition in the Indo-Pakistan Subcontinent*. Delmar, NY, 1978.

—'Shari'at and Ḥaqīqat', in Ewing, ed., *Shari'at and Ambiguity in South-Asian Islam*, pp.63–76.

Nanjiani, Sachedina. *Khojā Vṛttānt*. Ahmedabad, 1892; repr. 1918.

Nehru, Jawaharlal. *The Discovery of India*. Calcutta, 1946.
Nizami, Khwaja Hasan, *Fatimi daʿwat-e-Islam*. Delhi, 1338/1919.
Nut, Hugo G. 'Syncretism', in David Carrasco, ed., *Oxford Encyclopedia of Mesoamerican Cultures*. Oxford, 2001, pp.177–181.
Offreddi, Mariola. *The Banyan Tree*. Delhi, 2001.
Oberoi, Harjot. *The Construction of Religious Boundaries – Culture, Identity and Diversity in the Sikh Tradition*. Delhi, 1994.
Pande, Susmita. *Birth of Bhakti in Indian Religions and Art*. New Delhi, 1982.
—*Medieval Bhakti Movement*. Meerut, 1989.
Pandey, Gyanendra. 'The Appeal of Hindu History', in Dalmia and von Stietencron, ed., *Representing Hinduism*, pp.369–388.
Pinto, Desiderio. *Piri-Muridi Relationship – A Study of the Nizamuddin Dargah*. Delhi, 1995.
Prashad, Vijay. *Untouchable Freedom*. Delhi, 2000.
Qureshi, Saleem. 'The Politics of the Shia Minority in Pakistan: Context and Development', in Vajpeyi and Malik, ed., *Religious and Ethnic Minority Politics in South Asia*, pp.109–138.
Rattansi, Diamond. *Islamization and the Khojah Ismaʿili Community in Pakistan*. Unpublished Ph.D. thesis, McGill University, Montreal, 1987.
Rizvi, Sayid Athar Abbas. A *History of Sufism in India*. Delhi, 1978; repr. 1986.
Rose, H.A. *A Glossary of the Tribes and Castes of the Punjab and North- West Frontier Provinces*. Delhi, 1919; repr. 1990.
Roy, Asim. *The Islamic Syncretistic Tradition in Bengal*. Princeton, 1983.
Ruhela, S.P. *Sri Shirdi Sai Baba the Universal Master*. New Delhi, 1994.
Saffronised Substandard (n.a.), Delhi, 2002.
Sarkar, Sumit. 'Indian Nationalism and the Politics of Hindutva', in Ludden, ed., *Making India Hindu*, pp.270–294.
Schomer, Karine and W.H. Mcleod, ed. *The Sants – Studies in a Devotional Tradition of India*. Delhi, 1987.
Shackle, Christopher and Zawahir Moir. *Ismaili Hymns from South Asia. An Introduction to the Ginans*. London, 1992; repr. Richmond, 2000.
Shekhawat, Sobhagya Singh. *Shekhāvāṭī ke vīr gīt*. Jodhpur, 1991.
Shivadas Sathyabai and Rao R. Prabharakara. *Narayana Guru: The Social Philosopher of Kerala*. Mumbai, 2002.
Shodhan, Amrita. 'Legal Formulation of the Question of Community: Defining the Khoja Collective', *Indian Social Science Review*, 1 (1999), pp.137–151.
Shokoohy, Mehrdad. *Bhadresvar – The Oldest Islamic Monuments in India*. Leiden, 1988.
Sikand, Yoginder. 'Another Ayodhya in the Making? The Baba Budhangiri

Dargah Controversy in South India', *Journal of Muslim Minority Affairs*, 20 (2000), pp.209–225.
—*The Origins and Development of the Tablighi-jama'at (1920–2000): A Cross-country Comparative Study*. Delhi, 2002.
Sontheimer, Gunther D. and Hermann Kulke, ed. *Hinduism Reconsidered*. Delhi, 1991; repr. 1998.
Somani, R.V. *The History of Mewar*. Jaipur, 1976.
Srinivas, M.N. *Religion and Society among the Coorgs of South India*. Oxford, 1952.
Stutley, Margaret and James Stutley. *A Dictionary of Hinduism*. London, 1977.
Tajjdin, Mumtaz 'Alī. 'Ramdeo Pir: A Forgotten Ismaili Saint', *Sindh Review*, 32 (1995), pp.24–29.
Thapar, Romila. 'Syndicated Hindhism', in Sontheimer and Kulke, ed., *Hinduism Reconsidered*, pp.54–81.
—*Somatha: The Many Voices of a History*. Delhi, 2004.
Titus, Murray. *Indian Islam*. London, 1930.
Tod, James. *Annals and Antiquities of Rajasthan*. 1829–1832; repr. Delhi, 1983.
Troll, Christian W., ed. *Muslim Shrines in India – Their Character, History and Significance*. Delhi, 1989.
Turner, Victor. *Process, Performance and Pilgrimage*. New Delhi, 1991.
Uberoi, J.P.S. *Religion, Civil Society and the State – A Study of Sikhism*. Delhi, 1996.
Vajpeyi, Dhirendra and Yogendra K. Malik, ed. *Religious and Ethnic Minority Politics in South Asia*. Delhi, 1989.
—'Muslim Fundamentalism in India', in Vajpeyi and Malik, ed., *Religious and Ethnic Minority Politics in South Asia*.
Van Gennep, Arnold. *Rites of Passage*. London, 1960.
van Skyhawk, Hugh. 'Nasiruddin and Adinath, Nizamuddin and Kanipanath: Hindu-Muslim Religious Syncretism in the Folk Literature of the Deccan', in Heidrun Brückner, Lothar Lutze, and Aditya Malik, ed., *Flags of Fame – Studies in South Asian Folk Culture*. Delhi, 1993, pp.445–468.
Varteji, E.J. *Ismaīlī āftāb sahitya śrenī*. n.p., 1930.
Vaudeville, Charlotte. 'Sant Mat: Santism as the Universal Path to Sanctity', in Schomer and Mcleod, ed., *The Sants*, pp.21–40.
—*Kabir*. Oxford, 1974, vol. 1.
Virani, Shafique.'Vive l'Avatar: Quelques Hindous Musulmans de l'Inde', unpublished paper presented at Inde médiévale et moderne: textes et contextes, Ecole Pratique des Hautes Etudes, Sorbonne University, Paris, 8 February, 2000.

Volney, Constantin Francois. *Les ruines ou méditations sur les révolutions des empires*. Paris, 1791.

von Stietencron, Heinrich. 'Hinduism: On the Proper Use of a Deceptive Term', in Sontheimer and Kulke, ed., *Hinduism Reconsidered*, pp.11–28.

—'Religious Configurations in Pre-Muslim India and the Modern Concept of Hinduism' in Dalmia and von Stietencron, ed., *Representing Hinduism*, pp.51–81.

Wagle, Narendra K. 'Hindu-Muslim Interactions in Medieval Maharashtra', in Sontheimer and Kulke, ed., *Hinduism Reconsidered*, pp.51–66.

Zastoupil, Lynn and Martin Moir, ed. *The Great Indian Education Debate: Documents Relating to the Orientalist-Anglicist Controversy, 1781–1843*. Richmond, 1999.

Zelliot, Eleanor. 'Eknath's *Bharuds*: The Sant as a Link between Cultures', in Schomer and Mcleod, *The Sants*, pp.91–110.

Index